Private Markets in Health and Welfare
An International Perspective

Edited by
Norman Johnson

BERG
Oxford/Providence, USA

First published in 1995 by
Berg Publishers Limited
Editorial offices:
150 Cowley Road, Oxford, OX4 1JJ, UK
221 Waterman Street, Providence, RI 02906, USA

Library of Congress Cataloging-in-Publication Data
A catalogue record for this book is available from the Library of Congress.

British Library Cataloguing in Publication Data
A catalogue record for this book is available from the British Library.

ISBN 0 85496 822 9 (Cloth)
1 85973 097 3 (Paper)

Printed in the United Kingdom by WBC Book Manufacturers, Bridgend,
Mid Glamorgan.

Contents

Contents

List of Tables

List of Figures

Notes on Contributors

Daniel Cohn is a graduate of the Master of Social Science Programme offered by Stockholm University's International Graduate School. He is currently studying towards a PhD in political science at Carleton University (Ottawa, Canada). His MSc thesis, *Reforming Health Care in Canada and Sweden 1975–1990*, was published as part of the International Graduate School's Stockholm International Studies series.

André-Pierre Contandriopoulos is a full professor and chairman at the Health Administration Department, University of Montreal. His main areas of teaching and research are in the fields of Medical Care Organisation, Health Planning, and Health Economics. He has published widely in these areas. He is also a member of the Interdisciplinary Health Research Group (GRIS).

Patrizia David is a researcher in Sociology at the University of Ancona, Italy. Her publications include work on the personal social services, family and gender roles and the female labour market.

Neil Gilbert is Chernin Professor of Social Welfare at the School of Social Welfare, University of California at Berkeley, and Co-Director of the Family Welfare Research Group. Gilbert served as a Senior Research Fellow for the United Nations Research Institute for Social Development in Geneva in 1975. Fulbright research awards enabled him to study the changing structure of social services in the UK in 1981 and European social policy in 1987, when he was a Visiting Scholar at the London School of Economics and Political Science and at the University of Stockholm Social Research Institute. In 1982, Gilbert was a Visiting Fulbright Lecturer at Tel Aviv University. His numerous publications include *Capitalism and the Welfare State*, and (with Barbara Gilbert) *The Enabling State*, and he is editor of the Prentice-Hall Series on Social Welfare and the Praeger Publications Series on the Social Services. In 1987 he was awarded the University of Pittsburg Bicentennial Medallion of Distinction.

Stanisalawa Golinowska is Director of the Institute of Labour and Social Studies, Warsaw. She has served as an expert on the Government Commission for Economic Reform, the Team on Social Services, and the

Team of the Ministry of Culture and Science. From 1991 to 1992 she was Head of Department at the Institute of National Economy, and Research Director at the Institute of Culture. The author of eighty papers, her current areas of research interest are into the effectiveness of state social policies in Western and Central Europe; social policy and labour economics in the transition; the role of the state in socio-economic development in industrialised nations, and ageing and the labour market in Poland and Eastern Europe.

Sven E. Olsson Hort is Assistant Professor in the Department of Sociology at Stockholm University. His extensive publications in both Swedish and English include a second and enlarged edition of *Social Policy and Welfare State in Sweden*, and *Scandinavia in a New Europe* (co-edited with Thomas P. Boje). He has also recently contributed to *Social Security in Sweden and Other European Countries – Three Essays.*

Pierre Huard is a professor in the Faculty of Economic Sciences at the University of Aix-Marseilles 2. He is a specialist in health economics, and his main field of research and publications have been into current changes in the French health system.

Majda Černič Istenič is a researcher at the Institute for Social Sciences in the Faculty for Social Sciences at the University of Ljubljana. Her main fields of interest and publications are family sociology and social policy. She participated in the national project on the quality of life in Slovenia, and in research into the reconstruction of social services in Slovenia.

Norman Johnson is Professor of Public Policy at the University of Portsmouth. He has particular interests in welfare pluralism and comparative social policy. His main publications include *The Welfare State in Transition: The Theory and Practice of Welfare Pluralism* and *Reconstructing the Welfare State.*

Anne Lemay is a health economist in the Health Administration Department at the University of Montreal. Her research specialisations include the financing and cost of the health care system, the utilisation of health care services, and medical staff level planning. She has published a number of papers in these areas.

Frédéric Lesemann is Professor of Social Policy at the University of Montreal. He has researched and published extensively in the areas of poverty, family and social policy and social gerontology, in Canada, the United States and France. Among his most recent publications are: *Home-*

base Care – The Elderly, the Family and the Welfare State: An International Comparison and (with others) *Home-care . . . A Love Affair*. He is Director of the PhD program in Applied Social Sciences and Scientific Director of the Research Institute in Social Gerontology, Montreal. He is also editor of the *Revue Internationale d'Action Communitaire*.

Philippe Mossé is a research economist at the Laboratory for the Study of The Economics and Sociology of Work at the National Centre for Scientific Research at Aix-en-Provence. He is also a member of the board of the French Social Economics Association. His main publications have been in the field of health economics.

Eva Orosz is a senior lecturer in the Social Policy Department at Eotvos Lorand University. Her main teaching and research interests are in the areas of health policy, inequalities in health, comparative health care policy and health care reform in Hungary. Among her publications is a book entitled *Health Care Systems and Reform Endeavour*.

Guy Roustang was a Director at the National Union for Employment in Industry and Commerce before becoming Deputy Director and then Director of the Laboratory for the Study of the Economics and Sociology of Work. In 1979 he took up his present post as Research Director at the National Centre for Scientific Research at Aix-en-Provence. His research is mainly in the fields of employment, economic growth and society. He founded the Regional Group for the Study of Work, which endeavours to improve the interaction between human and technical resources in business. His main publications have been in the field of employment, society and economic growth.

Kwong Leung Tang is a lecturer on the Social Work Programme at the University of Northern British Columbia, Canada. He recently completed his doctoral studies in the School of Social Welfare at the University of California, Berkeley. He was a community worker in Hong Kong before becoming a lecturer at Hong Kong Polytechnic. He has edited two books about social security and industrial social services in Hong Kong.

Katarzyna Tymowska is a researcher and teacher in the Faculty of Economic Sciences at the University of Warsaw. She is Director of Postgraduate Study in Health Economics. She has acted as expert and consultant to a number of governmental and parliamentary bodies in Poland, including House and Senate Committees on Health. In 1989 she co-authored the proposal for the reform of the health care system in Poland. She also co-founded the Association of Health Service Managers, where she is a member of the board and editor of its monthly magazine on economic and management issues. Her publications are in the field of health economics, health sector financing and comparative studies of health service systems.

Giovanna Vicarelli is a researcher in sociology at the University of Ancona. She is the author of numerous papers on health policy, family studies and policies relating to migrants.

–1–

Introduction
Norman Johnson

Put at its simplest, markets are a means of bringing together buyers and sellers for purposes of voluntary exchange. The items involved in this exchange may be raw materials, agricultural produce, manufactured goods, labour or capital.

Markets consist of networks of dealings in which the outcomes are determined by the apparently uncoordinated actions of large numbers of individuals and firms. The classical view is that prices are determined by the relationship between supply and demand. The equilibrium price is that at which demand and supply are identical. In conditions of perfect competition, no single buyer or seller controls enough of the market to be able to affect prices by his or her own actions, so that large numbers of competing separate firms, seeking to maximise their profits, adjust their outputs to the known market price. When the equilibrium position is reached, no participant can improve his or her position without someone else losing; perfect competition, therefore, ensures the most efficient allocation of resources. Any interference with perfect competition will lead to a loss of efficiency and is therefore to be deprecated: trade unions (except as friendly societies), cartels, monopolies and monopsonies (a single or dominant buyer) are equally condemned.

The neo-classical approach to markets is criticised by economists of the Austrian school for being too static and taking too little account of entrepreneurship. The Austrians place less emphasis on prices and more on competition, and argue that the market is characterised by disequilibrium. The competitive process can be expected to produce a number of monopolies (a reward for competing successfully) but, provided that competition is unhindered, these will be relatively short-lived.

Both of these approaches come from groups of economists who are firmly committed to free markets. They share the view that unfettered markets, in which individuals pursue their own self-interest, lead to the best results for society as a whole. As we shall see, there are others who stress the potentially damaging effects of unrestricted markets, arguing that markets should be subject to regulation, and that some goods should be removed from the operation of the market altogether.

As the individual chapters in this book show, the extent and degree of market regulation vary from one country to another, as does the range of goods left to the market.

Advantages of Markets

A case for markets may be made on two grounds: efficiency and morality. The efficiency arguments usually receive most attention, and we will begin with these.

The neo-classical argument that perfect competition in free markets guarantees the most efficient allocation of resources has already been referred to. Producers, seeking to maximise their profits, compete with each other for a bigger share of the market. There is an incentive to reduce costs to a minimum and to improve the quality of the product. Producers who can achieve neither will eventually be forced to close down.

As Novak (1991, p.106) observes, competitive markets also encourage innovation:

> In a market system things move; wealth grows; opportunities open; breakthroughs are made; new groups rise to wealth. Practical intelligence assesses existing arrangements in order to invent others, to offer new services, to meet unmet needs, to discover better ways. The inventiveness encouraged by market systems may be their most important characteristic.

Another advantage claimed for markets is that they are an effective way of processing and transmitting information in the form of prices. If the supply of a particular product, material or service is insufficient to meet demand, its price will rise; if, on the other hand, supply exceeds demand, the price will fall. A higher price is a signal to current and potential producers that there are profits to be made, and this will be an incentive to increase output. A lower price will have the opposite effect. Estrin and Le Grand (1989, p.3) stress the importance of the conjunction of information and incentives: 'When they [markets] work well, they are an excellent way of processing information, while simultaneously providing incentives to act upon it.'

Gray (1992) also stresses the importance of information and incentives, and claims that the market is immeasurably superior to central planning in both respects. As evidence of this, Gray cites the economic failure in the former Soviet Union and in the former communist states of Central and Eastern Europe. According to Gray, the failure of central planning is partly to be explained by 'the absence of the benign incentives provided by the disciplines of market competition and the presence of incentives to mismanagement and mal-investment' (p.6).

Gray, however, emphasises the epistemic problems facing central economic planners – problems stemming from the limitations of human knowledge. Without the information provided by prices, central planners are at a grave disadvantage. The work of Hayek (1976), Polanyi (1951) and Shackle (1972) is used by Gray to substantiate this claim. According to Hayek, it is not simply a lack of knowledge on the part of planners that creates problems, but the nature of the knowledge possessed by those making economic decisions. Frequently this knowledge is intuitive and local, and it is constantly changing. Such knowledge is not available to central planning agencies, and it can never be made available. Polanyi makes a similar point when he writes of tacit and local knowledge, much of which remains unarticulated and may not be capable of articulation. Shackle's main argument is that the future is entirely unpredictable, and central planners are therefore reduced to guessing. This is no less true of participants in markets, but the consequences of wrong guesses are less far-reaching than are errors in central plans.

So far, the discussion has been restricted to the advantages of markets in terms of efficiency. A discussion of some of the sources of possible inefficiencies will be postponed until the next section. I now wish to turn to the moral or ethical case for markets.

Miller (1990, p.72) says that 'much liberal thinking in recent years has been dominated by the principle of neutrality.' He defines an institution or practice as neutral 'when, as far as can reasonably be foreseen, it does not favour any particular conception of the good at the expense of others' (p.77). Miller claims that markets act neutrally with regard to people's conceptions of the good which are based on the possession, use and exchange of commodities, but that they are less able to deal neutrally with conceptions of the good which extend beyond the private enjoyment of commodities. Notions of the good life that include community and fellowship ideals, for example, are not treated neutrally, and Miller, a market socialist who favours workplace co-operatives, says that markets actively discriminate against co-operative work relations.

In spite of these reservations, Miller (1989) maintains that markets permit industrial democracy, whereas planned economies require conformity with centrally determined targets, forms of management and work practices.

Miller (1989) also argues that markets may be supported on the grounds that they promote greater freedom to choose the products that one wishes to buy and the supplier one wishes to patronise. They also allow some choice as to the type of work one does and the place in which one does it.

Freedom in relation to markets is an issue addressed by Gray (1992) and Plant (1992). Gray rejects the classical liberal view of freedom as merely the absence of coercion or constraint. This negative formulation of freedom is, he says, 'a dead end' (p.21). There is nothing *intrinsically* valuable about the absence of coercion, and 'the value of negative liberty must therefore be theorised in terms of its contribution to something other than itself, which does possess intrinsic value' (p.22). Gray concludes that the chief value of negative liberty is to be found in the contribution it makes to the positive liberty of autonomy, which he defines as:

> the condition in which a person can be at least part author of his life, in that he has before him a range of worthwhile options, in respect of which his choices are not fettered by coercion and with regard to which he possesses the capacities and resources presupposed by a reasonable measure of success in his self-chosen path among these options. (p.22)

Writers from a wide variety of political perspectives are agreed that autonomy is of immense value in a society, and that markets make a major contribution to it. Miller (1990, p.46) puts the point most strongly, stating that, when freedom is defined positively as self-determination, then markets are 'a practically indispensable means of ensuring that people make autonomous choices about matters such as work and consumption'.

There would be less agreement about the most appropriate scope of markets, about the need for regulation and about the range of welfare provision thought necessary to enable people to exercise their autonomy. Some of these issues will be addressed as the chapter progresses. We now turn to the possible limitations of markets.

Limitations of Markets

Again the arguments will be divided into two groups: efficiency and ethics. In part, this section will consider the conditional nature of some of the advantages claimed for markets.

For example, some of the efficiency advantages claimed for markets are conditional upon competition. The greatest advantages occur when there is perfect competition in which many suppliers compete for the custom of knowledgeable consumers. For a variety of reasons, however, market failure may result from imperfect competition. The development of monopolies, in which a single supplier or a very small group of suppliers controls the entire market, is the most obvious example of imperfect competition. When there are only a few producers, cartels to regulate output or prices may be formed. Market imperfections also arise when there is a monopsony.

There are several instances of 'natural monopolies' when it would be wasteful or prohibitively expensive to duplicate units of production – gas, water supply and electricity distribution come into this category. Local monopolies may also arise, even when there is a large number of suppliers nationally, if mobility problems and the cost of travel render the use of alternative facilities impractical.

Perfect competition also requires knowledgeable consumers, and, in the vast majority of transactions, people do have the necessary knowledge to enable them to make reasonable decisions about which goods and services to buy from among those available. However, there are certain very technical or professional services which most people have to take on trust, although independent advice services, consumer protection agencies and legislation help to reduce the danger of exploitation.

A second source of market failure is the problem of externalities. Levacic (1991, p.36) says that 'externalities occur when the actions of one economic agent affect the welfare of others in a way that is not reflected in market prices.' There are external costs and external benefits. An example of the former is pollution from productive processes, and an example of an external benefit might be the benefit to a rural community of keeping an uneconomic railway line open. Prices reflect only the costs and benefits to those directly involved in the transaction. The market, by ignoring external costs and benefits, tends to overvalue goods which incur external costs and undervalue goods which confer external benefits. This leads to over-production of the former and under-production of the latter.

Another form of externality is concerned with goods which confer general benefits from which people cannot be excluded – defence, law and order and public health are the most obvious examples. This is one of the reasons why responsibility for the provision of such services often falls upon public authorities. It is worth noting, however, that the growth of private security firms and the opening of private penal institutions in the United States and the United Kingdom indicates that markets may arise even in the most unpromising areas.

The arguments advanced in the previous section about the serious deficiencies of centralised economic planning are incontrovertible, but this does not necessarily mean that all planning is to be avoided. Planning which is decentralised, democratically controlled and participative in nature might be feasible, and might avoid some of the grave shortcomings of centralised planning. Most of the support for new forms of planning comes from socialists. Walker (1984), for example, argues for decentralised and participative social planning, and market socialists Estrin and Winter (1989) argue for what they call indicative planning, although they are at pains to stress that 'indicative planning is a valuable complement to, but not in any sense a substitute for, the market as the principal mechanism for allocating resources' (p.115). Estrin and Winter describe indicative planning as 'a decentralized, and preferably democratic, process of consultation and discussion concerned exclusively with plan construction and elaboration' (p.116). The plan would not contain prescribed methods of implementation, which would be left to negotiation among individual agents. The French system is cited as an example of this form of planning.

Some of the ethical arguments relating to markets will be considered more fully when we come to consider the role of markets in health and welfare, where they have particular relevance, but some general ethical considerations need to be addressed by way of preface to the more specifically focused material.

A common criticism of markets is that they respond to demand backed by the ability to pay, rather than to need, and that this may lead to an allocation of resources that devotes too much to satisfying the wants of the rich and too little to meeting the needs of the poor. It is, of course, possible to increase the purchasing power of poor people by means of transfer payments or vouchers.

Experience suggests, however, that transfer payments and vouchers are often set at minimum levels, and do little to reduce the basic inequality. Without doubt, unregulated markets produce great inequality, but this is of little concern to free-market liberals and conservatives, such as Gray, (1989, 1992), who are dismissive of egalitarianism, claiming that it has no ethical foundation and has little to do with social justice, which should take account of merit and desert. On the other hand, inequality remains a major preoccupation of socialists, who are more prepared to contemplate the regulation of markets and to support redistributionist policies. This is not the place to enter into this debate, but, given the emphasis placed on autonomy in the ethical justification of markets, one is forced to ask what level of welfare provision is necessary to guarantee the autonomy of poor and deprived people, chronically sick and disabled people, and deprived children.

Markets in Health and Welfare

As the succeeding chapters demonstrate, there has been a significant growth in private market provision of health and welfare services over the last twenty years. Stoesz and Midgley (1991, p.38), in a study of the radical right, state that:

> Within democratic-capitalist states, the commercialization of human services has proceeded rapidly during the last two decades. Proprietary firms have

exploited markets in nursing care, hospital management, health maintenance organizations, child day care, and even corrections.

The pace and extent of the development of commercial services has differed from one country to another. Chapter 9 on Sweden, by Hort and Cohn, indicates very modest development in that country, whereas in the United States (Chapter 10, by Gilbert and Tang) and the United Kingdom (Chapter 2, by Johnson) there has been more substantial development. The development of private markets in health and welfare in Central and Eastern Europe is of much more recent origin.

How are these developments to be explained? Separate explanations are needed for the former communist countries of Eastern and Central Europe and for the capitalist countries of the West. In Eastern and Central Europe, markets in health and welfare came into being as a consequence of political unrest and the overthrow of what had become unpopular regimes (Dahrendorf, 1990; Glenny, 1990). Deacon (Deacon et al., 1992, p.9) says:

> The revolutions of 1989 were clearly at least partly motivated by the wish of significant sections of the population to join in the fruits of Western capitalist consumerism. A more or less rapid introduction of market mechanisms with a pluralization of forms of property is an inevitable outcome of these social changes.

Deacon sees these changes as having two effects upon social policy: 'a shift in the pattern of social inequality from those based on bureaucratic privilege to those based on market relations', and 'an incursion of market relations directly into the welfare sphere' (pp.9–10). However, Chapter 5 by Orosz in this book, and a paper by Szalai and Orosz (1992), indicate that the changes in Hungary have been less far-reaching than the rhetoric would suggest, and that the erosion of the old regime, and the institutions associated with it, began well before 1989.

In relation to the capitalist countries of the West, Glennerster and Midgley (1991, p.ix) see the rise of the radical right as the most significant factor:

> During the 1980s, the welfare consensus was severely shaken by radical right-wing political leaders who popularized the idea that state-sponsored welfare is inimical to national well-being and to economic and social progress. These leaders drew political support from disaffected elements within the established conservative movement who had come to believe that economic growth, cherished traditional values, established beliefs and national pride had been undermined by the insidious spread and docile acceptance of socialist ideas during the post-war era.

The rise of the radical right to positions of influence in the late 1970s and the 1980s has been charted by several writers (Mishra, 1984; King, 1987; Gamble, 1987; Glennerster and Midgley, 1991). There are different interpretations and differences of emphasis, but all commentators are agreed that among the aims of the radical right were: the destruction of the social democratic consensus; a diminished role for the state; reduced public expenditure, and the privatisation of welfare. This is not an exhaustive list, but it includes those elements of radical right philosophy which have most relevance for a consideration of markets in health and welfare. All four aims would be served by a declining role for the State in the provision, finance and regulation of health and welfare services.

Important theoretical backing for the radical right's ideas about the role of government came from adherents of the public choice school (Downs, 1957, 1967; Buchanan and Tullock, 1962; Niskanen, 1971, 1978), who sought to apply economic theory to the behaviour of governments. More particularly, they argued that the methods employed in the analysis of markets could be applied to the public sector. The behaviour of bureaucrats was just as self-interested as the behaviour of individuals in the market. The difference was that bureaucrats were not subject to the discipline of the market and the necessity of making a profit.[1]

However, it was not only the radical right who were advocating a reduced role for the state in the sphere of welfare: more moderate voices were also to be heard from the political centre and from the middle-left (Gladstone, 1979; Hatch, 1980; Hadley and Hatch, 1981; Gilbert, 1983; Gilbert and Gilbert, 1989). Again, these commentators represent a variety of views, but they all support a more pluralist form of Welfare State, with the state playing a smaller part in direct service *provision*, but retaining its role in finance and regulation. The welfare pluralist case frequently begins with a critique of state-provided services, which are depicted as over-centralised, over- bureaucratic and too dominated by administrators and professionals. In short, state provision is disempowering and unresponsive. Although there is no space to deal with it here, it should be noted that Le Grand (1991), freely adapting the work of Wolf (1988), has attempted to construct a theory of government failure comparable to the theory of market failure. Le Grand is careful to emphasise that 'a study of government failure does not imply that governments always fail; still less that markets always succeed ... Governments sometimes succeed: a fact that should not be lost to view in the current glare of the market's bright lights' (p.19).

---

1. For an overview of public choice theory see McLean (1987). A critical analysis of public choice theory is provided by Dunleavy, P. (1991).

If the state is to provide less, then other forms of provision must compensate if levels of service are to be maintained. This means that greater responsibility will fall upon voluntary (non-profit) organisations, commercial undertakings, and families, friends and neighbours. I have written elsewhere (Johnson, 1990) of some of the problems associated with policies designed to transfer service provision from the state to other agencies, but we are here concerned only with commercial provision. It is worth noting, however, that commercial provision, whilst necessary to a fully pluralist system, may be damaging to the voluntary or non-profit sector on which both moderates and the radical right set such great store. Stoesz and Midgley (1991, p.37) say that:

> To the extent that welfare is beyond the means of the family and the informal sector, the radical right prefers that assistance be provided through the organized voluntary sector which embodies virtues that are dear to traditionalists such as neighbourliness, self-reliance and community solidarity.

If this is true, then the relationship between market and voluntary provision becomes a matter of some importance, although the radical right has paid little attention to it.

Market provision could damage the voluntary sector directly (through the diversion of funds or takeover) or indirectly (through its effects on values). The market economy's effect on values has been a matter of some debate. Ware (1990, p.204), for example, argues that 'the general effect of the expansion of the market system has been to corrode altruism', whereas Gray (1992, p.24) maintains that 'The prejudice that markets promote egoism, while collective procedures facilitate altruism, is, if anything, the reverse of the truth.'

Even if markets are recognised as the most efficient means of allocating resources in most circumstances, there may still be a case for removing some goods from their operation. Plant (1992, p.120), after agreeing with Gray's rejection of central economic planning on epistemological grounds, continues:

> However, this is only part of the task of trying to work out the proper role for the market in a liberal society. This second task of trying to work out the appropriate moral limits to markets is also centrally important because the market is only likely to appear legitimate and command loyalty if it is seen to have a definite sphere of legitimacy and that it is constrained from spilling over into spheres of human life within which we do not wish to see goods treated as commodities.

An interesting example of goods perhaps inappropriately treated as commodities is the donation and selling of blood. Titmuss's (1973) five-country study of blood donation raised questions not only about the appropriateness of commercial systems, but also about their efficiency. He concluded that:

> In commercial blood markets the consumer is not king. He has less freedom to live unharmed; little choice of determining price; is more subject to shortages in supply; is less free from bureaucratization; has fewer opportunities to express altruism; and exercises fewer checks and controls in relation to consumption, quality and external costs. Far from being sovereign, he is often exploited. (p.233)

Titmuss used his study to illustrate a general proposition that markets do not always produce a better service. However, a major problem of attempting to demonstrate that one form of provision is more efficient than another in health and welfare is the difficulty of measuring efficiency. What, in the first place, constitutes an efficient service? Is it one that provides an adequate service at minimum cost, or is it one that most nearly meets the needs of its recipients? Is it one that most fully implements government policy, or one that empowers users and involves them in its management?

It is easy to reduce public expenditure on a service by transferring the costs to users or carers. But this does not reduce costs, it merely redistributes them. The transfer of a public service to outside contractors may appear to produce savings, but this may not lead to greater efficiency if the savings are made at the expense of lower standards of service and poorer pay and conditions of work for employees. The lowest bid in a system of competitive tendering may not be the best option.

There are also problems of measuring output and agreeing appropriate criteria for appraising services. What is the output of a home providing residential care for elderly people? There is always the danger that only the measurable will be taken into account. In a residential home, for example, the physical facilities are quantifiable, but they are less important than the quality of the human relationships that characterise the home. A great deal of ingenuity and effort is being put into devising performance indicators in a number of countries, but the results to date have not been notably successful. The question arises whether social services have any features that make judgement by ordinary commercial criteria inappropriate.

No apologies need be made for resurrecting Titmuss's (1967) refutation of the assumption that medical care had no characteristics which differentiated it from goods in the private market. Titmuss's argument for treating medical care differently from other goods rested on the high degree of uncertainty and unpredictability which characterises the consumption of medical care. He also stressed the lack of knowledge of consumers in this sphere, and their reliance on professional advice.

Lack of knowledge is particularly obvious in medical care, but it also affects other areas of social provision, as Glennerster (1992, pp.20–1) points out:

> Where a producer is making a standard product that can be tested comparisons are possible. What characterises most social services is their highly personal nature, and this makes simple, widely available measures of quality difficult to produce ... Individual consumers thus face a more difficult prospect operating in these kinds of market than the everyday high street shop. The reasons all have to do with limited and uncertain information.

Markets in health and welfare may create greater inequality in a variety of ways:

1 by excluding poor and disadvantaged people from its benefits;
2 by creating a two-tier service;
3 by affecting the distribution of services and enabling more prosperous areas to attract better and more resources.

There are ways of tempering these features of markets. For example, income-related cash benefits or service-specific vouchers could be paid to those who would otherwise be unable to participate in markets except on the most disadvantageous of terms.

Improved and more accessible sources of advice and information would also help, as would tighter consumer protection legislation. Regulation by statutory agencies – monitoring commercial providers and setting minimum standards – may reduce the possibility of exploitation, although regulation is extraordinarily difficult to enforce and can be costly. Regulation may be slightly easier when government enters into specific contracts with commercial providers to supply a particular service at a particular cost. If the firm fails to deliver, or if there are complaints from consumers, then the contract may not be renewed. This assumes, of course, that there are alternative suppliers, which may not always be the case.

Contracting out is one method by which the state financially supports private-market provision of health and welfare. Less formally, the state may pay fees for the use of services and facilities without the benefit of a contract. Other methods of state support include:

1 tax relief on the contributions to private pension schemes, mortgage repayments, private health insurance or school fees;
2 certain costs being borne by the state; in the UK, for example, most of the costs of training doctors, nurses, teachers and social workers

are met out of public expenditure with the private sector contributing very little.

Certain aspects of market ideology have permeated the public sector. The term 'quasi-markets', which has been applied to this process, suffers from a degree of imprecision, but includes any measures designed to introduce or extend competition in public services – competitive tendering, vouchers, internal markets and opting out of state control. Bartlett (1991, p.2) defines quasi-markets in the following way:

> In general terms, the quasi-markets revolution involves a process of separation of state finance from state provision of welfare services, alongside the introduction of competition in the provision of services between independent agencies. These agencies may be under private or public ownership, and may have profit or not-for-profit objectives, but are no longer to be under exclusive public control. The agencies involved are to operate systems of service delivery that involve the extension of public choice and competition between private, voluntary or public suppliers within a framework of rules and funding set out by the state.[2]

Conclusion

Over the last decade, markets have enjoyed a great deal of favourable publicity. Even committed socialists have come to accept the value of markets, and the countries of Central and Eastern Europe and the former Soviet Union have also now embraced the market system. Barry (1991, p.231) claims that 'One of the most striking features of the development of social science over the last decade has been the re-establishment of the intellectual respectability of the decentralized market exchange system as a social institution.' Later in the same paper he says that 'The market at the moment is on the threshold of a new era of intellectual popularity.' He attributes this not merely to changes in fashion, but to 'the observed failures of alternative social and economic arrangements' (p.241).

Taylor (1990, p.5) takes an entirely different view of the apparent popularity of markets. He suggests that 'It may be the international growth of consumerism as such which has achieved "popularity" rather than the fact that such consumerism is presently being fed, in many western societies, by "deregulated" free market institutions.' This echoes

---

2. This paper by Will Bartlett is one of a series produced by the School for Advanced Urban Studies, Bristol University, under the general title of *Studies in Decentralisation and Quasi-markets.*

Deacon's (Deacon et al., 1992, p.9) comment, referred to earlier in the chapter, that the 1989 revolutions in Eastern Europe were 'partly motivated by the wish of significant sections of the population to join in the fruits of Western capitalist consumerism'.

But the major debate is no longer about the relative merits of a market system as compared with a centrally planned system. The major questions now revolve around such issues as the most appropriate size and scope of the market, the degree of regulation that is thought to be desirable and the degree to which government ought to intervene to enhance certain groups' ability to participate in the market and modify market outcomes. These are by no means new concerns in social policy, but they have gained particular significance in the light of recent changes in both Western capitalist countries and in Central and Eastern Europe. Many of the issues concerning markets are of particular relevance in the area of health and welfare services, and the remainder of this book looks at the ways in which nine countries are approaching the problem.

References

Barry, N. (1991) 'Understanding the market', in Loney, M., Bocock, R., Clarke, J., Cochrane, A., Graham, P. and Wilson, M. (eds) (1991) *The State or the Market: Politics and Welfare in Contemporary Britain* (2nd edn), London, Sage, pp.231–41.

Bartlett, W. (1991) *Quasi-markets and Contracts: A Market and Hierarchies Perspective on NHS Reform*, Bristol, School for Advanced Urban Studies.

Buchanan, J.M. and Tullock, G. (1962) *The Calculus of Consent*, Ann Arbor, University of Michigan Press.

Dahrendorf, R. (1990) *Reflections on the Revolution in Europe*, London, Chatto and Windus.

Deacon, B., Castle-Kanerova, M., Manning, M., Millard, F., Orosz, E., Szalai, J. and Vidinova, A. (1992) *The New Eastern Europe: Social Policy Past, Present and Future*, London, Sage.

Downs, A. (1957) *An Economic Theory of Democracy*, New York, Harper and Row.

——— (1967) *Inside Bureaucracy*, Boston, Little, Brown.

Dunleavy, P. (1991) *Democracy, Bureaucracy and Public Choice*, Hemel Hempstead, Harvester Wheatsheaf.

Estrin, S. and Le Grand, J. (1989) 'Market socialism', in Le Grand, J. and Estrin, S. (eds) (1989) *Market Socialism*, Oxford, Clarendon Press, pp.1–24.

Estrin, S. and Winter, D. (1989) 'Planning in a socialist market economy', in Le Grand, J. and Estrin S. (eds) (1989) *Market Socialism*, Oxford,

Clarendon Press.

Gamble, A. (1987) *The Free Economy and the Strong State: The Politics of Thatcherism*, London, Macmillan.

Gilbert, N. (1983) *Capitalism and the Welfare State*, New Haven, Yale University Press.

Gilbert, N. and Gilbert, B. (1989) *The Enabling State*, New York, Oxford University Press.

Gladstone, F.J. (1979) *Voluntary Action in a Changing World*, London, Bedford Square Press.

Glennerster, H. (1992) *Paying for Welfare: The 1990s*, Hemel Hempstead, Harvester Wheatsheaf.

Glennerster, H. and Midgley, M. (eds) (1991) *The Radical Right and the Welfare State: An International Assessment*, Hemel Hempstead, Harvester Wheatsheaf.

Glenny, M. (1990) *The Re-birth of History*, Harmondsworth, Penguin.

Gray, J. (1989) *Liberalisms: Essays in Political Philosophy*, London, Routledge.

—— (1992) *The Moral Foundations of Market Institutions*, London, Institute of Economic Affairs Health and Welfare Unit.

Hadley, R. and Hatch, S. (1981) *Social Welfare and the Failure of the State*, London, George Allen and Unwin.

Hatch, S. (1980) *Outside the State*, London, Croom Helm.

Hayek, F.A. (1976) *Individualism and Economic Order*, London, Routledge and Kegan Paul.

Johnson, N. (1990) 'Problems for the mixed economy of welfare', in Ware, A. and Goodin, R.E. (eds) (1990) *Needs and Welfare*, London, Sage, pp.145–64.

King, D.S. (1987) *The New Right: Politics, Markets and Citizenship*, London, Macmillan.

Le Grand, J. (1991) *The Theory of Government Failure*, Bristol, School for Advanced Urban Studies.

Levacic, R. (1991) 'Markets and government: an overview', in Thompson, G., Frances, J., Levacic, R. and Mitchell, J. (eds) (1991) *Markets, Hierarchies and Networks*, London, Sage, pp.35–47.

McLean, I. (1987) *Public Choice: An Introduction*, Oxford, Blackwell.

Miller, D. (1989) 'Why markets?', in Le Grand, J. and Estrin, S. (eds) (1989) *Market Socialism*, Oxford, Clarendon Press, pp.25–49.

—— (1990) *Market, State and Community: Theoretical Foundations of Market Socialism*, Oxford, Clarendon Press.

Mishra, R. (1984) *The Welfare State in Crisis*, Brighton, Wheatsheaf Books.

Niskanen, W.A. (1971) *Bureaucracy and Representative Government* Chicago, Aldine-Atherton.

—— (1978) 'Competition among government bureaus', in Buchanan, J.M. (ed.) (1978) *The Economics of Politics*, London, Institute of Economic Affairs.

Novak, M. (1991) *The Spirit of Democratic Capitalism*, Lanham, Maryland, Madison Books and London, The Institute of Economic Affairs Health and Welfare Unit.

Plant, R. (1992) 'Autonomy, social rights and distributive justice', in Gray, J. (1992) *The Moral Foundations of Market Institutions*, London, Institute of Economic Affairs Health and Welfare Unit, pp.119–41.

Polanyi, M. (1951) *The Logic of Liberty*, Chicago, University of Chicago Press.

Shackle, G.L.S. (1972) *Epistemics and Economics: A Critique of Economic Doctrines*, Cambridge, Cambridge University Press.

Stoesz, D. and Midgley, J. (1991) 'The radical right and the welfare state', in Glennerster, H. and Midgley, J. (eds) (1991) *The Radical Right and the Welfare State: An International Assessment*, Hemel Hempstead, Harvester Wheatsheaf, pp.24–42.

Szalai, J, and Orosz, E. (1992) 'Social Policy in Hungary', in Deacon, B. et al. (1992) *The New Eastern Europe: Social Policy Past Present and Future*, London, Sage.

Taylor, I. (ed.) (1990) *The Social Effects of Free Market Policies*, Hemel Hempstead, Harvester Wheatsheaf.

Titmuss, R.M. (1967) *Choice and the Welfare State*, London, Fabian Society.

—— (1973) *The Gift Relationship*, Harmondsworth, Penguin.

Walker, A. (1984) *Social Planning: A Strategy for Socialist Welfare*, Oxford, Blackwell.

Ware, A. (1990) 'Meeting needs through voluntary action: Does market society corrode altruism?', in Ware, A. and Goodin, R.E. (eds) (1990) *Needs and Welfare*, London, Sage, pp.185–207.

Wolf, C. (1988) *Markets or Governments?*, Cambridge, Mass., Massachusetts Institute of Technology Press.

–2–

The United Kingdom
Norman Johnson

In the period following the Second World War there was a measure of cross-party agreement that the state had a responsibility for meeting the needs of its citizens. In spite of differences between the two main political parties over the *scale* of state activity, a stable welfare mix was established in which the state became a major provider of health and welfare services. These developments were by no means confined to the UK, as Glennerster and Midgley (1991, p.ix) explain:

> Although there are significant differences in the degree to which governments have allocated resources to the social services, or have managed to meet the needs of its citizens, state involvement in welfare has been ubiquitous and internationally accepted. Despite ideological differences between various political parties and governments, thinking about social welfare during the post-war era was dominated by what has been described as a 'welfare consensus', forged by the supporters of both the political right and left , which institutionalized the idea of government intervention in social affairs.

In the UK, the changes introduced by the Labour government between 1945 and 1950 were not, as some had feared, overturned by the Conservatives when they took office in 1951. Nevertheless, Glennerster (1990) is probably right in characterising the period from 1951 to 1958 as a period of retrenchment, in which the Conservative government sought to reassert individualistic values and move away from the universalist model of social policy. The attempt to restrict public spending was only partially successful, however, and at the end of the 1950s the period of retrenchment gave way to what Glennerster calls the period of expansion and convergence, which lasted until about 1970. The term 'welfare consensus' most closely fits this period, in which there seemed to be a much greater degree of agreement about the aims of the Welfare State, and there was considerable expansion in social spending, first under a Conservative administration, and from 1964 under a Labour government. In 1970 the Conservative Party was again returned to power, and, although it increased spending on health and education, it sought to introduce a greater degree of selectivity.

Despite these shifts in policy, the state-dominated welfare mix persisted throughout the 1950s and 1960s and into the early 1970s, and, although the degree of consensus may have been exaggerated, as both Taylor-Gooby (1985) and Glennerster (1990) claim, the more extreme criticisms of the principle of state-provided welfare from the radical right went largely unheeded until the mid-1970s.[1] Before that time, the critics from both the marxist left and the radical right were at the margins of political debate and had little significant influence.

A series of events combined to change this position, leading in the 1980s to a much more prominent role for the radical right in UK politics. The first jolt came in 1973 with the oil crisis and the ensuing world economic recession. A turning point came in 1976: with the UK economy in deep crisis the International Monetary Fund was brought in. The IMF, in return for its assistance, extracted an undertaking from the Labour government to restrict public expenditure. In fact, Mr Healey, the Chancellor of the Exchequer, had already begun the process of imposing greater financial restraint in the public sector before the IMF came into the picture. As a proportion of gross domestic product (GDP), public expenditure fell from 49 per cent in 1975 to 42 per cent in 1977; in the following year, however, the upward trend was re-established. The UK's economic position did not markedly improve, and in the winter of 1978–9 a series of strikes led to further economic disruption and the government seemed to have lost control. In 1979 came the general election.

In the meantime, Mrs Thatcher had assumed the leadership of the Conservative Party in 1975. She was already convinced of the wisdom of the radical right's prescriptions for the UK, and she immediately set about the task of moving her party to the right. Her election victory in 1979 gave her the opportunity to give effect to the ideas she had been pressing upon her party for the past four years.

Walker (1990, p.29) says of the period after 1979:

> The free market ideology of the New Right has been firmly entrenched in government in Britain for the last decade. The Conservative administration headed by Mrs Thatcher . . . has been the most ideologically committed government since the 1945–50 Labour Government . . . One of the chief targets for the Government's hostility has been the welfare state, because it represents the embodiment of the extended state created and legitimized by social democracy.

---

1. The term 'radical right' is used in this chapter in preference to 'new right'. Different writers attach a variety of interpretations to the two terms, but for most purposes they can be regarded as being interchangeable.

Gamble (1987) sees Thatcherism as an attempt to clear the way for the replacement of the already crumbling social democratic consensus with a new consensus based on a free economy and a strong state.

The Conservative governments of the 1980s used a variety of strategies in their attempts to privatise health and welfare provision. The most direct method was through the sale of assets; an obvious example has been the mandatory sale of council houses, either individually or of whole estates.

A second strategy was the contracting out of services, or parts of them, to independent providers – either for-profit or non-profit. Compulsory competitive tendering became a prominent feature of the National Health Service and several areas of local government during the 1980s.

The balance between public and private provision can be changed by a variety of financial measures. Prominent among these is the use of tax allowances. There are several examples in the UK:

1 tax relief on mortgage interest payments;
2 tax concessions on contributions to private pension schemes;
3 corporation tax relief on employers' contributions to private health insurance schemes, and certain concessions to members of private schemes who are over 60 or earning below a particular amount.

There are also instances of direct subsidies: the discounts to purchasers of council houses is one example, and the use of social security payments to meet the fees for residential accommodation for older people is another.

The final financial measure used during the 1980s was the increase in charges in the public sector. Obviously, if charges are introduced or increased in the public sector, the comparative cost of using the private sector is reduced. Massively increased prescription charges, the introduction of ophthalmic and dental consultation charges, increased public sector rents and increased charges for meals-on-wheels and home helps all had the effect of increasing the attractiveness of the private market sector.

An even more effective way of achieving the same result is to restrict the development or reduce the quality of public provision. Taylor-Gooby (1991) has identified great support among the general public for the National Health Service, combined with some dissatisfaction with the standards of service. So far this has not resulted in an exodus from the NHS, but continued under-funding could have this effect. Another illustration may be drawn from the personal social services: lack of adequate local authority community care services may persuade people to make their own private arrangements or to seek residential care which is increasingly dominated by the private sector.

A rather more indirect process of denigrating public services was also apparent in the UK during the 1980s. As Deakin and Wright (1990, pp. 1–2) observe:

> the Right has found it possible to launch a major ideological assault on the public provision of services and to cut, deregulate, privatize, and market them in the vocabulary of populist rhetoric. It has been possible to appeal to, and to nourish, an image of public services as bleak, unresponsive, and inefficient bureaucracies and to contrast them unfavourably with the private sector in these respects.

Johnson (1990) relates this to consumption sector theory, which holds that the main cleavages in UK society, cutting across class divisions, are based upon consumption patterns. Of particular significance is the distinction between those who obtain goods and services through the private market and those who are forced to rely on public services. Furthermore:

> the split between the private and the public sectors extends beyond consumption into employment, so that the use of private services and employment in the private sector are perceived as status enhancing, while the consumption of public sector goods and services and public-sector employment are perceived as stigmatising. (p.197)

Mrs Thatcher's attempts to control public expenditure met with little success in the early years of her administration. In 1982 public expenditure constituted 47 per cent of GDP – the highest level since the mid-1970s. Although there was a slight decline in the following two years, significant reductions did not occur until 1985. By 1988, however, public expenditure had fallen to 37.8 per cent of GDP, which was the lowest level since 1966. There were slight rises in 1989 and 1990, and in 1991 public expenditure was 40 per cent of GDP (Central Statistical Office, 1991, 1992, 1993).[2] These figures have to be set against what has been happening to the GDP itself. Between 1979 and 1981 the GDP fell by about 3 per cent. There were rises in GDP throughout the 1980s, the most substantial (4.5 per cent) occurring between 1987 and 1988. There was a slowing down in the rate of increase in 1989, and in 1990 growth amounted to slightly less than 1 per cent. In 1991, GDP declined by 2.4 per cent (Central Statistical Office, 1990, 1991, 1992, 1993).

Having sketched in the background to private market developments in the UK, we now turn to analysing services in more detail. The areas to be covered include health services, the personal social services, housing and pensions.

---

2. Public expenditure figures take account of the proceeds of privatisation.

Health Services

The National Health Service (NHS) occupies a particular place in the affections of the UK public. This explains the frequent assertion of Conservative Party leaders that the health service is safe in their hands. Despite this assurance, the government's approval of the private medical sector was made very plain, and they took practical steps to encourage it.

There are several issues to be addressed: compulsory competitive tendering; private practice within the NHS; private practice in the independent sector, and the likely effects on private medicine of the changes currently being implemented in the NHS under the National Health Service and Community Care Act of 1990.

Compulsory Competitive Tendering

'Competitive tendering' refers to putting contracts for non-clinical services out to tender, and, although this sort of contracting out was not new, it flourished in the enterprise culture of the 1980s. As Ascher (1987, pp.22 and 25) says:

> The popularity of contracting out as an alternative means of public sector service delivery grew dramatically between 1980 and 1986 in Britain . . . In 1978, the year before the Conservatives took power, the presence of contractors in both local government and the health service went virtually unnoticed. Very few contractors thought that public sector work would grow significantly, and none would have predicted the explosion that was about to occur.

The Conservatives encouraged contracting out in the NHS, but the first administration relied upon exhortation. When by 1983 this had clearly failed, they turned to compulsion. Health authorities were now required to invite tenders for cleaning, catering and laundry services. In-house bids would be considered alongside those from outside contractors.

Ascher (1987, pp.190–1) reports that 23.7 per cent of the contracts completed by the end of 1985 were awarded to external companies, who won 30 per cent of cleaning contracts, 25 per cent of laundry contracts and 5.5 per cent of catering contracts. Since 1985, in-house dominance has increased; the Department of Health (1989a, p.69) claims that, in the first five years of compulsory tendering, '85 per cent of contracts were won in-house, despite the keen competition.' Although, as one would expect, the Department of Health is anxious to stress the amount of competition in the tendering process, other evidence suggests that there is sometimes a shortage of outside bids. Milne (1987), for example, found that 63 per cent of a small sample of thirty-two contracts had no outside submissions when tenders were invited. There is a particular shortage of companies willing to bid for catering contracts.

Estimates of the savings as a result of tendering vary considerably and have to be treated with caution. The Department of Health (1989a) puts the savings at 17 per cent, whereas Milne (1987) identifies savings of one-third or more. Milne, however, found that in a majority of contracts, reductions in total expenditure resulted from changes in specification – a reduced amount of work being done and a lower level of service provided. Moreover, managers sometimes took the opportunity to reallocate work, so that nurses, for example, might be required to carry out work formerly done by ancillary staff.

This raises the question of the effect of tendering on working conditions. An inter-departmental review of tendering in central government (Treasury, 1986, p.33) was surprisingly blunt about this:

> Most of the savings from contracting out arise because contractors offer poorer conditions of employment . . . they eliminate costly bonus schemes and overtime working, provide little if any sick pay, and avoid national insurance payments by means of more part-time working.

Although this statement does not relate specifically to the NHS, the position in the health service is not dissimilar. Redundancies are also more likely, and many contractors will only employ non-union labour.

Private Practice Within the NHS

There has been a great deal of controversy surrounding the issue of pay beds, which the last Labour government had planned to phase out, establishing a Health Services Board to supervise the process. Between 1974 and 1979 the number of pay beds declined from about 4,500 to under 3,000. The new Conservative government sought to reverse this trend, and proceeded to abolish the Health Services Board under the Health Services Act of 1980. This resulted in a small increase in the number of pay beds, which stood at 3,138 in 1991 (Central Statistical Office, 1991, 1992, 1993). Private practice within the NHS is not restricted to in-patient treatment, and there has been a substantial increase in the number of out-patient consultations: between 1979 and 1986 the number of consultations increased from 132,400 to 261,600, an increase of 97 per cent (Central Statistical Office, 1990).

Further encouragement of private practice came about through changes to consultants' contracts in 1980. Full-time consultants were for the first time allowed to engage in private practice, provided that they did not earn more than 10 per cent of gross income from that source. Maximum part-time consultants could engage in unrestricted private practice provided they forfeited one-eleventh of their NHS salaries; formerly two-elevenths of salary had to be foregone in return for unrestricted opportunities for private practice.

Throughout most of the 1980s NHS income from private treatment fell in real terms, largely as a result of increased competition from private hospitals and clinics. In 1989, however, NHS income from private patients increased by 19 per cent, compared with only a 15 per cent increase in non-NHS hospitals and clinics. In the following year the position was again reversed, as the independent hospitals increased their income by 17 per cent, whereas the NHS private income went up by 14 per cent. In 1993, £1,114 million was spent on treatment in the independent hospitals, compared with £172 million on private treatment in NHS hospitals (Laing and Buisson, 1994).[3]

There is undoubtedly potential for the expansion of private income in the NHS, and the Health and Medicines Act of 1988 sought to encourage entrepreneurial activity by extending health authorities' freedom to earn income from treating private patients. So far this has led to the establishment and refurbishment of dedicated pay bed units, of which there are currently seventy – twenty of them being in Greater London. All of these are owned by health authorities, but five of the more recent ones are managed by private operators.

Partnership arrangements are also a way in which the NHS can generate income from private treatment. In return for a long lease of a ward or unit or of adjacent land on which to build private facilities, a private operator will invest capital and make regular, fixed payments to the health authority. Usually the independent partner will buy ancillary services from the health authority. However, one of the leaders in this field, Bioplan Ltd, ran into severe financial difficulties, and this could discourage others contemplating setting up partnerships.

Private Practice in the Independent Sector

Private health care during the 1980s was one of the few sectors of business to show consistent growth. In some years the growth was spectacular: in both 1980 and 1981, for example, expenditure in real terms grew by 30 per cent. The recession has had an impact, however, bringing the growth in real terms down to 6 per cent between 1989 and 1990.

---

3. The statistics in this paragraph and the ones which follow in this section and the next are mainly taken from Laing and Buisson (1994).

In 1979 there were 150 independent acute hospitals in the United Kingdom, with 6,671 beds overall. By December 1993, the number of hospitals had increased to 224, with 11,391 beds. The major expansion, however, occurred in the early 1980s: between 1980 and 1984 there was a net increase of fifty hospitals and 3,396 beds; between 1985 and the end of 1993 there was a net increase of twenty-four in the number of hospitals, and an additional 1,324 beds (Health Care Information Services, 1994).

Until the late 1980s the expansion of private health facilities was led by US companies, which controlled 50 per cent of the for-profit sector and 25 per cent of the entire independent sector by 1987. Most of the US for-profit hospital companies have now left the UK for more profitable outlets, or they have been taken over by European competitors; Humana is the sole survivor. The UK hospital market is now dominated by European companies, the biggest of which in terms of operating revenue is the French company, Compagnie Générale des Eaux. Foreign interests control 34.7 per cent of the UK hospital market. Another change is the greater dominance of the for-profit hospitals as a proportion of the total independent sector: in 1979, for-profit groups provided 41 per cent of the beds in the independent sector, but by January 1994 their share had increased to 62 per cent (Health Care Information Services, 1994).

The initial surge in private health care in the early 1980s was concentrated in the hospital sector, but more recently a small number of companies have begun to operate in the primary health care sector. There has also been a modest growth in private psychiatric care, reflecting a greater willingness on the part of medical insurance companies to provide cover for this type of care.

Much of the development of private medicine has been associated with an expansion of private medical insurance. Taking the figures relating to the three major provident insurers, who currently have a joint market share of 84 per cent,[4] the number of subscribers more than doubled between 1979 and 1990, increasing from 1.3 million to 2.7 million. The number of people insured almost doubled in the same period, increasing from 2.8 million to 5.4 million. Laing and Buisson (1994) say that in 1993 there were twenty-four private medical insurance companies with a combined total of 3.3 million policies covering 6.6 million people – 11.3 per cent of the UK population. The recession, combined with increased claims and higher medical bills, has brought an end to the years of very rapid expansion. Greatly reduced profitability between 1990 and 1993 has discouraged potential new entrants among insurance companies, and

4. The market share of 'the big three' has fallen in recent years: in 1985 it was 91 per cent.

those already operating in this area are imposing 'stringent new rules for medical treatment' under which 'subscribers must now get approval from their insurers before starting treatment' (Ferriman, 1992). The number of subscribers is now virtually static.

Most of the growth in private medical insurance has been in policies arranged by companies on behalf of their employees: according to Laing and Buisson (1994), 60 per cent of policies were purchased by companies in 1993, although in a minority of cases the company did not meet the full cost of the subscription. Laing and Buisson (1994), using data collected in the General Household Survey, show that private medical insurance is mainly the preserve of the top two socio-economic groups, of whom 27 per cent and 23 per cent respectively are covered by private medical insurance, compared with only 3 per cent of skilled manual workers, 2 per cent of semi-skilled manual workers, and 1 per cent of unskilled manual workers.

The NHS and Community Care Act

The reforms implemented under the NHS and Community Care Act of 1990 are likely to have the effect of encouraging private health care. Individual hospitals, while remaining in the NHS, have been given the opportunity to become independent of the district health authorities by forming self-governing Hospital Trusts, controlling their own funds and appointing their own staff. In June 1993 there were 292 trusts, and 145 under consideration for trust status in April 1994. The trusts are expected to compete for contracts with private and conventional NHS hospitals, and they have been encouraged to enter into joint arrangements with private companies and to extend contracting out by means of competitive tendering. At the same time, the slimmed-down district health authorities, in securing services for their populations, were encouraged to shop around for the best deal and to make use of private facilities wherever this seemed appropriate. The private health providers expected to gain considerably from these new arrangements, especially from picking up business from the health authorities. It appears, however, that health authorities have so far been reluctant to enter into contracts with private companies. An unnamed author in *Laing's Review* (Laing and Buisson, 1994, p.107) states: 'most health authorities have probably not even considered the option of contracting with independent providers for mainstream services.'

Another aspect of the NHS reforms also has the potential to benefit private health care providers. General practices of a minimum size (a list containing 7,000 patients in April 1992) could manage their own budgets, buying services for their patients from suppliers of the doctors' choosing.

The same unnamed author in *Laing's Review* (Laing and Buisson, 1992, p.81) says that 'in the first months after April 1991 many of the more entrepreneurial GP fundholders displayed a much greater readiness than health authorities to consider radically new options for the supply of at least some of their acute healthcare services.' It was reported in the *Guardian* on 25 March 1992 that some fundholding family doctors were spending up to 10 per cent of their budgets in paying for patients to be treated in private hospitals, although this practice was by no means universal among fundholders.

The picture in health services in the UK is one of rapid growth of private medicine during the 1980s, but much slower growth in the early years of the 1990s. It may be that this slower rate of growth is simply a consequence of the recession, and that the former buoyancy of the private sector will re-establish itself once the promised economic recovery occurs.

Personal Social Services

In the UK, responsibility for the provision of personal social services rests with local authorities, the kind of authority which has this responsibility varying from one part of the country to another. Local authority social services departments are responsible for the provision of a range of services, principally for children, older people and disabled people. In the interests of brevity, this section will concentrate mainly on older people, but references to other client groups will be made as appropriate. It is in services for older people that markets have made the greatest inroads. Demographic trends, with increasing proportions in the population of people aged 75 and over and aged 85 and over, will mean an increase in the proportion of older people requiring some form of support, and an expanding market for commercial suppliers.

Residential Care

Although government policy over several decades has expressed a strong preference for community as opposed to institutional care, the necessary resources have never been made available. Mainly for this reason, but also because some people prefer it, residential care has remained an important element in the provision of services for elderly people.

Private residential and nursing homes for older people experienced spectacular growth during the 1980s. In 1980, local authorities owned 45.8 per cent of all residential homes for older people and chronically sick and physically disabled people, and provided 62.7 per cent of the places; the private sector owned 34.7 per cent of the homes, contributing

17.4 per cent of the places, and the voluntary sector owned 19.5 per cent of the homes, and provided 19.9 per cent of the places. By 1993 the picture had changed dramatically: local authorities owned only 18.3 per cent of the homes, providing 31 per cent of the places; private homes constituted 68.44 per cent of the total, providing 53 per cent of the places, and the voluntary sector owned 13 per cent of the homes, contributing 16 per cent of the places. Between 1980 and 1993 the number of places in local authority residential homes fell, while the number of places in private homes more than quadrupled.

Until 1987 the figures for nursing home places combined private and voluntary provision: in 1980 the combined total was 26,900, and by 1986 this had risen to 47,900. The figures for later years indicate where the main expansion had taken place: in 1993, private nursing homes provided 168,200 places, compared with 15,100 in voluntary homes and 62,100 in NHS establishments.

The expansion of private provision came about through the mushrooming of small, usually family, businesses. However, in the last two or three years, some local authorities have sold their residential homes to private contractors, and this process is continuing. Another noticeable trend is the entry into the residential care market – especially nursing homes – of large companies with a diverse range of interests.

The rapid development of private residential and nursing homes could not have occurred in the absence of two sets of favourable circumstances. The first was the willingness on the part of banks and other financial institutions to finance the operation, and the second was the massive State subsidy in the form of income support payments. In 1979 the Department of Health and Social Security (DHSS) contributed £10 million to the fees paid by residents in private and voluntary homes, but by 1991 the bill had risen to almost £1.9 billion. Given the overwhelming dominance of private homes within the independent sector, the vast bulk of this money must have gone to private operators. In April 1992 the Department of Social Security (DSS) limits for residents in residential homes ranged from £175 a week for an elderly person who is not heavily dependent to £230 a week for someone who is physically disabled and below pension age. The limits for nursing homes were higher, ranging from £270 a week for an elderly person who is not very dependent to £305 a week for a physically disabled person below pension age. Those running the homes have frequently claimed that the amounts are inadequate, and residents in some instances are being asked to make up the difference between benefits and fees, and sometimes to pay for extras, which may include medical dressings, diabetic diets, nursing care during illness, chiropody and physiotherapy. In January 1994, the average weekly fee in private nursing homes was £319; in residential homes it was £227 (Laing and

Buisson, 1994).

The number of beds has been increasing at a much faster rate than would appear to be justified by demographic factors alone, and there is a danger of overcapacity. As the profitability of private residential care becomes less assured, the banks are now much less ready to give financial support. In April 1993, responsibility for paying for the care element in residential provision passed from the DSS to local authorities; this certainly introduced an added degree of uncertainty into the financing of private care. As one commentator notes, the new arrangements may actively discourage local authority provision:

> In order to prevent empire building by local authorities, the government has stated that local authorities will have to pay for the *full* cost of accommodating people in their own council run residential homes – but only the care element of costs for people they support in private or voluntary homes. Thus there will be a very strong incentive for local authorities to limit their own care home provision to the sort of special needs that are not met by the independent sector. (Laing and Buisson, 1992, p.167)

It is claimed that this will strengthen a trend already noted, of local authorities selling off their residential homes.

In the much longer term, several insurance companies and the major provident associations have introduced, or are planning to introduce, policies designed to cover fees for residential or nursing home accommodation or for private nursing. This development is in its infancy at present, and its full effects will not be felt for some years.

Residential care is not restricted to older people or to people who are physically disabled. There have been less substantial incursions of the private sector into other spheres. For example, a small number of private operators provide residential accommodation for people who are mentally ill or mentally handicapped. Private nursing home provision in the mental health field is still relatively undeveloped. There are also a few community homes for children and young people in the private sector.

Community Care

Social work in its several forms is the central activity of social services departments, although it is not their exclusive preserve. Voluntary associations have long employed professional social workers – the NSPCC and Barnardos are two examples of several organisations working in the area of child care and child protection. Profit-oriented agencies in social work are much less common, but there were some developments in this direction during the 1980s, and the new community care arrangements could lead to the employment of social workers by companies specialising in the field of domiciliary care.

Private consultants and trainers are more numerous than they were in the 1970s. The Children Act of 1989 gave rise to a deluge of training courses and training packs, and there are training companies specialising in such areas as race awareness and anti-discriminatory practice. There are consultants in every area of social work, but probably the best-known and most numerous are to be found in child abuse. Social work careers consultants advertise in the professional weeklies and, less grandly, there are employment agencies offering advice on full-time or part-time employment, and providing temporary workers and locums.

Most of these initiatives, however, are relatively small-scale, and in the absence of research it is difficult to assess their significance. Much more important in the long term are the new community care arrangements that came into effect in April 1993.

A great deal has been written about the Griffiths Report (1988) and the White Paper, *Caring for People* (Department of Health, 1989b), which followed it. Our concern is a fairly restricted one. Are the changes implemented in 1993 likely to lead to a more significant role for the market?

The new arrangements are based on a separation of roles into purchasers/commissioners on the one side and providers on the other. Local authority social services departments remain the lead organisations in community care, responsible for assessing needs in their areas and co-ordinating the response. They also control their community care budgets. They are to ensure that needs are met, but they are not obliged to directly *provide* services: they are expected to be enablers rather than providers, although provision, especially in the initial phases, is not ruled out. An implementation document prepared by the Social Services Inspectorate sums up the position:

> In future, SSDs will be responsible for identifying the needs of the population they serve and publishing a plan for the provision of community care services in their area. They will decide objectives and priorities; secure the delivery of services by developing their purchasing and contracting role as well as by acting as direct providers; and ensure overall quality and value for money. (Department of Health, 1991, p.4)

The Department of Health emphasises that the reorganisation of community care is intended to increase consumer choice. It is also plain, however, that privatisation lies at the heart of the proposals. Local authorities are to enter into contracts with commercial and voluntary providers. Where no such suppliers exist, the authorities are required to take steps to encourage their development. It was the shortage and uneven distribution of independent suppliers of non-residential care services that persuaded the government to stop short of compulsory competitive tendering. This may remain as a long-term aim, and for the present the government intends to monitor local authorities' progress in fostering provision by private companies and voluntary agencies through the annually updated three-year plans which the local authorities are required to produce for the Secretary of State's approval. The White Paper made this explicit:

> Social services authorities will be expected to make clear in their community care plans what steps they will be taking to make increased use of non-statutory service providers or, where such providers are not currently available, how they propose to stimulate such activity. In particular, they should consider how they will encourage diversification into the non-residential care sector. (Department of Health, 1989b, p.23)

The Secretary of State can refuse to endorse plans that, in his or her view, make insufficient use of independent suppliers.

It is not entirely clear how contracting will increase choice for consumers unless contracts are entered into for the provision of a particular service by a variety of suppliers. Furthermore, access to services will be mediated through social workers acting as care managers, who will devise packages of care for individual clients. If the local authority has entered into a contract with a particular supplier for certain services, then the care manager would be expected to use those services if he or she judges them to be necessary. The Social Services Inspectorate identifies the role of care managers in developing a mixed economy of care:

> As assessors and arrangers of service care managers have an important role to play in the promotion of a mixed economy of care. They should in effect act as brokers for services across the statutory and independent sectors. The major responsibility of care managers will be planning and purchasing individual care packages rather than direct service provisions. (Department of Health, 1991, p.8)

Although the profits in domiciliary care are unlikely to be astronomical, the prospects are sufficiently bright in some areas to have already stimulated the emergence of companies trading in domiciliary care – some from a base in the residential sector. The penetration of these companies is at present very slight and patchy, but at one time the same might have been said about residential care. Most of the current firms offer a variety of services, including home helps, the cooking of meals in the home, nursing auxiliaries and care attendants, and home nursing. Commercial alarm systems are already widely available, there is a large but highly informal market in domestic help, and other possibilities include day centres and meals-on-wheels.

At present the recession may be holding back the full development of commercial services, and it may be that some local authorities prefer to enter into contracts with non-profit rather than for-profit agencies. Local authorities have now published their community care plans, but it will be some years before a considered assessment will be possible. If past experience is anything to go by, community care plans tend to be an expression of hope rather than a description of what can realistically be achieved.

An important element in community care, sometimes forgotten in the discussion of care managers and contracts, is adequate housing at prices people can afford to pay. It is to housing that we now turn.

Housing

One of the distinguishing characteristics of the UK housing tenure is the large number of houses in public ownership – council houses built and owned by local authorities. There have been some long-term changes in housing tenure, the most striking feature of which has been a huge increase in owner-occupation and a marked reduction in privately rented housing. The proportion of the housing stock in owner-occupation increased from 29 per cent in 1951 to 43 per cent in 1961 and to 68 per cent in 1992. The proportion of housing that is rented from private land-lords has been declining since the turn of the century, when 95 per cent of dwellings were in this form of tenure: currently, the proportion is about 10 per cent. The proportion of housing rented from local authorities or new towns increased until 1979, when it reached 32 per cent, but then fell back during the 1980s, standing at 21 per cent in 1992. The number of dwellings owned by local authorities fell from 6.7 million dwellings in 1979 to 5.3 million dwellings in 1990. Public sector house-building has now almost ceased: between 1961 and 1970, local authorities and new towns completed an annual average of 161,000 dwellings, whereas in 1992 only 5,000 were completed (Central Statistical Office, 1992, 1993, 1994).

Since 1980 the government has been determined to privatise council housing. The Housing Act of 1980 required local authorities to sell their houses to any tenant who wished to purchase. The right-to-buy policy gave tenants of at least three years' standing the opportunity to buy their houses at a discount of 33 per cent after three years, rising to 50 per cent after 20 years. In 1984 the maximum discount was raised to 60 per cent and the qualifying period was reduced from three years to two. In 1987 the maximum discount on flats was raised to 70 per cent. In the summer of 1992 the government announced yet another scheme to encourage council tenants to buy their houses: this is the rent-to-mortgage scheme, under which tenants are entitled to the same discounts as under the standard scheme but continue to pay the same rent, which is treated like a mortgage.

By 1990 over 1.5 million local authority and new town dwellings had been sold, but by then sales had dipped sharply due to stagnation in the housing market generally, and continually rising unemployment. In 1992, 65,000 houses were sold as compared with 200,000 in 1982. Falling unemployment since 1993 has done nothing to revive sales. Two pieces of research (Forrest and Murie, 1984; Kerr, 1988) showed that it was the better properties with gardens that had been sold. Those with any history of rent arrears were denied the right to buy, and so purchasers were concentrated among the better-off. As the better-off tenants buy their houses, the proportion of poor, unemployed people in council housing increases and polarisation occurs. Forrest and Murie (1988, p.83) claim that 'The public housing sector is well on the way to becoming an unambiguously residual, second class form of housing provision serving some of the poorest sections of the population.' In spite of this change in the social composition of council tenants, rents have risen steeply in the last two years, and this has contributed to an increased number of rent arrears. A report published in 1990 indicated that 16 per cent of tenants, more than a million households, were in arrears with their rents (Berthoud and Kempson, 1990).

The government is continuing to encourage people to buy their council houses in the face of mounting repossessions and mortgage arrears. In 1991, repossessions reached an all-time record of 75,540. Although the number of repossessions fell to 68,540 in 1992, Janet Ford (1992) reports that in the first three months of the same year homes were being repossessed at the rate of 144 a day. At the end of 1992, the Council of Mortgage Lenders reported record numbers of borrowers at least six months behind with their mortgage repayments – 352,050.

Local authorities lost houses under two provisions of the Housing Act of 1988. The first of these, known as 'tenants' choice', allows for the transfer of whole housing estates to either private landlords, housing associations or tenants' co-operatives. Tenants are allowed to vote on the change of landlord in a system which counts abstentions as 'yes' votes. Most of the initiatives for change have come not from tenants, as the government had hoped, but from prospective landlords. The second provision allowed for the establishment of a small number of Housing Action Trusts, which take over run-down estates from local authorities. The trust becomes responsible for managing the estate, and particularly for improving the housing and the environment. After five years the trusts will be disbanded and the houses disposed of to new landlords, who could be a private landlord or company, a housing association or a co-operative.

These changes have been taking place against a backdrop of rising homelessness. The number of homeless households in the UK more than doubled between 1979 – when 57,000 households were homeless – and 1987, when the number of homeless households reached 118,000. In 1992 the number rose to 167,000. A hidden form of privatisation occurs as some families (13,000 in 1991) are accommodated by local authorities in private bed and breakfast establishments, and public funds are used to pay the rents. Fortunately, however, the number in bed and breakfast fell by 40 per cent in 1992.

Housing in the UK has undergone considerable change since 1979. When the combined effects of the reduction in building, the sale of council houses, the transfer of tenancies and the introduction of Housing Action Trusts are considered, the diminution of public sector housing is seen to be substantial.

Pensions

The current UK retirement pension scheme came into being in 1978, with all-party agreement, under the Social Security Act of 1975. The Act provided for retirement pensions comprising two elements: a basic flat-rate state pension and a State Earnings-Related Pension Scheme (SERPS). Contributors would receive from SERPS 25 per cent of their average revalued earnings for the twenty years when their earnings were highest. Clearly, the scheme would not become fully operative until 1998, since that was the date by which the first entrants to the scheme would have completed twenty years. Occupational pension schemes which fulfilled certain conditions could contract out of the earnings-related element of the State scheme. Contracted-out employees paid lower National Insurance contributions – in effect a rebate of 5.4 per cent. In 1990, 60 per cent of employees were members of occupational schemes, but there were big differences among socio-economic groups: 77 per cent of the intermediate non-manual group were members of employers' pension schemes, and the professional group achieved only one percentage point less, but only 43 per cent of unskilled manual workers belonged to an occupational scheme (Central Statistical Office, 1993). Since most non-manual jobs carry occupational pensions, and many self-employed professionals take out private pensions, the majority of people on SERPS are manual workers.

The government undertook a major review of social security in 1984, the results of its deliberations being published in Green Paper form in June 1985, and six months later in White Paper form. The Social Security Act of 1986 gave legislative form to the proposals. Our concern is with the effects of all this activity on retirement pensions.

The government was greatly concerned about the cost of SERPS, and recommended the abolition of the scheme in the Green Paper. The outcry was so great, however, that they had to withdraw the proposal and settle for considerable modification of the scheme, reducing its scope, rather than complete abolition. The changes were designed to make SERPS less expensive and, crucially, less attractive; they were to begin to come into effect in 1999 and be phased in over the following ten years.

The scheme is being changed for the worse in three ways. First, calculation of pension will in future be based on a lifetime's earnings, rather than the twenty years when earnings were highest. Second, the amount paid will be 20 per cent of average earnings, rather than 25 per cent. Third, widows will be entitled to only half of their husband's pension rights, rather than the whole of them as at present.

One of the objectives of the changes was to make private pensions relatively more attractive. The government, however, decided that positive inducements might also be required to achieve a switch from state to private pensions. They took two steps. First, the National Insurance rebate for those contracted out of the state scheme was increased from 5.4 per cent to 5.8 per cent. Second, for five years the Department of Social Security would add a further 2 per cent to the employee's own contributions to a personal private pension. The same subsidy was also available to people transferring from occupational to private pensions.

The incentives to transfer from SERPS to personal private pensions were rather more effective than the government had ever anticipated. The expectation had been that between 500,000 and 1.5 million people would make the switch, but nearly 5 million did so, and this considerably inflated the cost to the Exchequer. Joanna Slaughter (1992) points out the irony in this:

> The encouragement of private pensions was intended to reduce the future cost of SERPS, but by 1993 the National Insurance Fund's bill for the exodus from the scheme will be £9 billion, while the corresponding saving on future SERPS benefits will be only £3 billion.

The rebate/subsidy scheme was due to come to an end in April 1993, and it was feared that people over thirty would then revert to SERPS. The incentives were heavily biased in favour of young people, whose premiums for a personal pension were much lower than those payable by older workers. In order to encourage older workers to continue with their personal pensions, the Social Security Secretary announced in February 1992 that, as from April 1993, people over thirty years of age would receive an annual rebate of 1 per cent from their National Insurance contributions for a period of five years. This may be the first step in replacing a flat-rate rebate with an age-related one.

Conclusion

The push towards market provision of health and welfare services during the 1980s was not simply the work of Mrs Thatcher, although she was the prime mover. But her successor, Mr Major, was a leading member of Mrs Thatcher's governments, and indeed one of her protégés. We should not, therefore, expect any dramatic changes in policy under the present government, although a distinct change in style is very obvious. The Conservative Party is still dominated by those who have undiminished faith in the capacity of markets to meet social need.

Thus the changes in the NHS and in community care which, it has been argued, facilitate market provision, are proceeding according to timetable. New measures to encourage the sale of council houses have been introduced, and private pensions are being promoted at the expense of state provision. Two new areas for market provision have been found – school inspection and prisons.

The very deep and protracted recession may have contradictory effects on the further development of markets in health and welfare. On the one hand, the government has warned of severe restraint in public expenditure. The Economics Editor of *The Guardian*, commenting on government spending plans announced in November 1993, said that total public spending in 1994/5 will fall by 1.3 per cent in real terms, followed by a rise of 0.9 per cent in 1995/6 and of 1 per cent in 1996/7. (Hutton, 1993) This could result in declining standards in public services. People may feel forced to turn to market provision.

On the other hand, the recession, and its accompanying high level of unemployment, will reduce people's capacity to purchase private services. The sale of council houses has already fallen substantially, and the growth of the private sector in health, and particularly medical insurance, has slowed down. The profitability of residential accommodation is now less assured, and, in some parts of the country at least, there may be surplus capacity.

However, the private market sector now has a firmer base in the UK Welfare State, and once the recession is over, it may begin to expand at its previous rate. Nevertheless, the main components of the Welfare State are still in place, although much modified since 1987.

Public support for the Welfare State did not decline during the 1980s – in fact, quite the reverse. Taylor-Gooby (1985, 1989, 1990, 1991) who, more than any other commentator, has added to our knowledge of public attitudes towards the Welfare State, concludes a recent survey in the following way:

The 1980s have been a decade of rapid and profound welfare reform. The forty-year tradition of the state as the dominant agency in welfare provision has been challenged by cuts, by the privatisation of ancillary services, and by new policies which emphasise the importance of market forces in creating greater efficiency, flexibility and responsiveness to 'consumer' demands. The 1980s have also seen a widening gap emerge between the rich and poor which many people felt would erode support for the traditional pattern of state welfare provision. Yet the evidence from this series, and from the latest survey in particular, is that, far from a reduction in support for health and welfare expenditure, the 1980s have seen a strengthening of public endorsement of centralised, tax-financed state welfare. (1991, p.41)

Support for health, education and pensions is strong across all social classes, whereas support for social security benefits shows a class gradient, with greater working-class than middle-class support. Respondents were asked whether the government should reduce taxes and spend less on health, education and social benefits, keep taxes and spending at the same level as at present, or increase taxes and spend more on health, education and social benefits. There was some social class variation, but between 61 per cent and 51 per cent chose the third option, and between 2 per cent and 4 per cent favoured reducing taxes and spending less.

There is, then, wide support for state welfare, and this provides the context within which market provision has to operate. Taylor-Gooby points out that there is no inconsistency in simultaneously supporting increased state spending on health and welfare and believing that private market provision should be allowed. He writes:

there is little support for the belief that income inequalities undermine support for mass welfare services as the better off transfer to the private sector. However there is a strong current of support for allowing people to choose between the state and private market, and this support is expressed rather more forcibly by those in the best position to benefit from such arrangements. The better off value state provision, but they wish to be able to complement it from the private sector. (Taylor-Gooby, 1990, p.13)

There appears to be strong public backing for a mixed economy of welfare, but this leaves unanswered the question of how big a role the market should play.

References

Ascher, K. (1987) *The Politics of Privatisation: Contracting Out Public Services*, London, Macmillan.

Berthoud, R. and Kempson, E. (1990) *Credit and Debt in Britain*, London,

Policy Studies Institute.

Central Statistical Office (1990, 1991, 1992, 1993) *Social Trends*, nos 20, 21, 22, 23, 24, London, HMSO.

Deakin, N. and Wright, A. (eds) (1990) *Consuming Public Services*, London, Routledge.

Department of Health (1989a) *Working for Patients*, Cm 555, London, HMSO.

—— (1989b) *Caring for People*, Cm 849, London, HMSO.

—— (1991) *Purchase of Service*, London, HMSO.

Ferriman, A. (1992) 'Private patients swamp hospitals and insurers', *Observer*, 21 June.

Ford, J. (1992) Report prepared for Shelter, *Roof*, June.

Forrest, R. and Murie, A. (1984) *The Right to Buy? Need, Equity and Polarisation in the Sale of Council Houses*, Bristol, School for Advanced Urban Studies.

—— (1988) 'The Social division of housing subsidies', *Critical Social Policy*, vol.8, no.2, pp.83–93.

Gamble, A. (1987) *The Free Economy and the Strong State: The Politics of Thatcherism*, London, Macmillan.

Glennerster, H. (1990) 'Social policy since the second world war', in Hills, J. (ed.) (1990) *The State of Welfare: The Welfare State in Britain Since 1974*, Oxford, Clarendon Press, pp.11–27.

Glennerster, H. and Midgley, J. (1991) 'Preface', in Glennerster, H. and Midgley, J. (eds) (1991) *The Radical Right and the Welfare State: An International Assessment*, Hemel Hempstead, Harvester Wheatsheaf, pp.ix–xv.

Griffiths, R. (1988) *Community Care: Agenda for Action*, London, HMSO.

Health Care Information Services (1994) *The Fitzhugh Directory of Independent Healthcare*, London, Health Care Information Services, cited in Laing and Buisson (1994).

Hutton, W. (1993) 'Draconian assault on spending', *The Guardian*, 1 December.

Johnson, N. (1990) 'Problems for the mixed economy of welfare', in Ware, A. and Goodin, R.E. (eds) (1990) *Needs and Welfare*, London, Sage, pp.145–64.

Kerr, M. (1988) *The Right to Buy: A National Survey of Tenants and Buyers of Council Houses*, London, HMSO.

Laing and Buisson (1994) *Laing's Review of Private Healthcare, 1994*, London, Laing and Buisson Publications.

Milne, R.G. (1987) 'Competitive tendering in the NHS: An economic analysis of the early implementation of HC(83)H8', *Public Administration*, vol.15, no.2, pp.145–60.

Slaughter, J. (1992) *Observer*, 1 March.

Taylor-Gooby, P. (1985) *Public Opinion, Ideology and State Welfare*, London, Routledge and Kegan Paul.

—— (1989) 'Welfare privatization: The British experience', *International Journal of Health Studies*, vol.19, no.2, pp. 209–20.

—— (1990) 'Social welfare: The unkindest cuts', in Jowell, R., Witherspoon, S. and Brook, L. (eds) (1990) *British Social Attitudes: The 7th Report*, Aldershot, Gower, pp.1–26.

—— (1991) 'Attachment to the welfare state', in Jowell, R., Brook, L. and Taylor, B. (1991) *British Social Attitudes: The 8th Report*, Aldershot, Dartmouth Publishing Company, pp.23–42.

Treasury (1986) *Using Private Enterprise in Government: Report of a Multi-departmental Review of Competitive Tendering and Contracting for Services in Government Departments*, London, HMSO.

Walker, A. (1990) 'The strategy of inequality', in Taylor, I. (ed.) (1990) *The Social Effects of Free Market Policies: An International Text*, Hemel Hempstead, Harvester Wheatsheaf, pp.29–47.

-3-

Canada

André-Pierre Contandriopoulos, Frédéric
Lesemann and *Anne Lemay*

Introduction

Canada is the second largest country by area in the world, with a population of 26.5 million scattered along the United States border. It is a confederation of ten provinces and two territories. The Canadian constitution, which originated with the British North American Act of 1867, was repatriated from London to Ottawa in 1982. It is currently the object of heated discussion, but for the moment it still governs the relationship between the federal government and the provincial governments, establishing the areas of jurisdiction of the two levels of government.

> The act assigned in 1967 all matters of national concern, plus those activities likely to be costly, to the Federal Government, which had the broadest tax base; Ottawa was given jurisdiction over such items as railways, canals, coinage and, in the health field, quarantine, marine hospitals and health services for native people and the armed forces. The provinces were given authority for those local concerns which were at that time thought unlikely to be costly – including roads, education and the Establishment, Maintenance and Management of Hospitals, Asylums, Charities, and Eleemosynary Institutions [charitable institutions] in and for the Province, other than Marine Hospitals.

Municipal governments have only such powers as are delegated to them by the provinces (Vayda and Deber, 1984, p.191). These provisions are where the power of the provinces in the health and social services field originates.

In spite of its efforts to introduce a universal health insurance scheme in 1919, and again in 1945, the federal government had to wait until 1958 to persuade the provinces to introduce a universal public hospitalisation insurance scheme, and until 1968 to extend it to medical services.

To obtain the participation of the provinces, the federal government undertook to assume half the cost of the insured services, and the provinces, in return, agreed to comply with five basic requirements. In 1984 the Canada Health Act empowered the federal government to apply economic sanctions against provinces which did not comply with the basic requirements:

1 'Public Administration: the provincial system must be administered on a non-profit basis by a public authority appointed or designated by the government of the province and subject to audits of its accounts and financial transactions.'
2 'Comprehensiveness: the system must deliver all insured health services provided by hospitals, medical practitioners or dentists and, where authorized, services provided by other health professionals.'
3 'Universality: 100 per cent of the insured population of a province must be entitled to the insured health services provided by the plan on uniform terms and conditions.'
4 'Portability: when people take up residence in another province, the province of origin must pay the cost of insured health services during a minimum period of residence (less than three months). Portability also means that the province of origin agrees to the coverage of services provided outside the province.'
5 'Accessibility: insured health services must be provided on uniform terms and conditions, and Canadians must be guaranteed satisfactory access to insured health services without any direct or indirect barrier such as extra billing and/or user fees. Accessibility also means that reasonable compensation must be provided for all insured health services rendered by doctors or dentists and that adequate payment must be made to hospitals in respect of the cost of insured health services' (House of Commons, Canada, 1991, p.15).

The Canada Health Act also specifies that provinces which do not respect these conditions are liable to financial sanctions. The federal government can, in fact, reduce the amount of its contribution, in accordance with the Established Program Financing Act of 1977, by an amount equal to the extra billing amount or the user fees. All this legislation ensures that funding of nearly 80 per cent of health services in Canada is the responsibility of the public authorities (Contandriopoulos et al., 1988).

In the field of personal social services, the federal government has made a major financial contribution since the Canada Assistance Plan of 1966. Each province, however, retains extensive autonomy in defining the services offered, the methods of distributing them, and the people covered. The degree to which the health services and social services are integrated varies greatly from one province to another (Tsalikis, 1982).

This outline of the organisation of health and social services in Canada makes it clear that, financially, there is not one Canadian system, but rather a discrete socio-health system in each province. Also, since the end of the 1960s, in all Canadian provinces, public health insurance and social insurance schemes have been introduced that are nearly 80 per cent financed by the state. This situation reflects the fundamental role of the state in Canada.

This role has traditionally been exercised not only in the area of health, welfare and educational services, but also in business and industry in general, to the point that, in 1984, the government of Canada was sole owner of 179 companies, and was also joint owner with the private sector of even more.

It should at once be noted that these figures, though impressive when compared with the situation in the United States, are much lower than those in the major European countries (Stein, 1988; Economic Council of Canada, 1986; Stanbury, 1989).

The impressive number of Crown Corporations in Canada is essentially the expression of the fundamental role played by the federal state since the end of the Second World War and later – in particular at the end of the 1960s and during the 1970s – in the economic development of the country. Since its creation in 1867, Canada has always been a country obsessed with maintaining its coast-to-coast political cohesion and distinct cultural identity in the face of its extremely powerful southern neighbour. With this in mind, it invested in culture (CBC Radio and TV; National Film Board) and telecommunications, as well as transport (Air Canada, Canadian National Railways, Trans-Canada Highway) and energy. In industry, the federal government has not hesitated to show strong leadership in developing leading-edge industries, new technology and direct protection of Canadian industrial and financial interests as a bulwark against intensive penetration by US investments. Between 1867 and the beginning of the 1980s, the Liberal Party of Canada was in power in Ottawa, and pursued a protectionist economic policy, with a nationalist orientation for the economy and culture, and with a policy of expansion of the Welfare State with regard to education, health and welfare.

It was precisely this dual orientation – of protectionism on the economic front and expansionism of public services – that the Liberals themselves were preparing to change when they were ousted from power by the Conservatives in 1984. The Conservatives decided to accelerate the process. From the moment it came to power in 1984, the Conservative Party of Canada started promoting privatisation with great enthusiasm as a 'matter of good management' (McDermid, 1989).

Two major political events symbolised the fundamental reorientation of the economy and the role of the State in the mid-1980s: the work of the Royal Commission on the Economic Union and Development Prospects for Canada (the Macdonald Commission), with the lengthy report it published in 1985; and the negotiations with the United States subsequent to the work of the Macdonald Commission, with a view to establishing a free-trade agreement between the two countries, which began to come into force progressively on 1 January 1989.

The Macdonald Report dealt very briefly (II, 385) with the privatisation of Crown Corporations, emphasising that it was equally relevant to consider selling them, and that it was no longer a good idea to limit foreign (especially US) investments or nationalise certain sectors of investment. While the report's observations are rather vague when dealing with privatisation, the general philosophy that inspired it nevertheless preaches the virtues of renewed liberalism, reduced State intervention, opening up of markets, controlling inflation and the public debt, and deregulation of economic activities – all perspectives that correspond to the orientations of privatising public enterprises.

In the area of social policy, a document published by the C.D. Howe Institute (Courchene, 1987), entitled *Social Policy in the 1990s: Agenda for Reform*, expressing a philosophy close to that of the Macdonald Report, stated very clearly the consequences of new economic paths for the social policy system. Today, the Welfare State programmes and the economic system can no longer be separated. As a result, there are three underlying challenges reflecting the economic environment:

1 the fiscal challenge (deficit, tax cuts), which strongly limits the spending capacity of government;
2 the economic technological challenge and its necessary search for efficiency and competitiveness;
3 the socio-demographic challenge that implies modifying current priorities of programmes in progress to reflect the increasing number of elderly people.

These challenges, in turn, correspond with three trade-offs: between adjustment versus security (or efficiency versus entitlements), decentralisation versus centralisation, and private sector versus public sector.

Regarding the service sector, the Macdonald Report pointed out, albeit briefly (II, 809), the potential value of the 'privatization of service delivery on a supervised, but profit-making basis'. But the Commission at once went on to express 'some reservations about an overly enthusiastic application of this approach', pointing out in particular that, in the area of nursing-home facilities, 'private markets work best when consumers are both well informed about alternative sources of service and mobile. Since neither condition usually obtains for nursing-home residents, governments must, at the very least, continue to play a major supervisory role' (p.809).

Thus, in the mid-1980s, those in Canada found themselves in an economic and political context that was highly favourable to devolution of the role of the state, with privatisation of companies being one of the main ways of achieving this. And yet, paradoxical as it may seem, only a small number of public concerns have so far been privatised and, in the socio-health sector, privatisation, in the sense of selling or handing over public organisations to commercial companies or transferring public financing to private financing, has remained very limited. Everything that has happened so far suggests that the idea of turning over all or part of the service sector to for-profit privatisation has had very little concrete effect.

Health Services

The five basic requirements to which the provinces are subject, together with the fact that the organisation of the care system is under provincial jurisdiction, mean that in Canada there are ten different health care systems sharing common characteristics. The most important one is that in each province there 'is a government-run insurance plan, which uses public funds to pay for a private system' (Vayda and Deber, 1984, p.191).

To begin with, we will analyse the development of the place of the state and the private sector in the financing of health care services, going on to deal with how the quest for profit, in the financial sense, plays a major role in the public health care system (Champagne et al., 1984).

Financing of Health Care Services

Canada's total health care expenditure is high compared with that of other developed countries, whether seen as per capita expenditure or as a proportion of the Gross Domestic Product (GDP) – between 8.5 per cent and 10 per cent of GDP between 1985 and 1991 (Champagne et al., 1991; Government of Quebec, 1991; Moreau et al., 1991). The share of public funding in total health care expenditure is 74.1 per cent, putting Canada in a similar position to the average European country. However, this percentage varies from one province to another. Quebec is the province in which the State has the largest role.

In the rest of this section, given that we cannot really speak of the organisation of the Canadian health care system as a whole, we will be focusing our analysis on the situation in Quebec, comparing it with that in Ontario and Canada as a whole. This is justified by the important role of the State in this province, and by the fact that profit should therefore play a less important role here than in the other Canadian provinces.

In a way, Quebec had represented the lowest common denominator of the provinces as regards the role of the private sector in the health care system until 1987, the latest year for which data on overall health care services used by Quebecers is available (Health and Welfare Canada, 1990). In that year expenditure totalled $C11.676 billion, or $C1,770 for each Quebecer (Champagne et al., 1991). This amount is 17 times higher than the amount for 1960 ($C103). However, although the average Quebecer's contribution in today's financial terms has increased considerably since the pan-Canadian health insurance scheme was set up at the beginning of the 1970s, the share of collective funds going to the health sector peaked in 1983 and then decreased. The share of the GDP devoted to the health care sector in Quebec reached a maximum of 9.34 per cent in 1983. For subsequent years, the health care sector shows a decrease compared with the average for other sectors of the economy. In 1987, the health care sector's share in the economy was 8.86 per cent; and in 1986, for the first year since 1965, the amount devoted to health care in Quebec was lower than the average for Canadian provinces.

When you use an expenditure indicator that takes into account factors that are external to the health care system, such as demographic growth, development of economic production and inflation, you find that, since the beginning of the 1980s, health expenditure in Quebec has stopped growing. This indicator of relativised expenditure (Contandriopoulos et al., 1989) is obtained by bringing down the amount of actual health expenditure per capita (in constant 1981 Canadian dollars) by a GDP growth index for the base year 1981. This method of analysing health care expenditure shows that each Quebecer consumed an average of $C1,094 in 1987 (Champagne et al., 1991). With the constant increase in prices and the GDP, this is about the same as in 1971 ($C1,088). Since the mid-1980s, the financial contribution of Quebecers to health care has been reducing. In 1987, the relative portion of the GDP that went to health care was, for all practical purposes, the same as it was 20 years earlier.

Sources of Financing

Essentially there are five sources of financing for health care expenditure. Funding for four of them comes from various forms of direct or indirect taxation – federal, provincial, municipal and CSST (occupational health and safety) – all public financing sources. The fifth form of financing is that assumed by the private sector, and is the financial contribution made by the user when paying for certain services not covered by public insurance schemes, private insurance companies, or the foundations of various organisations for the acquisition of equipment and funds (Rochon Commission, 1988, p.350).

Until hospitalisation and health care insurance schemes were set up, the private sector was the main source of health care financing, both in Quebec and other Canadian provinces (Figure 3.1). Subsequently, its role steadily decreased in importance until 1977, a period corresponding to the fiscal accords that began federal government detachment from the financing of programmes for health care and post-secondary education.

After 1977 the size of the private sector contribution to funding health care expenditure once again began to show moderate growth. This phenomenon of privatisation in the health care sector, observed since 1987, is more widespread in Quebec than the other provinces (Figure 3.1). In 1987, 23 per cent of the health care budget was directly defrayed by

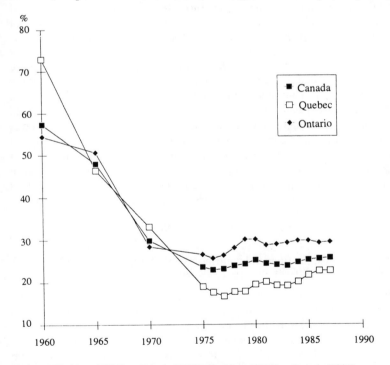

Sources: Health and Welfare Canada (1990); Health and Welfare Canada (1991).

Figure 3.1 Relative Contribution of the Private Sector to the Funding of Total Health Care Expenditure, Quebec, Ontario, Canada, 1960–87

the private sector. Given the public finance crisis (debt, limiting tax increases, etc.), the financing capacity of the federal and provincial governments became severely mortgaged. The Social Welfare Committee (House of Commons, Canada, 1991) found that: 'Total cash payments made by the federal government . . . under the terms of the 1977 fiscal accords could disappear a few years from now' (p.22). From 1975 to 1987, Quebec government funds constituted the main source of financing for health care services, with the exception of federal transfer payments. In 1987, the provincial government was financing 46 per cent of the budget and the federal government 30.6 per cent, while the contribution of the municipalities and the CSST remained marginal, for all practical purposes, throughout this period.

In addition to these four sources of funding, we should also take into account the health care services offered by members of society who are not paid for them. The value of health care services provided under the aegis of community organisations (non-subsidised), domestic help and volunteer agencies is not accounted for. We do not know exactly the extent or value of services provided in this form. However, the Conseil des Affaires Sociales du Quebec (Morin, 1990) quotes the Pontbriand study (Chicha-Pontbriand, 1983), which estimates the value of health care services provided in the guise of domestic work at $C9.3 billion for the year 1988/9. This amount corresponds to 6.7 per cent of Quebec's GDP.

In this same study, Le Conseil des Affaires Sociales estimates the value of services provided by volunteers at $C604 million in 1988. Even if valuation of health care services provided by unpaid workers is still in its infancy, owing to the shortage of relevant information, the fact remains that services offered by unpaid workers represent a considerable contribution to the health care system because they provide services whose value is almost as great as the services officially accounted for.

The Role of Profit in the Health Care System

The development of private financing of the health care system by category of expenditure is shown in Table 3.1.

Hospitals Figure 3.2 shows that, since the mid-1960s, hospitals have been 90 per cent financed by public authorities. In addition, it shows that, since the beginning of the 1980s, the proportion of private expenditure has slightly increased. In Quebec this increase is due to an explicit desire to encourage hospital directors to increase the revenues of their own hospitals (through fees for private rooms and parking facilities, for example). However, this trend is still marginal. Most of the funds are paid to hospitals in the form of a prospective overall budget (Contandriopoulos et al., 1989).

	1960 $CM	1970 $CM	1980 $CM	1985 $CM	1987 $CM
Institutional Services					
Hospitals	27.59	6.13	8.02	9.37	9.41
Other institutions	57.34	31.74	17.24	24.41	24.22
Other	0.00	69.14	1.57	0.87	0.90
Professional Services					
Doctors	86.08	22.65	6.21	5.57	4.35
Dentists	98.81	94.49	85.08	87.47	88.66
Other professionals	97.74	89.10	37.90	38.65	39.81
Medication and Prostheses					
Prescription medication	98.19	95.85	55.70	48.38	49.51
Non-prescription medication	100.00	100.00	100.00	100.00	100.00
Optical prostheses	100.00	99.66	98.49	98.65	98.63
Auditory prostheses	100.00	100.00	86.30	81.57	91.25
Other prostheses	70.37	73.85	47.61	33.29	30.78
Other Expenditure					
Administration	81.99	25.08	35.68	47.84	46.00
Public health	0.00	0.00	0.00	0.00	0.00
Capital expenditure	48.30	36.32	43.34	34.35	35.06
Health research	32.79	14.22	31.49	28.11	36.13
Other	57.14	61.28	69.58	67.38	70.83
Total Expenditure	57.26	29.81	25.27	25.31	25.80

Sources: Health and Welfare Canada (1990); Health and Welfare Canada (1991).

Table 3.1 Contribution of the Private Sector to Funding of Health Care Expenditure, by Category of Service, Canada, 1960–87

Under these conditions, and because the hospitals are non-profit corporations, there is virtually no way in which profit can really play a part. However, it is quite possible that this situation will change in future years. With the difficulties of the economic situation and public finances, the Ministre de la Santé Publique explored the possibilities of privatising some hospital support services (catering, admissions, laundry) in a consultative report entitled *Un financement équitable à la mesure de nos moyens* (Gouvernement du Québec, 1991).

Other Institutions This category consists essentially of nursing and residential homes. As shown in Figure 3.3, the proportion of private expenditure varies a good deal from province to province. However, in this sector, it is not so much the payment mechanism of these centres that

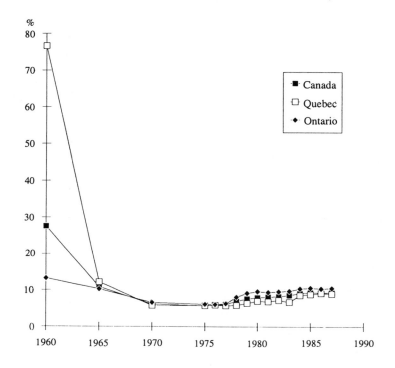

Sources: Health and Welfare Canada (1990); Health and Welfare Canada (1991).

Figure 3.2 Comparative Contribution of the Private Sector to the Funding of Hospital Expenses, Quebec, Ontario, Canada, 1960–87

is important but rather their administrative status. A sizeable proportion of these homes are run in recognised private establishments, most of which are profit-oriented.

At present, no serious study has been able to demonstrate the advantages or disadvantages of the competition between the two categories of state-funded institutions.

In Quebec, the bases for financing are the same for both categories of establishment. These private establishments generate profits directly from the state subsidy by trimming the administrative structure as much as possible and, in a way, leasing their immovable assets to the state. The budget for clinical activities is protected so as to guarantee the quality of care.

Medical Services   Figure 3.4 indicates that, from the mid-1970s, the public insurance scheme for medical services was applied in all Canadian provinces. This scheme is 90 per cent financed by the state. In spite of this – and here we find a major distinctive feature of the Canadian health insurance system – it is organised in such a way as to respect the professional liberty of physicians (right to participate in the scheme, right to choose their speciality, place of practice, type of practice, clientele) (Champagne et al., 1984). In addition, patients are free to consult the physician of their choice (general practitioner or specialist) wherever they prefer (private office, hospital or community centre). Patients do not have to hand over any money to obtain medical services; they simply show their health insurance card, rather like using a credit card, and a third party, financed by the state, settles the bill from the physician directly. These repayment tariffs are negotiated by the organisations representing doctors and the Ministry of Health. No extra billing is allowed.

Doctors are thus paid for each consultation by a third party, which pays

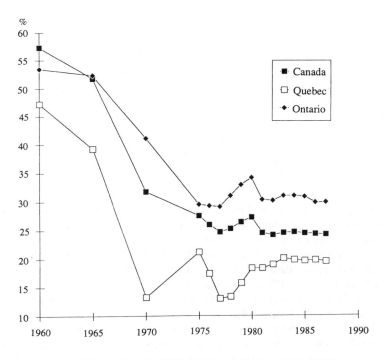

Sources: Health and Welfare Canada (1990); Health and Welfare Canada (1991).

Figure 3.3 Comparative Contribution of the Private Sector to Financing Expenditure in Other Institutions, Quebec, Ontario, Canada, 1960–87

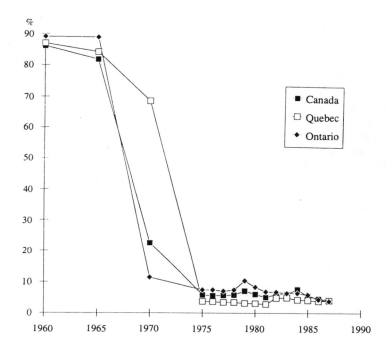

Sources: Health and Welfare Canada (1990); Health and Welfare Canada (1991).

Figure 3.4 Comparative Contribution of the Private Sector to Financing Expenditure on Medical Services, Quebec, Ontario, Canada, 1960–87

on the basis of negotiated rates (in Quebec, less than 15 per cent of doctors earn a salary in community centres). Under this type of system, the motivations associated with doctors' quest for profit are expressed in various ways.

Most of the studies in this area have been concerned with the impact of variations in the fee schedule negotiated on the volume and type of service claimed (Lomas et al., 1989; Labelle et al., 1989; Barer et al., 1988; Gabel and Rice, 1985; Contandriopoulos, 1976 and 1980; Evans, 1974; Lemay, 1985; Rochaix, 1990). All these studies show that doctors react to rate changes, but how they react and to what extent is hard to predict.

Research into the choice of location and speciality, however, shows that purely financial considerations are secondary (Eisenberg and Cantwell, 1976; Moscovice, 1983).

It is in the organisation behind the production of medical services that the quest for profit has a major influence. The fact that doctors working in private practice have to assume the operating costs of their offices has a twofold effect. The first is that private offices, notably in Quebec, are relatively poorly equipped. Doctors usually ask their patients to go and have tests (X-rays, laboratory tests) at hospitals. But increasingly, given the financial constraints experienced by hospitals, access to diagnostic departments is being reduced and waiting time has increased considerably. Faced with this situation, doctors have formed groups and opened large health centres providing a wide range of diagnostic and specialised services, of which a small but growing proportion are paid for directly by patients. The typical example of this trend is the acquisition of CAT scan equipment by a private clinic in the Montreal area (see pp.58–60).

Other Professionals   Figures 3.5 and 3.6 show that the share of private funding for health professionals other than doctors (dentists, pharmacists,

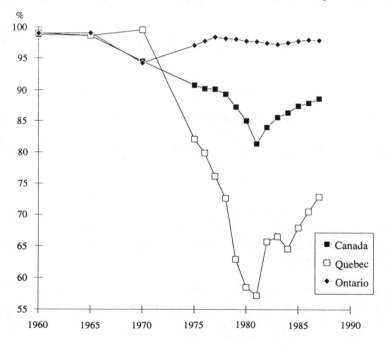

Sources: Health and Welfare Canada (1990); Health and Welfare Canada (1991).

Figure 3.5 Comparative Contribution of the Private Sector to Financing Expenditure on Dental Services, Quebec, Ontario, Canada, 1960–87

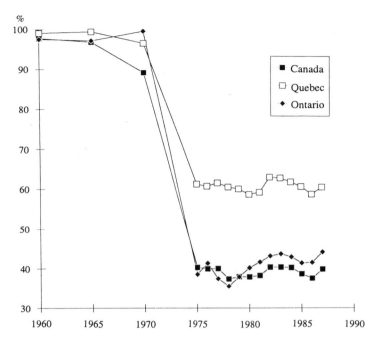

Sources: Health and Welfare Canada (1990); Health and Welfare Canada (1991).

Figure 3.6 Comparative Contribution of the Private Sector to Financing Expenditure on Professional Services (Other than Dentists and Doctors), Quebec, Ontario, Canada, 1960–87

optometrists, chiropractors, etc.) varies greatly from province to province. Broadly speaking, we can say that these are sectors in which the market plays a major role, with the State simply ensuring that the poorest people are not excluded.

Health Research   Figure 3.7 illustrates an interesting development. Until the beginning of the 1970s the state's role in the funding of research was growing, but during the 1970s private funding was increasingly resorted to. After a period of stagnation in the 80s, it continued to increase. The impact of this development on independent fundamental research is in need of further analysis, as is the importance of having applied research that is directly oriented to the implementation of innovations (CIAR, 1988).

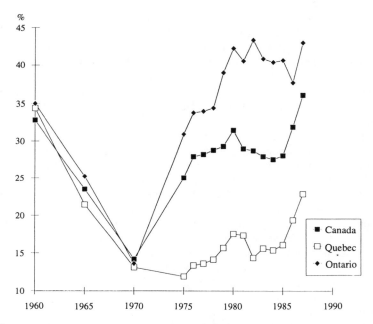

Sources: Health and Welfare Canada (1990); Health and Welfare Canada (1991).

Figure 3.7 Comparative Contribution of the Private Sector to Financing Expenditure on Health Care Research, Quebec, Ontario, Canada, 1960–87

To sum up, the Canadian health care system seems to have succeeded in maintaining, within a universal and accessible system, areas of decision where the competition and rivalry associated with profit-making are exercised. Among the characteristics that have enabled this balance to be maintained, we should note: decentralisation at the provincial level; decisions affecting the organisation of services; tax-based funding that has allowed for generous financing of the system but has also enabled its growth to be controlled, and a tradition of negotiation that has so far allowed us to succeed in reaching negotiated agreements between the various participants and governments, despite great tensions.

Personal Social Services

The primary responsibility for providing social services rests, as we have seen, with the provinces, who share the cost of funding these services with the federal government, under the Canada Assistance Plan (CAP) of 1966. The provinces also control how the services are organised, in accordance with the CAP, which explicitly encourages the non-profit delivery of services. So two main organizational models exist: some provinces, including Quebec for example, have created institutions for the delivery of services that are legally autonomous but 100 per cent government-funded; others, essentially the English-speaking provinces, have traditionally contracted out most services to private, non-profit, charitable agencies.

Two provinces did undertake to develop contracts with for-profit agencies, from the beginning of the 1980s. These were Ontario and British Columbia. It is surprising to find how little-known, little-publicised and little-documented these initiatives are. No doubt this is an indication of the reluctance of certain provincial governments to publicly acknowledge a preference for commercialisation of services. Presumably they feared disapproval, especially at the beginning of the 1980s, and even sanctions from the federal government, which, as will be recalled, shared the cost of social services. Also they were wary of the possible disapproval of a major segment of the public, traditionally very attached to its universal system of socio-health services, and certainly of professional groups, unionised workers and academics associated with the health and social services field.

For the province of Ontario, in 1984 the Social Planning Council of Metropolitan Toronto (SPCMT) produced one of the few studies of commercialisation of the social services, *Caring for Profit* (SPCMT, 1984). This shows the extent to which the Conservative government in this province allowed the development of for-profit agencies, starting in the late 1970s. While the image of an essentially public health care and social service system prevails, this study surprisingly revealed that in 1983 over 90 per cent of the province's 322 nursing homes were operated for profit; over half of Ontario's beds for elderly people were provided for profit, compared with 27 per cent in the rest of Canada; almost half of Ontario's 70,000 licensed day care spaces were in the commercial sector; and half of the contracts for home-making services purchased by Ontario's local Home Care Programs were with commercial agencies (SPCMT, 1984, ch.3). For overall home-making services in Ontario, the development of for-profit services was particularly marked during the 1980s: in 1982 the commercial services represented 23 per cent of total home-making services, but by 1989 this percentage had increased to 43 per cent, and reached an estimated 50 per cent in 1992. In the case of long-term care facilities, the majority are for-profit (Workshop on Long-term Care in Toronto, 1991).

The study Workshop makes a point of emphasising the 'substantial risks associated with expanding the role of the commercial sector . . . in relation to its effects on accountability to service users and to government; influence on public policy; quality of service; equity and cost-effectiveness' (SPCMT, 1984, ch.5). It also warns of the potentially negative consequences of widespread commercialisation of social services, based on a critical analysis of the US experience in this area (SPCMT, 1984, ch.4). These reservations accurately reflect the widespread Canadian political and moral stance in favour of the Welfare State. It is also interesting to note that, in spring 1985, when Ontario elected a minority Liberal government that had to rely on the support of the New Democratic Party (Labour), there was a subsequent slowing down and even halt in the trend toward privatisation for profit in health care and social services in this foremost Canadian province, except for home-making services and long-term care facilities. The election of the New Democratic Party in 1990 has helped to strengthen this resistance to privatisation.

Since 1983, the province of British Columbia has been practising purchase of service contracting (POSC) with private commercial agencies for the organisation of a limited section of the social services. According to Veit (1990), who uses the definition coined by Kettner and Lawrence (1987), this POSC is

> a legally binding agreement between a government contracting agency (with responsibility for serving clients and the resources to serve them) and a contractor (with appropriate service delivery capability) in which the contractor provides care or services to clients of the government contracting agency in exchange for funds or other resources.

POSC can cover such diverse services as: income assistance administration; child protection; homes and services to mentally handicapped people; day care; single persons' hostels; achievement centres, and home-makers (Veit, 1990, p.200). Veit points out that the attraction of POSC has increased in line with the trend toward de-institutionalisation or non-institutionalisation of various categories of clientele, and also the trend toward decentralisation of many operations and attempts to reduce the scale of government efforts. The POSC budget in British Columbia reached $C170 million in 1986/7, out of an overall Ministry of Social Services and Housing budget of $C1.4 billion. This $C170 million represented 1,900 contracts signed by this ministry, through its 160 district offices, mostly with non-profit agencies, individuals or small proprietary businesses in all the required types of social services (Veit, 1990, p.203). The proprietary agencies are thus a new phenomenon in the social welfare sector in that they introduce a logic of profit and competition between the for-profit and non-profit agencies. But, according to Veit, we must distinguish between these small proprietary agencies and traditional profit-making companies (p.209), because:

> to say that small proprietary agencies are interested in making a 'profit' through the provision of social services often seems to overstate the case . . . And it is true that these agencies are very often owner/operator individuals or couples who agree to take in one or two foster children . . . The establishment of a proprietary agency becomes a creative job-development option. (p.210)

In all cases the ministry monitors, evaluates and reports on the quality of service provided, and retains responsibility for these clients.

On the basis of these two major examples of privatisation of social services, we can state that the favoured method of government privatisation consists of contracting out a given volume of services. It is never a question of selling equipment or whole programmes to the private sector: this would be part of a totally independent commercial philosophy.

A recent report by a group of experts appointed by the Quebec Health and Social Services Department (Quebec City, 1991), indicates that, in Quebec,

> more than one third of places in residential homes are the result of collaboration with the private sector: intermediate resources (foster families and homes), nursing homes and recognized private hospital centres (99 institutions with 7,292 places), and subject to the same standards as the public sector. Private self-financing nursing homes (4,500 places) receive no public funding. (p.82)

The same report also emphasises the development of constantly increasing direct susbidies for the purchase of home care services related to daily and domestic activities. Of funds paid in Quebec in 1990 for home care, 17 per cent went to 'direct subsidies'.

In general, we find that privatisation is very common in nursing homes, management of beds or spaces in day care centres, for people mostly defined by a temporary dependence report (day care for children or elderly people) or chronic care (handicapped and elderly people, for example). This phenomenon is mainly related to the steep growth in the number of elderly people at a time when the state is financially and politically unable to invest in this fast-growing service sector. The same applies to the child care services sector, whose development is partly the result of women having increasing access to the job market, even when they have very young children.

In so far as residential care is one of the main features of the development of the for-profit social services sector, it is interesting to note that, in most provinces, many for-profit home care agencies, and especially home-making services, have been established in the last ten years in response to the growing demand for such services. This demand is related to restricted access to nursing homes and the increasing number of dependent elderly people. Home care services clearly represent a 'new' growth sector in services, in which provincial governments hesitate to become too actively involved at a time of budget restrictions, especially as the legal status of these services is not clear because they provide a service whose content usually goes beyond the bounds of a strictly medical or para-medical service. They are thus no longer the concern only of universal protection as accorded by public health insurance schemes, but also of CAP programmes. Services offered by a private undertaking can easily be swallowed up in the legal vacuum currently surrounding the definition of the status and limits of home care. The swift expansion of for-profit home care service agencies in Canada, though it is real, is very hard to document with precision, given the wide range of services offered, methods of organisation used, current legal statuses, and the regulatory constraints that vary from province to province. Recent research (Nahmiash and Reis, 1991) identified about 350 major private for-profit agencies in Canada. But this research gives us no precise information about the volume of services provided, or the number and socio-economic profile of clients.

A potential growth area for for-profit agencies is found in the increased technology now being used to keep dependent people in their own homes. Emergency response systems which automatically dial the prearranged numbers of a social supporter, or the supply of complex services involving advanced equipment previously administered only in a hospital setting are examples of technological development often introduced by commercial agencies (Nahmiash and Reis, 1991, pp.10–11).

Housing

The question of public housing can be dealt with here since it is more and more closely associated with the question of public responsibility for dependent people. Canada's public housing stock is very limited. The Canadian Mortgage and Housing Corporation (CHMC) is the federal body responsible for building public housing. Created at the end of the Second World War in order to provide demobilised soldiers with adequate and affordable housing, the CMHC has not, in fact, been very active in building public housing, following the North American idea that housing is a matter for private initiative rather than the public sector. Over the last ten years, existing public housing, rather than being privatised, has been gradually designed to respond to the needs of single-parent families, and elderly people finding it increasingly difficult to live alone, as an alternative to early institutionalisation.

Conclusion

It is therefore surprising to find how poorly represented are the theory, and especially the practice, of privatisation for profit in the social services sector, with the exception – as we have seen – of two provinces and the area of residential care and home-care services.

Of course, if this investigation had covered the practices of non-profit privatisation, then the whole area of community resources, co-operatives, volunteer work, self-help groups and families would have been dealt with, and a much more impressive picture of the current transformations of the Welfare State (at the federal and provincial levels) would have appeared. Most social programmes today include references to community funding, partnership, complementarity, the interface of formal and informal resources, and the role and responsibilities of families and the home as the place where caring begins. This is a quite distinct dimension of privatisation which so far has clearly predominated in re-defining public action.

Generally speaking, and with the exception of a few neo-liberal economists or managers, for-profit privatisation in the area of socio-health services finds only limited support, when it is not rejected out of hand. This is probably because it is perceived as a potential threat to the universality of health and social protection programmes. Many Canadians certainly regard these programmes as a pillar of national integration, or even collective identity, that distinguishes them in a positive way, and is a bulwark against their southern neighbours. Because of this, the issue of privatisation in health and welfare services is much more than just an economic and fiscal question. It is a profoundly political issue, for it touches symbolically the distinctive cultural identity of Canadians.

The Acquisition of Costly Technology in the Private Sector: A Case Study

Here we describe how a private clinic in the greater Montreal area has succeeded in acquiring axial tomography (CAT scan) equipment, in spite of major constraints, and in promoting its use within both the public health network and the general public.

The Clinic: A Brief Description

This clinic now has about 100 general practitioners and specialists, dentists, psychologists, psychotherapy department (psychoanalysis, group therapy and relaxation), and a minor surgery department. In addition, it has a radiology department that also performs ultrasound and laboratory tests. The clinic was established in 1973. All the physicians are also shareholders. It is one of the largest organisations of its kind in the Montreal area.

The Decision Process for the Acquisition of Axial Tomography Equipment

The decision to acquire a CAT scan machine at this clinic was based on two kinds of motivation. The first motivations were linked to the desire to respond to patient needs not satisfied by the public sector. The clinic's doctors wanted to provide a service in addition to that provided via the hospitals. This would avoid patients having to wait because of long waiting lists, provide better access, and enhance relations with the patients. Unlike the public sector, the private sector is able to set up appointments in under two to three days, instead of several months. Results of examinations are also available much sooner. The second category of motivations was linked to the desire of members of this organisation to possess the latest technology. The doctors wanted to be able to compete with the public sector to show that they really knew what they were doing. Finally, as with any profit-making organisation, profitability was also a factor.

A market study commissioned by the clinic's managers showed that there was indeed a sizeable clientele. It consisted of patients covered by the Occupational Health and Safety Commission (CSST), or the Quebec Auto Insurance Board (RAAQ), and patients not covered by public or para-public health insurance, such as employees of General Motors, or members of the general public. Nearly half the doctors at the clinic (42), both general practitioners and specialists (especially radiologists and neurologists), therefore decided to invest in the best CAT scan equipment then available, at a cost of $C1.5 million.

In 1987 the clinic's directors met with the Deputy Minister of Health and Social Services to tell him of their decision to buy a CAT scan machine. The project was not formally opposed by the department. The CAT scan machine was acquired in December 1988. This was the first time in Canada that such equipment had been bought by and for the private sector. However, under law, the provision and coverage by the private sector of services already provided by the public sector is illegal. The clinic therefore forfeited the clientele covered by the other public agencies for these services (Worker Compensation Agency and Automobile Insurance Board). During 1989 and the first half of 1990 the project showed a loss of $C350,000. Subsequently, CAT scan services were excluded from the Act respecting unprovided services, and the project became profitable.

At the present time the clinic undertakes fifteen to seventeen CAT scan examinations every day. Of the patients using the CAT scan service, 70 per cent are insured under the public and para-public system. These are patients from Montreal area hospitals to which the clinic is under contract, and CSST and RAAQ beneficiaries. The clinic charges a lower fee than public sector hospitals in the market in which certain hospitals buy services. In 1989, the examination cost $C200 at the clinic, compared to $C230 in other Montreal hospitals offering the service. The remaining 30 per cent of patients consist of people paying for the examination themselves or through their insurance company. It seems that 60 per cent of private insurance companies are currently covering this type of service. Insurance companies responded to the demand by doing so.

Postscript

In October 1993 the political landscape of Canada was transformed. In the general election the ruling Progressive Conservative Party suffered a humiliating defeat, winning only two seats compared with its former 169. The Liberals now have a parliamentary majority, and have formed a new government under Prime Minister Jean Chrétien. The new government's first task was to address Canada's economic problems, attempting to bring down unemployment and reduce the federal budget deficit of $C36 billion. The precise impact of these changes upon health and welfare services in Canada is still unclear.

References

Barer, M.L., Evans, R.G. and Labelle, R. (1988) 'Fee controls as cost controls: Tale from the frozen north', *The Milbank Quarterly*, vol.66, no.1, pp.1–64.

Champagne, F., Contandriopoulos, A.P., Fournier, M.A. and Laurier, C. (1984) 'Pursuit of equity, respect of liberties and control of health care costs', *Journal of Health and Human Resources Administration*, vol.7, no.1, pp.4–31.

Champagne, F., Contandriopoulos, A.P., Preker, A. and Lemay, A. (1991)

Evaluation and projection of social welfare and health-care services expenditure in Quebec, GRIS, University of Montreal, R91–08.

Chicha-Pontbriand, Marie-Thérèse (1983) *The Extension of the Accountable Approach to the Economic Surplus: Conceptual, Qualitative and Pragmatic Aspects*, PhD Thesis, McGill University.

CIAR (1988) *Innovation and Canada's Prosperity: the Transforming Power of Science Engineering and Technology*, Canadian Institute for Advanced Research, Toronto.

Commission of enquiry into health and social services (1988) *Report*, Government of Quebec.

Contandriopoulos, A.P., Lemay, A., Tessier, G. and Champagne, F. (1989) 'Methods of financing and control of the costs of the welfare system; the example of Quebec', *Sciences, Sociales et Santé*, vol.7, no.4, December, pp.113–37.

Contandriopoulos, A.P. (1988) 'Prospective budgeting of hospital costs and related measures: The evidence from the Canadian provinces', paper presented to the International Symposium 1988: *Controlling Cost While Maintaining Health: The Experience of Canada, the United States of America and the Federal Republic of Germany with Alternative Cost-containment Strategies*, 27 and 28 June, Bonn.

Contandriopoulos, A.P. et al. (1988) *The costs and financing of the health and social welfare system*, Commission of Enquiry into the health and social services, Quebec official publishers, Quebec, 1988.

Contandriopoulos, A.P., Lemay, A. and Tessier, G. (1987) *The costs and financing of the services provided by the health and social welfare system*, Thematic record of the Commission of enquiry into the health and social services, November 1987.

Contandriopoulos, A.P. (1980) 'Economic incentives and the utilisation of the medical services', *l'Actualité Economique*, April–June, pp.265–96.

Contandriopoulos, A.P. (1976) *A pattern of the performance of doctors in their role as suppliers of a service*, doctoral thesis, Department of Economics, University of Montreal.

Courchene, T.J. (1987) *Social Policy in the 1990s: Agenda for Reform*, C.D. Howe Institute, Toronto.

Economic Council of Canada (1986) *Minding the Public's Business*, Ottawa.

Eisenberg, B.S. and Cantwell J.R. (1976) 'Policies to influence spatial-distribution of physicians – Conceptual review of selected programs and empirical evidence', *Medical Care*, vol.14, no.6, pp.455–66.

Evans, R.G. (1974) 'Supplier-Induced Demand: Some Empirical Evidence and Implication', in Perlman, M. (ed.) (1974) *The Economics of Health Care*, Conference of International Economic Association,

Tokyo, pp.162–53.

Gabel, J.R. and Rice, T.H. (1985) 'Reducing expenditures for physician services: The price of paying less', *Journal of Health Politics and Law*, vol.9, no.4, pp.595–609.

Government of Quebec, (1991) *Fair financing according to our means*, Ministry of Health and Social Services, Quebec.

Health and Welfare Canada (1979) *National Health Expenditure in Canada, 1960–1975*, Ottawa.

Health and Welfare Canada (1987) *National Health Expenditure in Canada, 1970–1985*, Ottawa.

Health and Welfare Canada (1990) *National Health Expenditure in Canada, 1975–1987*, Ottawa.

Health and Welfare Canada (1991) *National Health Expenditure in Canada, 1975–1987*, special computer printout, Ottawa.

House of Commons, Canada (1991) *The Health Care System in Canada and its Fundings: No Easy Solutions*, First Report of the Standing Committee on Health and Welfare, Social Affairs, Seniors and the Status of Women, Ottawa, Queen's Printer for Canada.

Ismael, J.S. and Vaillancourt, Y. (eds) (1988) *Privatization and Provincial Social Services in Canada*, The University of Alberta Press, Edmonton.

Kettner, P.M. and Lawrence, L.M. (1987) *Purchase of Service Contracting*, Newbury Park, Sage Publications.

Labelle, R., Hurley, J. and Rice, T. (1989) 'Financial incentives and medical practice: Evidence from Ontario on the effect of changes in physician fees on medical care utilization', paper prepared for Physician Payment Review Commission, Washington.

Lemay, A. (1985) *The influence of hospital resources on the geographical distribution of Quebec's doctors*, Thesis, Department of Economics, University of Montreal.

Lomas, J., Fooks, C., Rice, T. and Labelle, R. (1989) 'Paying physicians in Canada: minding our Ps and Qs', *Health Affairs*, Spring, pp.80–102.

Macdonald Commission (1985) *Report of the Royal Commission on the Economic Union and Development Prospects for Canada*, Ottawa, Supply and Services.

Moscovice, I.C. (1983) 'Policy Approaches for Improving the Distribution of Physicians, *Health Services Research*, vol.18, no.2, pp.270–4.

McDermid, J. (1989) *Privatization: A Matter of Good Management*, Conference Office of Privatization and Regulatory Affairs, Ottawa.

Moreau, Y., Berthod-Wurniser, M. and Béckon, C. (1991) *Health costs: an international view*, Report to the Prime Minister, Paris.

Morin, G. (ed.) (1990) *The financing of the health services. A breakdown for the 1990s*, Council for Social Affairs.

Nahmiash, D. and Reis, M. (1991) *An Exploratory Study of the Private/ Non-governmental Home-care Services in Canada*, Health and Welfare Canada, Seniors Independence Research Projects, Ottawa.

National Council for Social Welfare (1991) *The dangers which threaten the financing of health and higher education*, Ottawa.

Québec (1991) *Towards a new balancing of age, Experts' report on the elderly*, Ministry of Health and Social Services.

Richardson, J.J. (ed.) (1990) *Privatization and Deregulation in Canada and Britain*, Dartmouth, Aldershot.

Rochaix, L. (1990) *Joint Price Quantity Regulation in the Market for Physician Services: The Quebec Experiment*, paper presented at the First European Conference on Health Economics, Barcelona, 19–21 September.

Social Planning Council of Metropolitan Toronto (1984) *Caring for Profit, The Commercialization of Human Services in Ontario*, Toronto.

Stanbury, W.T. (1989) 'Privatization in Canada: Ideology, symbolism and substance', in MacAvory P.W. et al. (1989) *Privatization and State-owned Enterprises: Lessons from the US, Great Britain and Canada*, Kluwer Academic Publications, Boston, pp.273–360.

Stein, K. (1988) 'Privatization: A Canadian perspective', in Walker, M.A. (ed.) (1988) *Privatization: Tactics and Techniques*, The Fraser Institute, Burnaby, BC.

Tsalikis, G. (1982) 'Linking health care and social services: international perspectives', in Hokenstad, M.C., Jr and Ritvo, R.A. (eds) *Social Services Delivery Systems, An International Annual*, vol.5, Sage Publications.

Vaillancourt, Y., Bourque, D., David, F. and Ouellet, E. (1988) *The Privatization of the social services*, Report presented to the Rochon Commission, Quebec Publications, Quebec.

Vayda, E. and Deber, R.B. (1984) 'The Canadian health care system: An overview', *Social Sciences and Medicine*, vol.18, no.3, pp.191–7.

Veit, S. (1990) 'Purchase of service contracting in the social services in Canada', in Richardson, J.J. (ed.) (1990) *Privatisation and Deregulation in Canada and Britain*, Dartmouth, Aldershot, pp.199–207.

Walker, M.A. (ed.) (1988) *Privatization: Tactics and Techniques*, The Fraser Institute, Burnaby, BC.

Workshop on Long-term Care in Ontario (1991) University of Toronto, 14–15 September.

–4–

France

Pierre Huard, Phillipe Mossé and *Guy Roustang*

This chapter will begin by looking at the for-profit hospital sector and the way that administrative constraints affect its growth. It will then consider: the role of the professionals in the process of privatisation; the privatisation of costs; diversified social cover, and commercial professional practices. Finally, it will examine the provision of services for elderly people, day care for the young, and housing in the context of privatisation.

Health Services

The two main ways of organising social welfare to be observed in Western Europe – statutory centralisation and collaboration between social partners – are both found in the French system. Hence French health care depends largely upon negotiation between the actors concerned – health care professionals and health insurance funds; nevertheless, the strong presence of the public authorities is very obvious, providing a framework, and often intervening in a somewhat authoritarian way. It could be supposed that such intervention by the state would result in a system that was fully regulated, leaving little place for market force activity. In reality, comparisons with other European countries reveal that France currently takes the lead in health expenditure as a proportion of GDP; in the share of those expenses paid directly by the users, and probably in the volume of private for-profit hospital care.

In this section, interest will be focused on the importance of the implementation of a system based on market forces and the conditions and mechanisms necessary to put it into place. This examination will cover more particularly the field of hospital care, the activity of health professionals, and social services for elderly people and infants.

The For-profit Hospital Sector

The private hospital care industry cannot be considered as an homogeneous grouping, either from the point of view of its objectives or from its operating principles, and cannot be totally associated with market forces.

More precisely, according to currently used nomenclature, the hospital system can be divided into two broad sectors: the public sector (much the larger) and the private sector. The private sector can be further subdivided as follows:

1 non-profit private hospitals participating in the Hospital Public Service (PHSP);
2 non-profit non-PHSP hospitals;
3 for-profit hospitals.

The for-profit sector may be defined initially by the legal status of the establishments: public companies, non-trading companies and limited companies; whilst the non-profit private sector includes the mutual companies, foundations and associations governed by the Act of Associations Law of 1901.

In the private non-profit sector, a supplementary subdivision appears between those participating in the PHSP and those outside it. To be a participant signifies that an establishment accepts being bound by the same obligations and having the same rights as the public hospitals, particularly as far as emergencies and financial regulation are concerned.

An alternative subdivision emerges if we use the criterion of the method of financing. There are still two distinct groups: first, the public establishments and the private PHSP establishments (those participating in the public hospital service), which all have a 'global budget', that is they are pre-financed; and second, the private for-profit establishments and the private non-profit non-PHSP establishments whose operation is based on a cost per day, that is they are post-financed.

Among these various categories, it is obviously the for-profit establishments which respond most directly to market forces. These establishments have several distinguishing features:

1 They have private status; that is, they belong either to private individuals (doctors, groups of doctors, shareholders unconnected with the medical profession) or to various types of legal entities, among which are to be found financial organisations or industrial companies.
2 They are authorised to make profits and to distribute them among their owners.
3 Their activity is financed by means of contracts with the National Health Insurance system, which covers the entire costs, on a daily basis, of the insured person (excluding medical expenses, which are paid

directly to the private doctors and not to the establishments they work in).

In principle, therefore, use of these for-profit establishments is no more costly for the user than use of public hospital care.

For-profit health care establishments may be compared with companies in the commercial sector to the extent that, in the same way, they have as their principal objective a return on their invested capital. However, the context of their activity is not exactly the same as that of the free market, since the health system is strictly administered through tariffs, nomenclature for operations, regional hospital master plans, and various other regulations.

Whatever the constraints, however, these establishments will use the margins of freedom that they possess to develop strategies aimed at profitability: for example the choice of orientation of their medical activity: developing their own particular disciplines and specialities; the use of facilities to achieve higher productivity (beds, equipment, medical competence), and the rationalisation of structures (optimal size, groupings, specialisation).

The generally intensive use of facilities often appears as a dominating preoccupation which has repercussions on the number of patients admitted, and on the level of consumption of treatment per patient. This propensity probably has varied consequences: it certainly leads to an intensification of the use of capital, but it may also have several adverse effects, such as medical over-consumption; the proliferation of inessential medical treatment; medical care that is essentially technical, with the emphasis on speed, and contracts between clinics and doctors imposing a minimum level of activity or growth in the number of treatments.

The Place of For-profit Hospital Care

Measured in complete hospital care beds, private commercial hospital care represented less than 20 per cent (19.3 per cent = 18.7 + 0.6) of the whole of the private and public hospital care sector in France at 1 January 1990. The total number of beds (public and private combined) is 558,693. Figure 4.1 gives a more detailed breakdown. Figure 4.1 also shows that the for-profit establishments hold the greater share (55 per cent) of the private hospital care sector. (3,450 + 104,170 = 107,620; 107,620 / 195,578 = 55 per cent)

The for-profit sector is mainly oriented towards surgery and obstetrics, to which it devotes more than three-quarters of its beds. Furthermore, 85 per cent of full-time private surgeons work in this field. In addition, the number of beds for these two disciplines has slightly increased

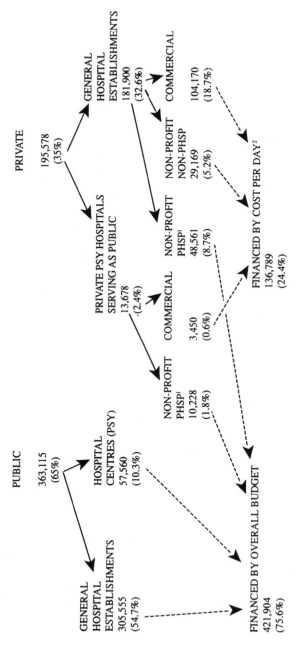

Figure 4.1 The Place of Private For-profit Hospital Care, France 1990 – Number of Beds

Notes:
1. Participating in the PHSP
2. The amount reimbursed to the hospital by the social security system

following a very slight overall drop during recent years, as compared with the other areas of private and State hospital care, where the decrease has been greater.

If we consider the public sector as including the private PHSP (that is to say, establishments participating in the public sector and financed by a global budget), and if we think of the private sector as corresponding to that financed on a daily basis, the changes in admissions for surgery between 1985 and 1988 can be presented as in Table 4.1. Thus, in the public sector, a decrease in admissions between 1986 and 1987 may be observed, with a similar decrease also to be found in obstetrics. Between 1987 and 1988 this trend was reversed, but the increase in private admissions was greater than the increase in the public sector. This difference in the increase in admissions is also apparent in non-surgical treatment, although we know that the share of the private sector remains much less than that of the public sector.

	1985/6 (%)	1986/7 (%)	1987/8 (%)
Public	2.4	–0.2	2.3
Private	5.7	3.6	4.4

Table 4.1 Changes in Surgery Admissions, France, 1985–8

In recent years, therefore, the for-profit private sector has been gaining ground, with increasing emphasis on surgery. A better understanding of the split may be provided, however, by an examination of the pathologies.

The main pathologies may be classified according to certain characteristic variables, such as:

1 the proportion of hospital stays made in the public and private non-profit PHSP sector;
2 the proportion of hospital stays during which surgery was involved;
3 the proportion of patients aged at least seventy;
4 the proportion of deaths among people of less than seventy years during their stay;
5 the proportion of patients resident in the catchment area of the establishment.

It is possible to compare groups in both the public and for-profit sectors (Choquet, 1991, pp.85–91).

The first group of pathologies, in which the private for-profit sector is significant (62 per cent of the patients), is constituted of those pathologies where surgery is of considerable importance (85 per cent). The pathologies concerned are those in which the risk to life is virtually nil, and where the number of elderly patients is low: appendicitis, the treatment of haemorrhoids and rheumatoid arthritis, dislocations, sprains, a great number of infections of the male and female genital organs, and disorders of the teeth and gums being among the most common.

There exists another group of pathologies which are mainly treated in the private for-profit sector (55 per cent). Surgery is once again significant in this group (60 per cent of admissions). Compared with the previous group, elderly people are more numerous and deaths not infrequent. The main reasons for admission are fractures of the neck of the femur, prostate gland treatment, varicose veins, cataracts, osteo-arthritis, and certain more accessible tumours: mouth, pharynx, rectum, breast and genital organs.

For the third group of pathologies, the public service proportion is 60 per cent, which is less than the average for hospital care as a whole. The patients are not elderly, and come frequently from the emergency services. Surgical interventions are common, with childbirth and minor traumatisms constituting the most frequent cases.

There are other emergency admissions which are treated almost wholly (92 per cent) in the public sector, with very few surgical interventions being undertaken. Poisonings, the more serious traumatisms, psychiatric disorders and acute breathing problems are particularly to be found in this group.

There remain three pathological groups in which the vast majority of cases are treated in the public sector. In the first of these groups, surgical interventions are relatively numerous. If the private share of the treatment is not large, it is because a certain number of them involve frontier technology – the prerogative of the CHRs (university teaching hospitals). Moreover, in this group, the proportion of patients who come from outside the local health region is greater. Neonatal pathology, congenital abnormalities, diabetes and kidney failure are among the main diagnoses of this group.

The second group are more serious pathologies, affecting at some time half of those aged at least seventy, where deaths are much more frequent. These are mainly the more serious tumours and heart and lung conditions.

The third group of pathologies (half of which affect older people, but in which the risk to life is less immediate) includes: stomach ulcers, intestinal occlusions, a large number of cardiac pathologies, chronic bronchitis and senile dementia. One admission in five in this group is an emergency.

These divisions indicate that the treatment of some pathologies appears to be more lucrative than others, doubtless because the private commercial sector is in a position to achieve a higher rate of real productivity. This is so because, in this sector, profit opportunities act as incentives for providers to produce services as efficiently as possible in terms of both resources and time. Indeed, the profitability of one or other medical activity is perhaps determined by the type of operation and its corresponding rate.

Finally, the development of the for-profit sector depends on the profitability of the field of activity that it selects; but this profitability itself has an impact upon the rules that govern the system. It would therefore be useful to consider the question of trends in relation to the administrative constraints surrounding hospital care, and their probable repercussions on the future of the private commercial establishments.

Administrative Constraints

As in all Western countries, the French public authorities have been seeking for a number of years to contain the expansion of health services and the resultant growth in expenses. As elsewhere, the main strategy has been that of fixed-price financing or pre-financing. This strategy was first applied to public hospitals (and to the non-profit PHSP hospitals) which were subjected in 1985 to global budgets. In the meantime, however, establishments in the for-profit sector retained the post-payment method of financing, based on the cost per day. It could be argued that the disparity in these methods of financing was in part responsible for the different development of the two sectors, the private taking advantage of the occasional opportunities for expansion unavailable to the state sector.

Since the Hospital Reform Act of 31 July 1991, this disparity in financing has ended. Following the passing of the Act, negotiations took place between the organisations representing the for-profit sector, the state and the Health Insurance Funds which led to a draft agreement based on three main directives: a national quantified objective (OQN); a regulatory mechanism, and reform of the fee structure.

The OQN concerns costs, with or without accommodation, for such treatments as dialysis, chemotherapy and out-patient surgery. This is added to hospital care costs, the cost of the purchase of apparatus, blood transfusion costs, and so on. The OQN, which is a base rate, in 1991 fixed a maximum annual increase for these expenses of 5.5 per cent.

The regulatory mechanism determines regional objectives in three-month periods, using the OQN as a basis, for such categories as medical treatment, surgery, gynaecology/obstetrics, average stay, psychiatry and long stay. At the end of each period the final shortfall is analysed and the rates are adjusted.

The reform of the fee structure introduced a long-term procedure based on the costs per pathology. The agreement (Article 10) stated that the new fee structure should 'make possible strict comparisons between public hospital care and private hospital care and the optimisation of the mechanisms for the allocation of resources between them'.

The transformation of the fee structure, however, is encompassed within the move towards rationalisation, which concerns as much the treatments that hospitals are able to offer as it does their facilities.

In the absence of effective evaluation, there can be no guarantee that the division of activities between the various components of the health system is optimal; hence the attention given over the last few years to the rationalisation of medical provision. This rationalisation may operate at two levels. First, there is the level of productivity: in other words, the relationship between, for example, the number of days a patient spends in hospital or the number of consultations he or she has, and the turn-over rate of the institution. Second, rationalisation may apply to results: that is the relationship between the effectiveness of the patient's medical treatment and the resources required to obtain this result.

In the first instance, the evaluation of the manner in which a service is produced, particularly in terms of cost per pathology, should provide a clearer comparison between patients in the state hospital sector and in the for-profit sector.

In the second instance, the medical effectiveness of the various services provided has yet to be evaluated. This should lead to their being separated into those which are medically justified and those which are of little or no medical use. Such an evaluation would highlight the incidence of each type of provision in the two respective hospital sectors.

However, neither of the above two forms of evaluation has yet reached an operational level because none of the producers of care has been encouraged to embark on such a process. Nevertheless, in as much as it can be predicted, it seems that in the short term the various components of the health system (public and private hospitals, out-patient medicine, biological analysis) will be subjected to similar forms of financial control. A comparison of the allocations, particularly when looked at in conjunction with the base rates, will be necessary. The legitimisation of allocative decisions will depend upon their being evaluated. As a result, the actors may be induced to draw up a realistic and objective evaluation of productivity and efficiency, rather than merely paying lip service to this ideal.

Even in these circumstances, however, technical difficulties, the necessary access to information, competence, and the possibility that some of the actors might prefer procedures of a political or corporatist bargaining nature, all need to be taken into account.

There exists in France, as in the majority of Western countries, a programme for hospital facilities covering the number of beds and the equipment. This programme, called the Regional Hospital Master Plan, dates from the Hospital Reform Law of 1970. Its operating principle consists of defining geographical areas or health areas and applying the bed/population ratios for the different medical specialisms to determine the hospital facilities required in each area. In fact, the ratios are often fixed in a rather arbitrary way, the local, political, corporatist and financial interests regularly succeeding in limiting the constraints of the Regional Hospital Master Plan.

Following the Hospital Reform Law of July 1991, a new regulatory plan has been created: the Regional Health Organisation Scheme (SROS). The aim is to take into consideration not exclusively the quantitative aspects of the hospital capacity of a region, as was the case previously, but also the more qualitative opportunities of reorganisation, which may occur through the regrouping, co-ordination, and redistribution of hospital provision. Special consideration should be given to the division between the public and private hospital sectors.

The various recent modifications in terms of administrative constraints on the for-profit hospital sector may, in time, affect its operation and profitability, and therefore its relative place in the French hospital system.

The question of profitability is crucial to the growth of the private for-profit hospital sector, and particularly so far as the financial investors are concerned. In fact, this category of hospital is generally 'medically' profitable: the doctors who practice in these hospitals and who own shares in the capital may receive satisfactory incomes from fees, payment for formal or real functions, and rental income. However, the profits distributed in the form of dividend to the shareholders are not always very high and, as a result, the investors who started showing an interest in the sector as early as 1985 have, it seems, become less active in recent years. This could be due to a realisation that it is difficult for them to control the activities of doctors.

While the reorganisation of the units of production is having a constrictive effect, a more specifically professional movement is developing which is contributing to the increase and strengthening of the role of commercial logic in the overall apparatus (Heinrich and Valerian, 1991). This will be examined in the next section.

Medical Professionals and Privatisation

The total number of health professionals is approximately 500,000. The majority are those with salaried contracts working in the State sector and those working in private practice, but distribution among professions is unequal. For example 24 per cent of the 80,000 general practitioners are salary earners, compared with 85 per cent of the 250,000 registered nurses. Overall, doctors constitute more than half of the health professionals paid on a fee-for-service basis.

Furthermore, the importance of the medical profession is highlighted by the fact that doctors are the determiners and authorisers of medical costs throughout the system. For this reason, their activity is subjected to complex and changing legislation. Control is essentially provided by an agreement negotiated regularly between the social security organisations, the state and the medical trade union. Its main function is to fix the charges for major services in order to provide a basis for the reimbursement of patients; for example in the context of the home visit the direct payment is generally around 20 per cent. The legislation is, however, subject to waivers which essentially aim at re-injecting commercial considerations into the very constraints which have been negotiated and put into practice by the majority of those taking part.

The phenomenon of privatisation is relatively widespread. It does not, however, affect the various forms of health provision, or the different professional categories, in an identical manner. Although the specialists may appear as the driving force behind this movement, in fact it is the specialism itself which influences the terms, conditions and speed of the process of privatisation within the health sector. The French medical profession is now, therefore, characterised by rapidly increasing specialisation, facilitated by the absence of any procedure to check it.

On the fringe of the official system there exists another form of production of care which is developing beyond any control in a market where the suppliers enter and move around freely, and where the prices are fixed according to the laws of supply and demand. These unqualified individuals, who include osteopaths and faith-healers, are not the subject of this paper. However, although they are situated outside the medical profession, they do contribute to shaping its evolution. These activities take place at the very limit of the regulated market, but in a health sector which is increasingly open to varied forms of private practices whose aim is to escape from constraints.

Common to all the above is the fact that they are able to increase in size and number thanks to a continual contraction of the forms, the circumstances and the context of the provision of state care. Faced with this phenomenon, and in an attempt to regulate it, the public authorities have instituted a mechanism which aims to limit entry to the ranks of the specialist. Despite the setting up of this 'closed shop', however, the movement continues through pseudo-specialisations accompanied by full-blown competition.

From the health professionals' point of view, the privatisation of the care system is taking place along two complementary lines, the economic effects of which are becoming more obvious. The first concerns the privatisation of financing with the increased contributions of users; the second concerns the evolution of the practices and modes of medical operation. Both of these will be considered in subsequent sections.

For the present it should be noted that, in a context of increased state control and of reforms in procedures, financing and reimbursements for care, the economic measures aimed at rationalising demand and increasing the participation and responsibility of the patients sometimes have immediate consequences on the choice of career for the medical professional and the direction it subsequently takes.

Privatisation of Costs

The proportion of costs borne by the patient, after having diminished during the 1970s, has not stopped increasing since. Today it amounts to approximately 20 per cent.

However, in analysing the extent of privatisation through financing, it is simply not enough to measure and add up the different forms of financial contribution. The situation in France is characterised by a recent and rapid increase in more subtle forms of charge. In fact, to evaluate and assess direct payments makes sense only when the provision of care remains unchanged. Nowadays the traditional forms of the use of care are diminishing, and the patient and his or her family are being increasingly requested to make greater efforts to contribute to the provision of care.

This contribution cannot be measured, and is not included in public accounts, the health budget or in social security. The following, therefore, contribute in unknown quantities to the increase in the privatisation of costs: the development of alternatives to hospital care; home nursing; out-patient surgery, and the opening of the doors of psychiatric hospitals. All these practices require of the patients and their family a certain availability, as well as know-how, accommodation and time, which not everybody has to the same degree. In this way the inequalities become obvious.

Given the increase in treatment at home, it might be expected that the proportion of home visits compared with consultations made at the doctor's practice is also increasing. In reality, this is not the case: patients are for the most part increasingly requested to make a contribution in the form of time spent on care and money spent on travel.

Elsewhere, the French social security system has since its inception made provision for the completely free treatment of certain pathologies. In this category are to be found accidents at work, work-related illnesses, and a list of around twenty illnesses reputed to be 'long and costly'. Table 4.2 shows that the number of people benefiting from free treatment has been steadily declining over the last fifteen years.

	1975	1980	1988	1990
Number of persons * reimbursed 100%	813.5			649.0
Percentage of consultations without direct payments		27		20

* Long-term illnesses, work accidents and illnesses

Source: Ministry of Health (1991), *Annaire des Statistiques Sanitaires et Sociales*, Paris.

Table 4.2 Number of Persons Reimbursed 100%, and Percentage of Consultations Without Direct Payment, France, 1975–90

Faced with this phenomenon, several explanations may be offered. Certain optimists would say that these statistics reveal the increasing efficiency of prevention policies. Others would point to the increasing disparity between, on the one hand, the classification system and the procedures used to obtain figures and, on the other hand, epidemiological change in the real world. Such critics would argue that the phenomenon observed is a fabrication.

Further research is required to demonstrate whether or not this decline continues unabated, and parallels the trend towards the privatisation of costs.

Thus, in a context where the overall demand for care is increasing regularly, the amount of medical treatment dispensed without financial contribution from the consumer is decreasing slowly but surely. This movement occurs automatically as a result of the recent declining share of the costs of care financed by social security.

Diversified Social Cover

In order to counterbalance the reduced cover from social security, more and more households opt for complementary insurance. Perhaps a strong aversion to the risks inherent in statutory welfare encourages people to look elsewhere for the very guarantees that the state is less and less inclined to offer.

The evolution of the structure of financing shows that the type of health insurance sought relates to its precise function. The consumer has to prepare him or herself to fill the increasing gap between what is covered by the national system and what remains his or her responsibility in the event of using care. The mutual insurance companies were founded many years ago, along corporatist or sectoral lines, to answer this need.

Nowadays, they are non-profit associations or holding companies whose role is to insure any member of the population. As a result they are generally to be found in competition with one another. Since affiliation is not obligatory, it is not surprising to observe that there is an uneven spread throughout the population. Overall, 80 per cent of the population take advantage of this kind of complementary health insurance as opposed to only 30 per cent in 1960, and the percentage varies according to income and social class.

For manual workers the impact of complementary insurance is to facilitate increased consumption of health care, whereas for non-manual workers, more of whom take out complementary cover, the impact is more qualitative, in that it facilitates more diversified forms of care.

Within this growing market for complementary health insurance, private and for-profit financial groups are beginning to appear. However, no figures relating to their market share are published by the Ministry of Health, and although it is difficult to estimate, this would seem to be relatively small. Nevertheless, this area of operation is likely to increase along with the momentum towards the individualisation of social cover already observable in the field of pensions.

One paradoxical consequence of declining support from the social security system is the growing participation of the state in the financing of health care. In fact, most of the health care delivered to poorer members of the community is financed by the national budget, and not by the social security system itself. The latter is financed from contributions taken from workers' salaries, while the state budget comes from more varied sources. With high and increasing rates of unemployment, the trend is for more health care expenditure to be financed from the national budget, which is less sensitive than social security to the vagaries of the labour market.

The French system works in such a way that the more the consumer is required to contribute, the more frequently assistance from the state – in the form of the *département* budget – is called upon. This contribution, however, remains marginal, and is not sufficient to compensate for the movement towards individualisation. The network of regulations and safety cover might lead to the belief that privatisation only affects the system partially and temporarily. Indeed, it is true that a swift appraisal of the recent history of financing health care leads one to think that these changes may not be irreversible. An upturn in the economy or a relaxing of budgetary constraints could reactivate the state's progress towards the expansion of national solidarity, which is today lying dormant, if not actually in decline. This belief perhaps explains the relative consensus which seems to accompany these changes.

However, along with these financial developments, certain customs and practices are becoming increasingly current amongst professionals. These changes may be termed 'structural', in that they tend to have a profound effect on doctor–patient relationships. It is to these that we now turn.

Commercial Professional Practices

The standard market and its classic modes of regulation are not totally absent from private practice in France; in fact, they are particularly relevant to the practice of medicine itself.

It is true that the unit price for the main services is fixed at national level within the context of agreements regularly and fiercely negotiated between the government, social security representatives and the professional trade unions. Nevertheless, various departures from this centralised form of control are possible, enabling the market to play a role in the allocation of resources within and to the health service. For example a number of doctors are permitted to charge a higher fee for their services than the basic rates negotiated for the calculation of reimbursement. In this case the consumer pays the difference, unless he or she is a member of a complementary mutual insurance company which agrees to settle the difference in cost.

The terms and conditions of this principle are themselves negotiated and have varied over time, especially during the last ten years; each new doctor entering the market has to conform to the current constraints. Succeeding generations of doctors have been free to a varying degree to determine their own charges.

Today there are three main forms of fee structure divided into sectors: Sector 1 covers doctors who opt for a strict application of the nationally and annually agreed basic fees. Within this sector, exceptions, which enable a practitioner with 'special skills' to charge higher fees, are being limited.

Sector 2, which is increasing dramatically, is a formula which enables a practitioner to charge for his or her services beyond the basic rate, the only limitation being an appeal to ethical standards and 'moderation'.

The doctors' wish to decide fees for consultations, and their acceptance by the majority of the population, is clearly reflected in the success of this formula. So much so that new negotiations in 1990 led to the strict limitation of access to this sector, restricting membership to certain categories of practitioner only. Despite this measure, however, the accumulated total of doctors engaged in relatively free determination of fees (Sector 2) amounts to 31 per cent of doctors, compared with 23 per cent in 1985 and 19 per cent in 1980.

This configuration sometimes creates inequalities in access to care, particularly since the positive features of classic market competition do not compensate for the freedom of doctors to make personal arrangements between themselves. Thus, areas of high population density are precisely those where the greatest percentage of doctors opting for Sector 2 and applying high fees are to be found. In Paris, for example, only 30 per cent of practitioners apply the negotiated, basic rates.

Affiliation to the national agreement and to one or other of its various conditions is not obligatory, even if the inducement is strong. Thus Sector 3 consists of a small group of doctors and clients choosing a totally commercial mode of relationship and exchange. Although this proportion may be low (less than 1 per cent of French doctors), it is nevertheless very sensitive to variations in conditions of the negotiated regulations and the room to manoeuvre that it leaves the professionals. After a continuous decline since 1980, the number of 'non-affiliated' doctors increased by 10 per cent between 1989 and 1990, following the redefinition of the conditions of access to Sector 2.

However, even within Sector 1, which encompasses the vast majority – doctors abiding by the annual nationally negotiated agreement – the proportion of fees charged within the context of the different conditions for the 'legal right to exceed' has risen from 4.9 per cent in 1980 to 8.5 per cent in 1990 (Table 4.3).

	1980	1985	1990
Doctors	4.9%	5.6%	8.5%
Dental surgeons	25.5%	32.3%	41.8%

Source: Social Security (1990), *Carnet Statistiques*, Paris.

Table 4.3 Share of Fees Outside Agreed Rates, France, 1980–90

Other branches of the profession have similarly evolved in the direction of a greater freedom of action by choosing practices which are more akin to the commercial sector. The most spectacular change has occurred among dental surgeons. The proportion of fees received over and above the agreed rates increased from 25 per cent to 42 per cent between 1980 and 1990. This is a sector where the percentage of professionals in private practice has always been high, and where the gap between the market price and rate of reimbursement has always been large.

The recent dynamics have therefore resulted from structural trends which have served only to accelerate these tendencies. This evolution is equally apparent in other fields. In this context, the increase in the percentage of professionals in private practice (and not as employees) is both an indicator and a predictor of the privatisation of health care. Table 4.4 shows that the proportion of private practice is increasing in all the health professions, both medical and paramedical.

	1980 (%)	1988 (%)	1990 (%)	2010 (%)
Nurses	11.8	13.7	14.1	
Physiotherapists	65.5	70.7		
Orthophorists	57.4	62.4		
Orthoptists	51.2	67.7		
Doctors	67	69	70	74

Source: Social Security (1991), *Carnets Statistiques*, Paris.

Table 4.4 Rate of Private Practice Activity, France, 1980–2010

Thus the extension of commercial logic from the very core of professional practice raises the question of the changing place of the consumer in the system of production.

Services for Elderly People

An analysis of services for the elderly and for young children will help pinpoint the changes in the division of responsibilities between the sphere of the layperson and that of the expert, and leads us to highlight the important role played by the family, alongside both the market and the public sectors. Similarly, given that dependence is not always, and certainly not principally, associated with illness, the boundaries between health and welfare are unclear.

In France, a very large majority of elderly people over sixty years of age live at home; in 1980 this was the case for 9,460,000 people. Those living in institutions were divided as follows: in a nursing or old people's home – 302,000; in a hospital – 60,000; in a religious community – 53,000; in a psychiatric hospital – 34,000. Residential centres (sheltered housing) accommodated 87,840 people in 1982. These are residential units consisting of small, autonomous dwellings provided with optional collective services: catering, meeting rooms, etc. (Audirac, 1987).

Nursing homes are public institutions where, in the past, could be found a mixture of the sick, the poor or the down-and-out. A law dating from 1975, dealing with the humanisation of hospitals, provided for the transformation of these establishments over a ten-year period so that they could provide comfortable accommodation for elderly people, particularly the dependent. In 1990, approximately one-third of the places still remained to be improved. From 1975 to 1982 the number of people living in old people's homes and nursing homes and residential centres doubled, but that still represented a total of only 4 per cent of the population over sixty. This proportion does, of course, increase with age. The role of the hospital has been expanded, from time to time taking over from the nursing home the accommodation of very elderly people. The number of residents in psychiatric hospitals is, however, stable.

According to a survey carried out in four *départements* in the South of France involving institutions accommodating elderly people, around six out of seven old people's homes and one residential centre out of two are likely to have private status. Unfortunately it is not possible to distinguish between the private non-profit and the private for-profit sectors (Sud Information Economique, 1990).

The number living in institutions, including residential centres, is therefore increasing rapidly; this movement will continue, given that the population as a whole is ageing, and that policies for home care have proved inadequate, despite their having being officially recognised since the VIth plan (1971–5) (Guillemard and Frossard, 1992). Even if the numbers in religious communities or psychiatric hospitals can be considered stable, the fact remains that the community is increasingly turning towards nursing homes, residential centres and old people's homes. They are now considered in a better light, thanks to the improvement in quality of accommodation, and currently they are attracting new social groups with high incomes.

In fact, elderly people are obviously a sought-after clientele, given their number and also the increase in their buying power over recent decades: 'between 1970 and 1984 the old age pensions of retired people over 65 have multiplied by an average 1.8 times in buying power, and the minimum pension has multiplied by an average of 2.6. In the same period, the average wage of a manual worker has only multiplied by 1.4 times' (Sud Information Economique, 1990, p.132). Furthermore, a study from the Centre for the Study of Revenues and Costs shows that, for men, the average monthly salary was 9,232 francs, whilst the average retirement pension of former wage-earners was 8,481 francs: not a very great difference (CERC, 1991).

It is impossible to obtain consistent and reliable information on the range of residential services made available to elderly people, mainly because no distinction is made between the various types of establishment offering for-profit and non-profit accommodation. It is equally impossible to obtain complete information on the available domiciliary services. Even when plans exist at the level of *départements* or regions, these are hardly ever followed. Public (residential accommodation developed by local councils) as much as private developments are built without authorisation and independent of the master plan (Ministry of Housing, Transportation and Space, 1992, p.250). Sometimes the authorisation granted does not correspond to the guidelines laid down. This is because the elected representatives of *départements* or local councils accept projects likely to encourage employment or provide highly visible examples of their power so that they may be well thought of by the electorate. It would seem that the schemes we have seen flourishing almost everywhere during the last few years are more often the work of the private for-profit sector (Ministry of Housing, Transportation and Space, 1992, pp.206 and 223). Certain residences for elderly people, created on the initiative of social workers and subsequently shown to be badly managed, have been taken over recently by private financial groups. This sort of accommodation is not within the reach of all budgets, and often those families who are the least well-off are forced to undertake the care of the elderly, either alone or with inadequate assistance.

A policy which meets the needs of elderly people more effectively and at the lowest possible cost is only likely to succeed if based upon a consistent approach involving the complete spectrum of organisations and the varying sources of financing. In reality, a division can be observed between the different ministerial departments (welfare, health, housing), between the state funds for the social security system (sickness, old age and family allowance payments, for example) and the complementary pension schemes, which are autonomous and follow their own policy. At the local level, since the decentralisation laws of 1982, the *département* governs matters of social policy, but it does not really succeed in co-ordinating the means:

> This splitting of responsibilities concerns legislation and control of institutions and services, the authorisation of new services and staff positions, the determination of tariffs for services, the allocation of the budget to the service-providing organisations . . . It should be emphasised that the majority of the organisations which finance these services do not directly supply them. (Henrard et al., 1991)

One of the main reasons for the inconsistency of the policy adopted in favour of the elderly comes from the rigidity deriving from the power of the health sector compared to that of the social sector. The report *Old People* from the VIth State Plan (1972–5) recommended that the health and social sectors should not be split (Henrard et al., 1991). In fact, the social law of 1975 institutionalised the dichotomy between the infrastructures belonging to the two sectors. A consistent and less costly policy would involve a redeployment of resources. At present, hospitals benefit from a concentration of means and financial resources at the expense of social establishments. Meanwhile, tens of thousands of beds in hospitals are thought to be occupied by elderly people who could just as easily be accommodated in institutions in the social sector. The present system of care is much more cumbersome and costly, but the power of hospital institutions, hospital directors and the medical profession has, until now, made any readjustment in the balance of resources impossible. Such a step would lead to a redistribution of resources and personnel from the hospital sector to the medical departments within the nursing homes or old people's homes, and to home care services.

The proportion of places with medical attention available represents little more than 20 per cent of the total of social sector establishments, which is obviously insufficient; and

> for the approximately 1,200,000 people living at home in need of assistance with everyday activities, only the home-help service has experienced a noticeable expansion (500,000 beneficiaries) . . . Of the 500,000 very dependent people in need of daily help, only 20 per cent benefit from nursing services at home. (Ministry of Housing, Transportation and Space, 1992, p.32)

Whilst the policy of home care has been constantly recommended for at least two decades, it is only modestly applied, mainly because of lack of resources. Nor is it always satisfactory, due to a lack of co-ordination between the different professions intervening at the home of the same person (Ministry of Housing, Transportation and Space, 1992, p.43). This results in admissions to social service institutions or to hospitals, which might have been avoided. The percentage of people admitted to an institution because their families had difficulty in taking care of them has increased constantly over recent years. Such people represented 15 per cent of admissions in 1968; this had doubled by 1989. Family difficulties can be explained by changing lifestyles: more frequent professional activity among women, distance between parents and children, greater demand for accommodation in towns and the greater desire for independence (Sud Information Economique, 1990).

There is a great need for much greater co-ordination of services for elderly people. Among the obstacles to this is that many local experiments seeking to remedy the segmentation of services are not aware of each other's existence. There is no real co-ordination which seeks complementarity and flexibility in order to adapt to the specific needs of each elderly person. Co-ordination cannot be decided from on high, it can only be constructed step by step through partnership between the different decision-makers: representatives of the *départements* and the local councils; the local offices of the different branches of the social security system including pensions; the health professionals; social services, and representatives of elderly people. 'The user of social services must be placed at the centre as an actor; his autonomy of decision-making must be maximised' (Guillemard and Frossard, 1992). It is a question of ensuring that we continuously adapt provision for an ageing society by co-ordinating the social services and care of elderly people; by facilitating their autonomy; and by supporting the efforts of the family or the neighbours. The liaison between the home care services and the institutions providing accommodation also needs to be improved. Numerous innovations in this direction exist in France, but they remain isolated, despite the fact that they are very much in line with the officially recommended policy (Planning Commission, 1991).

Day Care for Young Children

In France the education of young children is highly developed, with practically all (94 per cent) of children between three and six years old and more than one-third (35 per cent) of children from two to three years old attending a nursery school (Leprince, 1987). The Research Centre for the Study and Observation of Living Conditions had this to say:

> The policy for infant children which has been practised for several years aims at satisfying the theoretical criteria of the 'free choice' of parents through the joint development of several types of measure: aid to investment and the equipment of care facilities, reduction of the cost of services thanks to a certain number of social and fiscal allowances, and supplements in cash, such as the parental education supplement. (Hatchuel, 1989a and 1989b)

Since children over three years old attend school, the problem of day care only arises for children under three where both parents are working. At the beginning of 1986 there were estimated to be approximately 1,010,000 in this age group, a quarter of whom were looked after by their working mother; for example a farmer's wife, shopkeeper or professional person. The rest were spread as shown in Table 4.5.

The crèche (day nursery) is collective if care is provided in premises intended specifically for this use. Eighty per cent of collective day nurseries are neighbourhood crèches. Fifty-one per cent depend on the local council; some on the *département's* health and welfare services (19 per cent), and

Type of Centre	Share (%)
Formal Agencies	
Local crèches	12
Family-run crèches	6
Registered childminders	26
Total	44
Other Types of Day Care	
Grandparents	35
Non-registered childminders	21
Total	56

Source: Hatchuel (1989b).

Table 4.5 Distribution of Children in Day Care in France

10 per cent on non-profit associations. The remaining 20 per cent are crèches for the use of staff, generally located at the place of work: 16 per cent in hospitals, and the remaining 4 per cent in offices or private companies. What is remarkable is that in France there are no private companies offering commercial services for the day care of children. The commercial services are the exclusive domain of qualified and officially recognised nursery nurses, or unrecognised childminders taking young children into their homes for cash payments.

A family-run crèche is one where the day care is provided by qualified nursery nurses at their homes, and where the activity is co-ordinated and controlled by a responsible paediatric nurse. These day nurseries are managed mainly by local councils (82 per cent) and voluntary associations (11 per cent). The registered nursery nurses are controlled by the Mother and Child Protection Service.

The operating costs of a collective day nursery in 1985 amounted, on average, to 208 francs per day per child; those of a family-run crèche to 147 francs. The collective day nursery is subsidised to the tune of 20 per cent by the Family Allowance Fund, with 26 per cent of the income coming from the parents, and 54 per cent from the managing body – the local councils. It should be pointed out that, for the collective day nurseries, the financial participation of the parents is scaled in relation to their resources. For childminding by registered nursery nurses, the costs are mainly borne by the families, who only receive a 20 per cent subsidy from the local authority. Obviously, in the case of non-registered childminders working for cash payments, all the costs are borne by the parents.

When parents are asked which kind of day care would be the most satisfactory, the level of unsatisfied demand for collective day nurseries is high; but the rigidity of operation of these establishments, through such measures as restricted hours and the barring of children in the event of minor illness, results in their opting mainly for individual childminders.

The great majority of parents of young children (88 per cent) are in favour of cash benefits to enable the mothers of young children to give up work temporarily. They prefer such a cash allowance rather than benefits in kind, consisting of supplying certain equipment. The slow development of part-time work opportunities in France compared with other Western countries should also be taken into account. Of young mothers with children under three years old, one-third already work part-time, and another third would welcome the possibility of reducing their working hours, even if this meant a loss of salary (Hatchuel, 1989b).

For the day care of young children, parental day nurseries represent an original formula. A group of parents forms an association and engages one or several infant day care professionals. These parents profit from the assistance of the Family Allowance Fund; they contribute financially to the operation of the day nursery, and they participate in the childminding – between half a day and a day per family per week. This participation obviously reduces the operating costs. Thanks to help from the Federation of Parental Day Nurseries, which trains the parents, and government help in setting them up, the number of parental day nurseries, which stood at 200 in 1986, has risen to 800 in 1992, involving around 20,000 families.

As in the case of care for elderly people, a policy for pre-school children which would guarantee the maximum efficiency at the minimum cost would involve the consistent mobilisation of the resources of the non-commercial public sector, the commercial private sector and the domestic economy. For these types of inter-related services, it would be appropriate to incorporate the adaptation of the services to the needs and the aspirations of the users into the criteria relating to efficiency.

Housing

As in many other European countries, in the 1980s France engaged in a radical rethinking of its housing policy. In a context which can be considered as 'centralised', national policy has resulted in the acceleration of the movement towards private ownership. However, the first steps in this direction are taken at local or regional level, resulting in a rather complex procedure. For instance, the *départements* are responsible for implementing social housing policy, but they are not allowed to decide the market price nor draw up the legal framework within which they act. Nevertheless, it is clear that the major aim of French policy is to facilitate the expansion of the private market. For this reason there has been a significant shift away from help for private investors and builders to help towards individual home ownership.

Tenants have also been helped to buy property they have been renting in the private sector through nationwide control of prices, which has led to a further change in housing tenure. As a result, home ownership doubled between 1950 and 1990. Nevertheless, the 1990 figure of 56 per cent of owner-occupied property cannot be seen as a success for government policy when it is considered that France ranks only tenth among the twelve EU countries.

The eligibility of low-income groups for public social housing has been encapsulated in the law known as the *loi Besson*, which lays down the income threshold below which the needy or those with 'special difficulties' are entitled to claim. This law has resulted in the continuance of a high level of provision of social housing for rent: the figure is approximately 3.6 million dwellings – representing half of all rented houses in France. Of these, 1.8 million are in the public sector (generally managed at city level), while 1.5 million are owned by private, non-profit associations.

Such organisations, be they private or public, are today facing a dilemma. On the one hand they have the short-term objective of remaining financially solvent, while on the other hand they are being asked to support the cities' plans to reduce urban ghettos. Nevertheless, the overall result of housing policy is increasingly to divide households spatially according to their purchasing power.

Conclusion

The French health, welfare and housing systems, as we have shown, are characterised by a highly diverse range of modes of production and contexts within which care and services are meted out. The movement towards privatisation is developing within a system of constraints, centralised on a state supported by stable and powerful institutions. But, at the same time, those working within the system – especially health professionals, and more particularly the doctors – already have, and are further creating for themselves, wide margins for manoeuvre. Commercial considerations may, therefore, gain in strength and be used in the service of special interest groups, rather than for the benefit of the whole community.

Although most elderly people still live at home, the number and proportion moving into various forms of residential care, despite the avowal of policies of community care, is increasing. The figures are incomplete, but it is clear that a large proportion of residential establishments are independent, and that many of these are in the for-profit sector. This development of for-profit services is fuelled, as elsewhere in Western Europe and North America, by the increased relative prosperity of elderly people. At present, however, there has been little development of commercial provision of domiciliary services.

Similarly, there are no private companies offering day care for young children on a commercial basis. Nevertheless, 47 per cent of children receiving some form of day care are looked after by registered and unregistered childminders who are paid by parents. In addition, parents contribute fees, and sometimes labour, to other forms of day care.

The main thrust of housing policy has been the encouragement of home ownership, which doubled between 1950 and 1990. However, about 44 per cent of all dwellings are in the rented sector, and half of these are designated as social housing.

In France, health care has tended to overshadow social care. One of the major issues is the power exerted by the doctors and other health care professionals, and the difficulties which this causes for regulation of the services. In order to control the system as a whole, procedures of 'concerted control' are being introduced or planned, and the success of these will be important in determining future developments. The aim is to make the doctors more responsible by involving them directly in management and measurement operations. Such procedures towards rationalisation, backed by real progress in evaluation, should help to avoid a two-speed medical system and the introduction of commercial considerations which take no account of the wishes of the consumer, who, in the final analysis, is the best judge of services.

The development of corporatist strategies means that compartment-alisation is always possible; but it is more probable that the actors (public authorities, doctors and users) will choose to keep professional practices outside the field of the economic management of the health service.

We have identified co-ordination of provision as a major concern in health and social welfare in France. The emergence of private markets in these areas makes co-ordination even more significant. A balance between the commercial, informal voluntary and the statutory sectors is needed, but there is no agreement about precisely where the balance should be struck.

The overwhelming victory of the right and centre-right parties in the 1993 parliamentary elections is likely to lead to further privatisation, although much will depend upon the outcome of the almost inevitable clash between the Prime Minister and the President, and the result of the presidential election of 1995.

References

Audirac, P.A. (1987) 'Les personnes agées et leur famille'(Elderly people and their families), *Données Sociales.*

CERC (1991) 'Report from CERC', no.103, Paris.

Choquet, O. (1991) 'Le partage des soins hospitaliers entre le service public et le privé lucratif' (The share of in-patient care between the public and private sectors), *Solidarité Santé*, no.3, July–September, pp.85–91.

Guillemard, A.M. and Frossard, M. (1992) *Caring for the Dependent Elderly: French Old Age Policies and the Welfare Mix*, Vienna, European Centre.

Hatchuel, G. (1989a) 'Accueil de la petite enfance et activité féminine' (Children, day care and the involvement of women), *Collection of Reports*, no.61, May.

—— (1989b) 'Accueil des jeunes enfants: La course a la debrouille' (Coping with day care for young children), *Consommation et Modes de Vie*, no.41, July–August.

Heinrich, L. and Valerian, F. (1991) *La Santé Marchande, Cliniques Commerciales et Commerce des Cliniques* (Commercial Health, Commercial Clinic, and Clinics' Commerce), Rennes, Editions ENSP.

Henrard, J.C., Ankri, J. and Le Disert, D. (1991) 'Soins et aides aux personnes agées: Effet des caracteristiques structurelles du système sur la mise en oeuvre de la politique et la fonctionnement des services' (Care and Cure for elderly people: Effects of system characteristics on the implementation of reforms), *Sciences Sociales et Santé*, March.

Leprince, F. (1987) 'La garde des jeunes enfants' (Day care for young children), *Données Sociales.*

Ministry of Housing, Transportation and Space, (1992) *Vieillir Dans la Ville* (Growing Old in Cities), Paris, Editions L'Harmatan.

Planning Commission (1991) 'Dependance et solidarités: Mieux Aider les Personnes Agées' (Dependence and Support: Better ways of helping elderly people), *La Documentation Française*, September.

Sud Information Economique (1990) 'Les Personnes Agées' (Elderly People), *INSEE*, no.84.

–5–

Hungary
Eva Orosz

A reassessment of the role of the state and the privatisation of social welfare is the most significant international trend in social policy in the 1980s. Despite the numerous similarities, however, there are a number of important differences between the Western and the former state-socialist countries. In the context of Hungary, this chapter attempts to answer the following questions:

1 What are the most important differences?
2 How does the privatisation of welfare fit into the process of systemic change in politics and in the economy?
3 How relevant is privatisation as a means of solving the major problems of social welfare?
4 What are the specific individual features of social insurance, health care, personal social services and housing?
5 Exactly what are the participants creating, either actively or simply by their weakness and passivity?

Economic and Political Background

The so-called 'systemic changes' of 1988–90 were simply the completion of a previous long-term gradual erosion of the 'old rule' and of all its institutions, rather than the revolutionary beginning of potential radical social and conomic changes of the future. (Szalai and Orosz, 1992)

The second, or 'shadow', economy has in fact played a vital role in shaping the socio-economic changes of the past three decades, significantly eroding the state-socialist political and economic system. Since the late 1960s this dual structure – the 'official' and the 'shadow' economy – has been closely connected to the development of the social security system. Thus privatisation, and debate about the role of the market, started in reality well before 1990.

Political and economic change has involved the radical transformation of ownership relations in every sphere of the Hungarian economy (Matolcsy, 1991; Research Institute of Privatisation, 1992). The privatisation of welfare is part of this process. Factors which have directly influenced the welfare sector are:

1 privatisation in the economy;
2 the handing over of public health care institutions and social services to local government;
3 the return of former Church property;
4 the allocation of property to the Social Security Institute;
5 the setting up of new private institutions in the welfare sector.

The shift to a market economy presents a grave challenge, partly because it has been accompanied by deepening social problems (increased unemployment and poverty), and partly because the economic structure upon which the earlier social system was built has collapsed. That structure had been characterised by a labour 'market' adjusted to a non-market economy: in other words, by full employment in the state sector. Social insurance was connected to employment status. The level of wages, pensions and all social payments was set relatively low, because it was assumed that basic needs (for example housing, health, public transport, education) would be financed and provided fully or partly by state institutions, and free at the point of consumption. On the other hand:

> Through the gradual expansion of informal production, people had started to build their lives on two pillars: one in the formal, and another in the informal sector. In this manner a new way of life spread throughout Hungarian society, and two distinct clusters of motivation came to dominate people's daily activities. (Szalai and Orosz, 1992)

Today, those in the most desperate situation are people who obtained their income only from the state economy or from social welfare benefit, and who have not been able to enter the shadow economy.

The grave dilemma for the welfare sector is that, from a macro-economic perspective, the level of social expenditure is too high compared with countries at a similar stage of development (approximately 33–34 per cent of the GDP, including expenditure on education, housing and price subsidies). To improve the country's economic competitiveness, it would appear necessary to reduce social expenditure. On the other hand, even at present, welfare needs are not being met. The deepening recession of the early 1990s has dramatically increased this problem. It has led simultaneously to an increase in the burden of social expenditure on the economy, and to a decrease in the real value of financial resources available to the welfare sphere. At the same time, there has been a higher demand for social benefits and services. Economic transformation has, therefore, dramatically increased the need for social welfare provision, but simultaneously it has caused a financial and organisational crisis amongst social welfare institutions.

The retreat of the state does not simply mean a change in the proportion of provision between public and private. In the state-socialist welfare system, the state was the only agent (at least at the official, institutional level). Reassessment of the role of the state means a transition towards a system where several actors participate in the decision-making process; in other words, where the state is only one among many. This requires a fundamental transformation of the institutions and the decision-making mechanisms. The transformation of the political system in 1990–1991 has only produced the necessary preconditions at the level of macro-politics; it has not been sufficient to ensure the transformation of political and decision-making processes at lower levels in the political system, for instance within the sphere of welfare. It is a paradox that democratic reforms are being implemented by anti-democratic means.

Although debate about the desired reform of the different social welfare sectors has been going on for years, the possible alternatives have not yet been clarified. One reason for this is that the different options for public/private mix have not been defined. Decisions are mostly made on an *ad hoc* basis, without adequate consensus.

In many west European countries, privatisation has taken place without the basic characteristics of the Welfare State being dismantled (Johnson, 1987; Glennester, 1992). In Hungary, on the contrary, a radical overhaul of the public sector is envisaged, and it is questionable whether the present concentration on privatisation is the best solution: such a policy postpones decisions essential for the public sector, and creates a two-tier system.

There is the added complication that the evolving new government has to legitimise itself. This is one of the reasons why their handling of problems is characterised by excessive reference to ideology. Often the situation in the late 1980s and early 1990s is compared to the position in the 1930s or to the conditions under state socialism in the 1950s, in order to find reasons to justify current ideas and priorities. This greatly hinders the understanding and effective treatment of today's social problems. For example, the issue of returning to the churches their social and health care institutions, and the issue of abortion, have been given great attention, while statistics revealing deteriorating health, and horrifying revelations about pollution, have been ignored.

There is also a confusion of values. Government policy-makers see a number of the principles which constitute the basis of Western welfare programmes (such as universalism) as being identical to socialism.

However, the concepts of solidarity, social justice and equality have become discredited, partly as a result of the ever-widening gap between advocated values and reality which characterised the past decades.

The basic characteristics of state socialism have made developments like these inevitable. However, it is also necessary to look more closely at the changes of the recent past. The years 1990 and 1991 were characterised by wild illusions concerning the speed and feasibility of the introduction of a market economy. The view that had evolved over previous decades – that the market economy necessarily entails political democracy – was unassailable. It was also believed that the market would solve the grave inefficiencies in the field of welfare. However, privatisation has not proved to be a universal panacea, and expectations related to the market have considerably diminished. For the time being it is not clear whether the positive effects of the market will result in a more realistic and pragmatic policy, or whether diminishing expectations will offer ideological support to the emerging movement towards recentralisation.

It has now become clear, however, that a shift to a market economy is not simply a matter of changing the political regime, and that democracy does not automatically flourish along with the establishment of markets. It is also becoming apparent that the retreat of the state from social provision is not necessarily a blessing for the economy. It may mean just the opposite: the reduction of social income contributes to the contraction of the domestic market, which, in its turn, deepens economic recession.

Main Features of the Emerging Social Welfare System

It is very difficult to draw up a balance-sheet for the state-socialist welfare system. Although it played its role in maintaining the totalitarian political regime, it did provide relative security. Services and benefits, however, were provided in a paternalistic way, as 'gifts of the party-state'. As Ferge (1991, p.22) says: 'The whole notion of modern citizenship, and the civil, political and social rights on which it is based . . . were absent from state socialism.' On the other hand, many ingredients of the welfare system, such as universalism and adequate child care institutions, were enjoyed by the majority of the population and became part of everyday life. Hence, proposals under the present state of economic hardship to cut public expenditure and privatise these services are threatening the security of the worst-off.

The main function of the state-socialist system was to keep wages at a low level in order to concentrate resources in industrial development, rather than to provide social security and welfare. As a consequence of the non-market economy, support for unprofitable industries was unquestioned, and direct production objectives, not welfare goals, were the focus of the redistributive activities of the state (Szelenyi and Manchin, 1987).

This still continues today. Under state socialism, social services, health care, education and environmental protection were considered 'non-productive' – that is simply consumers of national income. This fallacy still prevails. The potentially significant role of these areas in promoting long-term economic growth and competitiveness has still not been recognised by the policy-makers.

A key question during our continuing socio-economic transition period must be: what kind of relationship is appropriate between the economy and social welfare in Hungary; how can or should elements forming this relationship be influenced, and is focusing on privatisation in the welfare sector constructive or diversionary?

A consideration of the emerging welfare system should distinguish between ideology, government decisions and actual events. As far as ideology is concerned, the 'social market economy' is the catchphrase of the day. The meaning, however, of a social market economy is unclear and much disputed. There are at least three different interpretations: (1) it might mean a Welfare State, predominantly funded and controlled by the state; (2) it might mean a free market with the minimum of public intervention, where social assistance is targeted only on the poor; (3) it might primarily be used to legitimise a hierarchical welfare system supported by a state bureaucracy.

Although it is yet to be seen which interpretation eventually wins the day,

> the more or less clearly formulated objective is to transform the current uniform system into dual or three-tier systems . . . The leading ideas may be spelt out: compulsory contributory schemes should strictly follow the 'equivalence' principle (that is, they should be as similar to private schemes as possible); the compulsory schemes should cover limited risks, so as to leave as much place as possible to private market arrangements; and if possible, universal solutions should be replaced by less costly targeted ones. (Ferge, 1991, p.23)

Economic exigencies, weakening popular support for the government, and the lack of a comprehensive, well thought out state programme, have led to vacillation between policies of withdrawal and policies of strengthening the role of the state. *Ad hoc* decisions are taken, influenced mainly by short-term interests and the power-struggles between leading figures of the central bureaucracy and the governing parties.

It is important to consider the issue of privatisation from the angle of the different interest groups. Representation of the different interest groups is still in its formative stage. They, too, concentrate mainly upon economic problems and inter-group conflict to the considerable neglect of social issues. For example, the self-government of social security has not been set up because the trade unions have been unable or unwilling to agree upon the issue of representation. Indeed, it seems that government is trying to slow down the evolution of representation, and to divide the possible representatives. Atkinson and Hills (1989) emphasise the role of administrative constraints in the shaping of the social security system: 'those engaged in the administration of social security constitute an interest group which may have an impact on the evolution of policy.' This is particularly true in the case of Hungary. The bureaucracy is partly interested in wiping out the debts of the welfare sector by transferring the financial burden to somebody else. On the other hand, the consolidation of power by a state wishing to retain a significant role is a strong motivating factor.

Nor can the common interests of local authorities be fully represented at the national level. Although they have several associations, each of them is individually weak. The government has the power to paralyse local authorities financially, and to limit their autonomy and activities. Social and health institutions have been transferred from the state to local authorities under the Act on Local Government of 1990, but their financing has been retained by the state. Formally, the local authorities are authorised by the Act to levy taxes, but the population cannot be burdened any further. Thus local authorities are forced to close down institutions and to privatise housing, even if they had previously had different plans. The adverse consequences of these measures, and the dissatisfaction of the population, obviously affect the local authorities. It is difficult to say how far government policy objectives are to be blamed, and how far it can be attributed to the fact that the majority of the local authorities have been led by the opposition parties.

The interest of employers, obviously, is to decrease social security contributions. The representative organisations of new enterprises are the main proponents of the plan that the comprehensive and compulsory social security system should be dispensed with and replaced by an enterprise-based insurance scheme. A new body called the Council for the Reconciliation of Interests, comprising representatives of the state, the employers and the workers, has been set up. It also discusses the main social policy proposals. Trade unions, on the other hand, do not have their own welfare policy. Moreover, the proliferating trade unions are divided and disorganised.

Social Insurance

Until 1988, social insurance revenues and expenditures were an integral part of the state budget. The creation of an autonomous social insurance system started in 1988, when the separate social insurance fund was created.

The Act guiding the social insurance system to self-government was passed in December 1991; however, the self-governing body, consisting of the representatives of employers and employees, was not set up until May 1993. This Act separated the social insurance fund into a pension fund and a health insurance fund. Before 1993, ten-member boards of control supervised both the pension scheme and the health insurance scheme. As the competence of these supervising committees was limited, the government virtually retained a free hand in forming the new system of social insurance, whereas the representatives of contributors did not get a real opportunity to participate in the making of basic decisions.

It is true that social security contributions mean a heavy burden on companies, but it is also true that services are unsatisfactory and do not offer a complete safety net. In 1991 the social security contribution was 54 per cent of wages (44 per cent was paid by the employers and 10 per cent by the employees). Behind the high percentage of contributions are relatively low wages, and low productivity. There are demographic considerations as well: for example the high percentage of elderly people in the population. In addition, it should also be emphasised that the changes made in the pension system in 1975 did not consider economic rationality – pensions were determined in too generous a way and the retiring age set too low (fifty-five for women and sixty for men).

The precondition for an increase in private insurance would obviously be a reduction in the high level of compulsory contributions. Yet even the present level of benefit does not offer adequate cover, and this is a reason for not making any radical cut. Inflation, which has been in double figures since the early 1980s, reached a peak of 35 per cent in 1991, and has been around 20/25 per cent since then. This, plus the lack of indexing, has caused a considerable fall in the real value of social insurance benefits, and of pensions in particular. The extreme financial instability of the social insurance fund is a factor at once forcing changes as well as narrowing the latitude for reforms.

These reforms have been dragging on for years. There has been very evident continuity between the ideas of the earlier regime and the present government. One of the aims of the reform of social insurance is to help private schemes to evolve and to enhance their role in the field of pension as well as health insurance. A further aim is to assert as much as possible the principle of equivalence, characteristic of both private and compulsory insurance – in other words, to reduce the principle of solidarity (redistribution among the social classes) to a minimum.

Disputes have been continuing as to whether liquidation of the uniform system (to be replaced by the pension funds of employers, branches, etc.) is needed, or whether it should be maintained but radically transformed. The liquidation of the uniform system is supported primarily by some liberal economists, by certain circles within the Treasury, and by the entrepreneurs. The departments concerned with public welfare, and the trade unions, represent the opposite point of view. However, no realistic proposal has been made as to how present pensions should be paid if the national pension fund were to be liquidated.

In late 1991 and early 1992 the first rather contradictory steps were taken towards the reform of the social insurance system. The changes are contained in the resolution of Parliament passed in October 1991, in the amendment to the Social Security Act of 1975, and the Act approving the 1992 budget of the Social Insurance Fund (*Magyar Kozlony*, 1991; 1992). The latter Acts were passed in February 1992.

Several forms of privatisation are evident in the changes that have taken place. The following deserve particular attention:

1 the limitation of state guarantees;
2 the introduction of an income ceiling for pension contributions;
3 the introduction of ten-day sick leave paid for by the employer;
4 the limitation of rights to health services.

Furthermore, the State Social Insurance Institution (which administers social security programmes, the pension scheme, sick pay, various maternity benefits and, since 1990, the financing of health care) may benefit significantly from privatisation, as it could share in the rewards obtained from the sale of state property.

A parliamentary resolution restated the decisive role of compulsory social insurance:

> Parliament agrees with the continuation of compulsory social insurance as the most comprehensive institution of social security, extending over the broadest possible circle of the population and which is to be guaranteed by the state in the future. The social insurance system realises the social protection of members of society in harmony with the other systems of state social provision and with the institution of unemployment insurance. (*Magyar Kozlony*, 1991)

However, the above wording is so general that it is open to a wide variety of interpretations. At present in Hungary, insurance does not cover the entire population: under new proposals, eligibility will be even more limited. Incomes below a certain level are not eligible for the pension scheme. Nor does health insurance cover everybody, whereas previously each citizen was entitled to it. As far as the role of the state is concerned, the resolution emphasises that:

> It is necessary that the state budget share financing. Its forms are direct (normative) and indirect budgetary support, the transfer of property, and a general state guarantee. The replenishment of the reserve funds of compulsory social insurance is necessary within the framework of the privatisation of state property in the form of the transfer of property free of charge. (*Magyar Kozlony*, 1991)

The parliamentary resolution sets the objective of an eventual three-tier pension system: (1) a flat-rate national pension; (2) an income-related pension; (3) voluntary complementary insurance. It stresses that a flat-rate pension 'can only be introduced at a high level of economic development, in the more distant future'. This may mean that the government did not wish to reject this proposal outright, but that it was actually removed from the agenda. This relegates the problem of elderly people who have no pension to the sphere of social assistance. In the case of income-related pensions, one of the main objectives is a gradual shift to pensions calculated on the basis of life-long earnings; the plan to raise the age of retirement for men was abandoned in 1994 in an attempt to gain electoral support. In 1992, the basis for the calculation of pensions was raised from three to four years. The age of retirement for women is to be raised by stages from 1993 onwards so that it will reach the planned sixty-two years after the turn of the century. If privatisation is interpreted broadly, then a part of the process must be the reduction in state allowances given in return for the same level of contribution.

The government intended to encourage the development of private pension insurance by setting an upper limit to the income after which compulsory pension contributions must be paid. But because this income ceiling is relatively high, it is relevant only in the case of a narrow stratum of the population. Furthermore, the upper limit applies only to the contribution paid by the employees and not to that paid by the employer. Therefore it can be considered as a symbolic political gesture aimed at the better-off. Obviously a lower income ceiling would have caused great difficulties for the Social Insurance Fund, because it would have further increased its already enormous debt. It should be stressed that this constitutes only one of the first steps in the transformation of the pension scheme.

The Social Insurance Fund, which had been a uniform one, has been divided into a Pension Fund and a Health Insurance Fund. The uniform contributions have also been divided. The most important change in the case of health care is that 'The curative/preventive services should be legally based on the grounds of insurance, with an obligatory payment of health insurance contribution determined by law' (*Magyar Kozlony*, 1991). This means that the former eligibility for health care based on a citizen's right has been eliminated, and replaced by eligibility for compulsory health insurance which does not cover the whole population. I will refer to this again.

Another fundamental change is that the different forms of ownership are acknowledged as equal. According to the parliamentary resolution, 'the services are purchased by the insurance company on the basis of performance, within the framework of a contract with health institutions owned by the state, the local governments, the churches, and by private individuals' (*Magyar Kozlony*, 1991).

The issue of state guarantee (the relationship between the state budget and the new Pension Fund and the Health Insurance Fund) is a fundamental issue, and constitutes one of the most critical points of dispute. This is also a key issue from the point of view of privatisation in the broadest sense. The Act on the State Budget passed in December 1991 only safeguards, up to 1 per cent, the Pension Fund; no guarantee has been provided for the Health Insurance Fund. In other words, it disregards the contents of the parliamentary resolution passed only two months earlier. No one can tell what will happen if either of the funds incurs significant deficit.

In the case of the pluralisation of the pension system, it should be remembered that complementary pension insurance appeared in the insurance market in 1988, primarily purchased by employers, but it is also available to private individuals. For the employers, complementary pension insurance has been one of the means of allocating tax-free income to their leading employees. As a result, no social insurance contribution was paid. Further, the individual had immediate access to additional tax-free income, as loans at a reduced interest rate could be taken up on the basis of the pension.

Since 1992, companies have been able to build up pension funds. According to the tax laws of 1992, payments to company pension funds enjoy a tax allowance. Twenty-five per cent of the sum paid to the pension fund by the employer and the individual may be deducted from taxable income, up to a specified maximum sum.

The Development of the Private Insurance Market

Changes in social insurance have influenced the demand for private insurance. There is no tradition of private pension and health insurance in Hungary, but the gradual development of two forms can be expected in the coming decades: (1) voluntary mutual insurance funds and (2) commercial insurance policies. The Act on Voluntary Mutual Insurance Funds was passed in late 1993 as a first attempt to encourage the development of voluntary mutual insurance schemes.

Until 1989 there had been only one personal insurance company in Hungary: the State Insurance Company. This could not be regarded as an enterprise, but much more as a department of the Ministry of Finance, and it had a monopolist position in offering life insurance (Karcsay, 1991). Now there are more than ten insurance companies, the majority of them operating with the participation of foreign capital. However, the State Insurance Company continues to dominate the market in the field of life and personal insurance to the extent of 80–90 per cent. Because of the previous monopoly of the State Insurance Company, there was an anti-insurance attitude.

Now, major companies and even trade unions have begun to design plans for the establishment of autonomous pension and health insurance funds. The attitude of the insurance companies is one of 'wait and see', while they exert pressure on the Social Security Institution. In fact, their sphere of activity will obviously be influenced in the future by the reform of social security and health care.

Privatisation of Health Care

Privatisation of health care has been taking place in all three major fields: regulation, finance, and services. But this has not affected public sector dominance. It should be emphasised that there is no clear-cut division between the public and private sectors. Thus it is not an issue of private institutions entirely separate from public ones, but much more of public institutions providing a background or basis for the operation of the private sector. This facilitation of private institutions leads to the assumption that the private is inherently better than the public service.

The expansion of the private sector is primarily influenced by the behaviour of the state. More precisely, factors independent of health policy are present on the supply as well as the demand side, and actions taken by the state are far more influential than the spontaneous processes of supply and demand.

The most important components of privatisation in health care are: (1) regulation of eligibility for compulsory health insurance; (2) reorganisation of primary care – that is, the introduction of the family doctor system; (3) emergence of private health insurance; (4) an increase in direct payment for prescriptions; (5) privatisation of pharmacies;

(6) development of private medical companies. Before discussing these processes, I wish to highlight some general issues.

First, it would be wrong to assume that current private health care started from nothing. Under state socialism there was always the phenomenon of the shadow private sector. Then there was the shift in emphasis in health policy which took place between 1990 and 1993. Finally, there are important legal and economic incentives and limitations. Unfortunately the available data relating to privatisation is rather limited.

To start with, the process of privatisation should not be studied ideologically, asking which is better: public or private. The real issue is what kind of public/private mix is best able to meet different objectives such as efficiency, equity, quality, local autonomy and individual freedom.

It would be misleading to present the current process simply as the transformation of over-centralised state health care into a mixed system of provision. It must be seen as the transformation of the previous dual system – official and shadow – into a system in which both are official, and still interwoven as they always have been. The majority of patients have always given 'gratitude money' to doctors. This phenomenon can be interpreted as a tacit contract between politicians, doctors and society. As their official salaries decreased, doctors were forced to accept 'gifts' which amounted to several times their salary. As a consequence, Hungarian health care has a dual system: shadow health care, similar to the shadow economy, functioning according to different rules; and official health care (Petschnig, 1983; Adam, 1984; Blasszauer, 1984; Kuti, 1984).

Thus, for a very long time, patients have been familiar with the idea that treatment is available for money, and there is considerable vested interest in maintaining this state of affairs. Indeed, it is a popular fallacy that state-socialist health care was driven by egalitarian aims: in fact, the system was not intrinsically committed to reducing inequalities; rather, the declaration of equality was merely the prime means of legitimising a monolithic power structure.

Today, the most distressing problem the health care system has to face is the dramatically deteriorating state of the nation's health. Comparisons of long-term trends in life expectancy and mortality show that there are not only quantitative differences between Western countries and Hungary, but that the trends have diverged from the mid-1960s onwards. (KSH, 1988; Orosz, 1990). The life expectancy of males at birth is now at the same level as in the late 1950s, and life expectancy at the age of forty is no higher than it was in the late 1930s.

Inequalities in health and mortality are widening along social and regional lines. In the 1990s, increasing social tension, unemployment and uncertainty will adversely affect those whose health deteriorated most during the 1980s.

To sum up: during the past few decades, uncontrolled and hidden privatisation has taken place in the health care sector, and we have to ask ourselves how to incorporate this into an institutionalised, regulated public/private mix. We must also consider: (1) how far privatisation can provide a solution to the grave problems which exist in the sector; (2) what would be the most appropriate mix from the point of view of financing and service provision; (3) what measures are needed in order to improve the efficiency and quality of services, widen freedom of choice, and improve the health of the population as a whole.

Health Policy and Privatisation

Under state socialism, only health personnel in full-time employment with the state had access to official private practice. In the late 1980s there were about 5,000 private practices; approximately half were dentists, the rest were mainly panel doctors, surgeons and gynaecologists. They were free to charge what they liked, yet the same tax regulations applied to them as to skilled manual workers. They arranged diagnostic tests for their private patients in the state hospitals, and in 1988 the regulation by which no social insurance subsidy was available for medicine prescribed by a private practitioner was repealed.

If the unofficial gratitude money is also taken into consideration, spending on private health care is estimated to amount to 25 per cent of total health expenditure. In 1990, public health care expenditure was 4.1 per cent of GDP, and total health care expenditure was estimated as 6 per cent. By 1993 the share of public health care expenditure increased to 6.6 per cent of GDP – unfortunately as a consequence of a fall in the GDP. If gratitude money is included, the proportion rises to 7.7 per cent of GDP. This means that the proportion of private expenditure is already higher than in several West European countries, and is increasing.

The only way of eliminating the payment of gratitude money might be to introduce a system of co-payment. Although this might mean that some feel they have paid for health care, several groups could be excluded, and it might lead to an increase in health expenditure.

Health care was not high on the agenda of the 1989 election campaign. Essentially, the policies of the new parties reflected the illusion that the market would be able to create a perfect system. In the resulting coalition government, the leading Hungarian Democratic Forum followed two conflicting approaches: in terms of its general aims, it adopted a social engineering approach; but its actual proposals, in terms of ownership and finance, supported the free market. On the one hand, it stated that 'health promotion concerns must play a role in every government decision', and 'the right to health is a human right for all'; on the other hand, its specific proposals were couched in the language of the market: there should be 'free competition for different forms of health insurance', and 'insured people must be influenced by economic means to practise preventative health care'. There should also be 'competition between different forms of ownership' of hospitals (Hungarian Democratic Forum, 1990).

The first general programme of the new government, the National Renewal Programme, did not make any distinction between privatisation in health care and privatisation in the economy. It stated: 'Government measures are planned to take effect in 1990 to implement the privatisation of health care together with economic privatisation' (Ministry of Welfare, 1990 p.125). This intention has not yet been fully realised. Nevertheless, during the 1990s, privatisation has made advances, particularly in the family doctor service.

In June 1991, the Welfare Ministry issued its *Action Programme for the Renewal of the Health Care System* (Ministry of Welfare, 1991). In the chapter 'A New Way of Functioning', the thrust seems to be whole-heartedly free-market-oriented: 'The real alternative to bureaucratic distribution can only be a control mechanism which rewards performance and which is based on the logic of the market.' Two paragraphs later, however, it suggests a very different approach: 'Control according to market principles means a fully regulated market'. Among its most important concrete measures is an attempt to re-organise primary care.

In 1975, under an order of integration, urban primary health care services and specialised out-patient institutions were united in a single unit under the supervision of the local hospital. Thus the development of primary health care was shaped by hospital departments. This hospital-centred health care is now being transformed into a separate system based on prevention and primary care and the establishment of a family doctor system.

The *Action Programme* states: 'In primary care, the characteristic form is the family doctor who is a self-employed practitioner and who enters into a contract with the health insurance institution.' However, instead of elaborating on economic, legal and organisational preconditions for the implementation of privatisation, the ministry has become entangled with a complicated indexing of the remuneration of family doctors and the problem of insurance cards, which is far more reminiscent of bureaucratic control than market principles. By the end of 1992, due to large-scale uncertainty, adverse economic conditions and lack of the necessary knowledge, only 120 family doctors out of approximately 6,000 chose this form of employment; the rest remained employed by local authorities. By January 1994, however, the number of self-employed doctors had grown to about 1,200.

Regulation of Eligibility for Compulsory Health Insurance

An amendment to the Social Security Act of 1975 ended a citizen's right to health care, and imposed detailed eligibility criteria. As a consequence, some of the most disadvantaged groups are likely to be left out. For example, those who receive unemployment benefit are entitled to health insurance, but when their unemployment benefit ends they may become uninsured. Different proposals for determining eligibility were ignored. The *Report on Social Security*, a comprehensive survey of the social insurance system presented by Fraternité Ltd collaborating with a distinguished group of intellectuals, emphasised that eligibility should be based on citizenship, and the insurance contributions of those without regular paid income should be paid from a specific state fund (Fraternité, 1991).

A telling example of ideology-driven reorganisation is the prominent 1991 slogan: 'no more automatic citizen's right to health care'. Policy-makers considered this an outstanding achievement. The belief that the citizen's 'right' was the cause of every problem stems from the failure to realise that the crux of reform is really the nexus between third-party payer and providers. Furthermore, health policy-makers hold the misconception that the citizen's right and financing through compulsory insurance are irreconcilable.

At the same time, private health insurance has not made significant advances. The only significant area so far in private health insurance has been cover for visits abroad. Few insurance companies offer a health insurance policy complementary to life insurance, and these policies only provide compensation for income loss in the case of sickness. There is no insurance policy offering compensation for medical costs. However, an increase in competition can be expected, similar to that in the field of pension insurance: several industrial firms and different associations are preparing to create their own health insurance funds.

The Development of Private Medical Companies

As a result of the decentralised practice of licensing and registering firms, statistics are scarce. According to Social Insurance Institution (SSI) estimates, there were between 150 and 200 private companies in health care at the end of 1991, and since then, this trend has become more pronounced. A considerable number, about 40–50 per cent, have contracts with state health care institutions. This might mean a medical company buying services from a public hospital and vice versa. In ten cases in 1991, state hospitals themselves set up new ventures.

The majority of private medical provision is financed by the consumers' direct payments and/or by state hospitals or out-patient clinics. An important minority are those enterprises which are financed directly by the SSI: such as the private ambulance units (which provide services in non-emergency cases only). Two of the most important enterprises, MAV-IMC Diagnostic Centrum and International Medical Services, were established by foreign investors who hold a 100 per cent share. There are other ventures with some foreign shareholders.

The money the SSI paid to private undertakings amounted to approximately 0.1 per cent of its health care budget in 1991, but this had grown to 1.8 per cent by 1994. This does not reveal the total amount paid from public funds for private care, because the money paid to companies by state hospitals also comes from the SSI budget. The SSI has individual contracts with medical companies, and is said to pay far more in fees to private providers than the cost of the same services in state hospitals.

Eighty private companies had their requests for reimbursement turned down by the SSI in 1991. The current decision-making mechanism is highly discretionary and lacks stringent standards. Consequently, personal relationships play an important role, as in the public sector.

The SSI has failed to elaborate its policy concerning the role of private medical care; furthermore, even the most elementary data on the cost of medical treatment provided in state hospitals is unavailable. Consequently there is a sharp contrast between the rhetoric of 'sectoral neutrality' and current practice. It is open to debate whether an unqualified sectoral neutrality is appropriate, or whether the SSI should contract only with state and non-private institutions.

These private enterprises are extremely heterogeneous, ranging from physicians working individually to foreign companies striving for an international presence. The example of Rolitron and Rolicare, at present operating as foreign joint stock companies, well illustrates the spontaneous nature of privatisation; the coexistence of the state and private systems; the ambiguities inherent in present legal and economic conditions; the rudimentary state of the decision-making mechanism, and the advantages and disadvantages accompanying privatisation.

Rolitron was founded in the 1980s by a small group of entrepreneurs as a workshop manufacturing dialysis equipment under the management of a well-connected engineer of enterprising spirit. Its expansion has been spectacular, and it now manufactures dialysis machines as well as office and computer equipment. In 1988 the company set up the first private dialysis centre on rented land belonging to a large Budapest hospital. The hospital also provided a professional backup service, such as in an emergency. The SSI paid Rolitron on a fee-for-service basis, but via the hospital administration: an illustration of regulatory inefficiency, which was compounded by frequent disputes over fees.

In 1990 a sister company, Rolicare, was set up to operate the dialysis centres, and in 1991, following lobbying by the company, the widespread privatisation of such centres was undertaken. By the end of the year more than one-third of all dialysis treatment in Hungary was undertaken by Rolicare. The directors of the centres are the heads of the nephrology departments of the hospitals to which the dialysis centres had been attached.

The privatisation of dialysis treatment has indeed led to higher standards, but increased costs for an increasing number of patients have led to resources being diverted from other areas of health care.

There has also been some privatisation in the pharmaceutical industry. Pharmaceutical companies and shops were previously owned by the state. A central organisation purchased from the factories and sent the medicines to the county centres, where the pharmacists obtained their supplies. These local centres also operated as professional supervisors.

Privatisation has proved very attractive to foreign investors: 40 per cent of one of Hungary's most important companies, Chinoin, with a turnover of $US188 million, was purchased by the French company Sanofi. The wealth engendered is of vital importance for Hungary from the point of view of research and development. However, privatisation has led to the reduction or ending of subsidised prices for medicines, and there has been a dramatic increase in direct payment for prescriptions from 0.2 per cent of GDP in 1989 to 0.5 per cent in 1993.

Government plans to transform the county centres into joint stock companies, the State Property Agency remaining the main shareholder, failed to materialise because of a fierce dispute between the State Property Agency (central government) and county authorities over the ownership of the pharmacies. Had these plans been implemented, they would have posed a number of questions, one being what would have happened to pharmacies in remote, 'unprofitable' areas.

Personal Social Services

There is a significant difference between services for elderly people and those for children. During the past decades, particularly in the 1970s, there was a marked increase in the quantity as well as quality of child care institutions such as nurseries and crèches, whereas services for elderly and handicapped people were ignored.

In the informal sector, families have always played a vital role alongside that of the state. Other forms of private provision have played only a marginal role. After the nationalisation of the early 1950s only a few religious institutions providing services for elderly and handicapped people survived, and these were subsidised by the state.

The 1980s saw the appearance of small enterprises in the field of personal social services, such as crèches, home care, nursing homes, etc. The state showed little interest in either regulation or funding, although individuals could sometimes obtain financial support from the local council or the ministry.

In the present chaotic economic and political circumstances the companies have rapidly forsaken their welfare role. At the same time, local authorities are forced to wind up or reduce their own provision because of the ending of subsidies, or the falling monetary value of these in real terms. The majority of families are unable to pay for expensive private services, thus the care role of the family is increasing, which may significantly alter the position of women in the labour market, their place in the family and in society in general.

The government has failed to elaborate an adequate, comprehensive social policy setting out clear ideas about the role of private providers and the relationship between public and private institutions. Promotion of the role of the Churches in the provision of social services has been a basic goal of the government, but at present they do not have a sufficient number of adequately trained workers.

A government decree of 1989 on social and medical private enterprise, sets out the requirements for starting a private business in the field of social welfare. No adequate standards regarding quality, however, have been laid down; indeed, even if there were such standards, a considerable number of state institutions would not meet them.

The present system of funding institutions was introduced in 1989, initiating a state subsidy on the basis of capitation payment in the case of the different social and educational services. The same capitation payment is granted to the private provider as is made to the state institution. The granting of subsidy is, however, discretionary, the ministry deciding whether a particular private provider should receive it or not. Payment for the services over and above the subsidy may be demanded, and the entrepreneurs are free to decide what fees should be charged. Consequently, demand for private services is rather limited, while there is a growing unmet need for state personal social services.

Non-profit institutions, which could bridge this gap, are finding their growth hampered by the lack of a Non-profit Act. The elaboration of such a bill was started years ago, during the previous government, but there are conflicting opinions, even within the government, about the role of non-profit institutions, regarded by some as only a form of tax evasion. The inability of the Churches to step in has already been mentioned.

Privatisation of Housing

In Hungary, housing has been the most serious social problem during the decades since the Second World War. A housing shortage has been abundantly evident, particularly in the cities. The price of flats in relation to income is one of the highest in Europe, and many families, particularly the urban newly-weds, have a diminishing chance of obtaining a home of their own.

It is no surprise, therefore, that the privatisation of housing arouses most interest in the population as a whole. In fact, the whole field of housing in Hungary is very different from other areas of social welfare. When residents buy a flat from the state they often call it a 'national gift' as a result of conditions laid down by the previous regime. Indeed, the gradual retreat of the state from housing provision began as early as the 1960s. A fifteen-year housing programme was launched with the aim of building one million flats, yet only 36 per cent were built by the state. The value of an owner's flat rises faster than the rate of inflation, which also contributes to wealth creation.

The state has never been the main provider of property, and the current fashion for privatisation gives it a further chance to shift a heavy financial burden. Nevertheless, the role of the state was decisively exerted through the limitation of disposition of property even while it supported the private market.

A housing policy which single-mindedly concentrated upon quantitative increase to the detriment of quality has resulted in a large number of small flats, from which those residents who could afford it soon wanted to move. The maintenance of the buildings was neglected, giving rise to the increasingly grave deterioration of the older flats owned by the state.

It was a significant feature of the flats built by the state that subsidy was linked to the flat and not to the occupier. The beneficiaries of housing continued to be primarily the political and power elites and the middle classes; it was they who populated the quality housing estates. The strength of the shadow economy has always provided the resources for the building of flats by private initiative, and this housing market became, in its own right, a driving force behind the shadow economy.

The state supported large-scale private initiatives by providing assistance for the purchase of plots, subsidising building materials, and providing long-term credit with low interest rates (Hegedus and Tosics, 1991). Of the flats built by the state, ever fewer were retained for social purposes. An increasing number were sold through the National Savings Bank or to housing co-operatives, the price of such flats containing significant subsidies. As rents also remained low in the state sector until the early 1980s, there were no real resources available to stem the decay in fabric.

From the mid-1980s onwards, the state withdrew still further from the field of housing, under the pressure of economic difficulties. Subsidies on building materials were ended, and the rents of state-owned flats were increased. At the same time, charges for electricity, water and fuel were repeatedly raised.

Nevertheless, during the 1980s a trend can be identified running counter to privatisation. The interest rate on credit granted for housing was fixed and very low (3.5 per cent), and the difference between this and the prevailing interest rate was paid by the state to the National Savings Bank. This form of state subsidy increased throughout this period. In 1991, however, the alteration in interest rates on housing credit resulted in a dramatic change. The introduction of market interest rates (32 per cent) applied also to credit granted earlier. The state attempted to stem the anticipated anger by offering to pay half the amount if the purchaser could pay the other half.

The main thrust of government housing policy had been, and remains, to encourage private provision, and various inducements were offered from the second half of the 1980s onwards to encourage tenants to buy state-owned flats: for example the purchase price of a flat was 15 per cent of the market value. In fact, even then, only the well-off were able to take advantage of this, or were living in flats worth buying. Thus this group in society were able to increase their personal capital to a significant extent.

Privatisation on a larger scale was accelerated in 1990 as the state maintenance company tried to get rid of the burden of reconstruction. Between 1982 and 1989, 70,000 people wished to purchase their rented flats in Budapest, whereas in 1990 alone this figure rose to 75,000. In Budapest almost one-third of all rented flats were earmarked for sale (Tausz, 1992). The rapid increase in the price of property, the chance of becoming owners, and fear of further increases in rent all strongly encouraged residents to purchase. Yet they remain uninformed and poorly advised. Speculation is one of the chief features of the present situation. In many cases private entrepreneurs transform the flats they have bought into shops, while many older people sell their flats for a low price in order to retain a life interest in the property.

The Local Government Act has handed over the state-owned flats to the local authorities, and central regulation has been wound up. Increases in rent, operation of subsidies, and the conditions for privatisation now depend on the decision of the individual local authorities.

The mayor of one of the Budapest districts wrote in a weekly newspaper about the disputes concerning the privatisation of flats:

It is a time bomb . . . if privatisation is continued under unchanged conditions, in a few years' time it would be the residents themselves who would have to face the reality of bankruptcy, neglected buildings – in other words the debt they purchased – and then they would blame the local authority for the entire problem. (Polinszky and Szabo, 1992)

The problem is compounded because the state companies for the maintenance of buildings were disbanded and private companies have not as yet been formed in sufficient numbers. In the meantime, the building of flats for social purposes has almost completely stopped. In 1991 only 100 new flats were available for rent over the entire country, and not a single one in Budapest. The local authorities can operate only with the existing stock because of the shortage of resources, but since flats are rapidly being sold, this possibility is also being restricted. Thus people who are unable to buy a flat in the market find themselves in a hopeless situation. The withdrawal of the state from the housing sector contributes to the growth of the number left without shelter: a significant proportion of those who had previously lived in the now-closed workers' hostels have become homeless.

No non-profit organisations exist in the housing sector because of the lack of legal norms allowing for their establishment (Tausz, 1992).

Conclusion

Three arguments are usually produced in Hungary to justify privatisation: (1) economic efficiency; (2) political interest and ideology; (3) justice.

The first argument, economic efficiency, ignores the fact that this is not necessarily increased through privatisation – for instance, where it creates a private monopoly in the place of a public one. The transformation of the general economic environment and the development of competition are also necessary for the promotion of efficiency.

The second, the political aspect of privatisation, gives rise to differences between Hungarian privatisation and that in the West. This is because the political circumstances in Hungary are so different.

Justice, the third argument, entails compensation for private owners' grievances suffered under state socialism. This ignores the fact that such groups as teachers and other workers also suffered injustice through having part of their wages appropriated by the state without the democratic right of a say in how this money should be used. These people were recompensed for only a fraction of the value of their work.

The historic transformation of the economy means a grave challenge for the social welfare sector, partly because economic recession is considerably greater and social costs are far higher than was expected, and partly because of the collapse of the economic base upon which the earlier social welfare system was built.

Ideological debates tend to formulate the question in an oversimplified way – namely, public *or* private. The real issues, however, are what kind of public/private mix should be developed, and what the core of social welfare policy should be. One option is to fundamentally reshape public control and regulation and create more efficient public financing. In this case, privatisation is to be considered as an important complementary method.

The other option is to concentrate efforts on privatisation and to expect it to remedy the shortcomings of the public sector. In this case we would have to accept the natural logic of private control: namely, that priorities are set by the rate of return on investment rather than need.

The above and similar questions have yet to be answered. The government has so far failed to elaborate an adequate concept of privatisation, even for the economy. Furthermore:

> Desirable changes in the structure of the state budget have failed to come about. In the budget of the Antall government, the expenditure on state apparatus, defence and police take priority just as they customarily did under the previous regime. Education, health care, culture and support of local government have continued to be the step-child of the state budget. (Bauer, 1992)

Lack of vision, and insensitivity to social problems, are characteristic of the current government. Decisions are mainly made by the decision-makers fluctuating between the desire to get rid of the debts accumulated under the previous regime and to consolidate bureaucratic power.

Privatisation may be an important means to promote innovation, and to meet those special demands which the public system cannot or does not want to meet. On the other hand, it may mean increasing inequalities, and the institutionalisation of a two-tier system. These phenomena are not new: they also existed under the previous state-socialist administration. The options now, however, lie between controlling them or making the situation worse.

The parliamentary election in May 1994, resulted in the defeat of the conservative coalition government with its somewhat traditional and provincial style. It has been replaced by the social-liberal coalition of the Socialists and Free Democrats. The new government's programme emphasises the need for a consistent, comprehensive reform of the public sector, in order to make it more efficient and responsive to social needs. Privatisation in service provision is regarded as a means of achieving this aim, but not as an end in itself. The current government is committed to universal entitlement to family benefit and health care. The next few years will show to what extent the government is able to achieve its promised goals.

References

Adam, G. (1984) 'Az orvosi halapenz koruli vitahoz' (To the debate on gratitude money), *Tarsadalmi Szemle*, 7–8, p.135.
Atkinson, A.B. and Hills, J. (1989) *Social Security in Developed Countries: Are There Lessons for Developing Countries?*, Welfare State Program, no.38, Suntory-Toyota International Centre for Economics and Related Disciplines.
Bauer, T. (1992) 'Az elszalasztott esely: az Antall-kormany ket everol' (The missed chance: On the two years of the Antall government), *Magyar Hirlap*, 26 March, p.8.
Blasszauer, B. (1984) 'Az orvosi halapenzrol etikai alapon' (On gratitude money – from an ethical point of view), *Valosag*, no.2, p.98.
Ferge, Z. (1991) 'Marginalisation, poverty and social institutions', Round Table organised by the International Institute for Labour Studies, Geneva, Paper No.4.
Fraternité (1991) *Report on Social Security*, Budapest.
Hegedus, J. and Tosics, I. (1991) 'Privatizacio a lakasrendszerben' (Privatisation in housing), *Esely*, no.3, p.60.
Hungarian Democratic Forum (1990) *Policy Document on Health Care*, Budapest.
HVG, 23 February, 1991 'A legertekesebb magyar cegben tobbsegbe kerul a Sanofi' (Sanofi becoming the main shareholder in the biggest Hungarian firm).
—— 8 February 1992 'Sappenz' (Kickback money) p.81.
JELENTES a magyar privatizaciorol, 1991 (1992) (Report on Hungarian privatisation, 1991), Research Institute of Privatization, Budapest.
Johnson, N. (1987) *The Welfare State in Transition*, Hemel Hempstead, Harvester Wheatsheaf.
Karcsay, R. (1991) 'A szemelybiztositas' (Personal insurance), *Figyelo*, 21 February, p.13.
KSH (1988) *Halandosagi Vizsgalatok 5* (Mortality Survey 5), KSH, Budapest.
Kuti, E. (1984) 'Az orvosi halapenzrol' (On gratitude money), *Valosag*, no.3, p.111.
Ladanyi, J. (1992) 'A lakasprivatizacio dilemmai' (Dilemmas of privatisation in housing), *Beszelo*, 18 January, p.33.
Losonczi, A. (1986) *A kiszolgaltatottsag Anatomiaja az Egeszsegugyben* (Anatomy of defencelessness in health care), Budapest, Magveto
Magyar Hirlap 3 October, 1991 'Ujgyarmatositas a hatso kapun?' (New

colonisation through the back door?)

—— 7 March,1992 'Otvenot milliard forint tartozas' (Debt of fifty-five forints).

Magyar Kozlony (1991) no.119 (Hungarian Official Gazette).

—— (1992) no.25 (Hungarian Official Gazette).

Matolcsy, G. (1991) 'Labadozasunk evei. A magyar privatizacio: trendek, tenyek, privatizacios peldak' (Years of our reconvalescence – The Hungarian privatisation: trends, facts and experiences of privatisation'), Research Institute of Privatization, Budapest.

Ministry of Welfare (1990) *The National Renewal Programme*, Budapest.

—— (1991) *Action Programme for the Renewal of the Health Care System*, Budapest.

Orosz, E. (1989) 'Az egeszsegugyi reform onkormanyzati alternativaja' (On the self-government alternative in the health care reform), *Tarsadalomkutatas*, no.2, pp.59–80.

—— (1990) 'Inequalities in health and health care in Hungary', *Social Science and Medicine*, no. 8, pp.847–57.

Petschnig, M. (1983) 'Az orvosi halapenzrol – nem etikai alapon'(On gratitude money – not from an ethical point of view), *Valosag*, no.11.

Polinszky, M. and Szabo, Z. (1992) 'Csodtomeg-gazdalkodas' (Crisis management), *Beszelo*, 15 February, p.33.

Research Institute of Privatisation (1992) *Report on Hungarian Privatisation*, Budapest.

Szalai J. (1986) *Az Egeszsegugy Betegsegei* (Diseases of the health care system), Budapest, Kozgazdasagi es Jogi Konyvkiado.

Szalai, J. and Orosz, E. (1992) 'Social policy in Hungary', in Deacon, B. (ed.) (1992) *The New Eastern Europe: Social Policy, Past, Present and Future*, London, Sage Publications.

Szelenyi, I. and Manchin R. (1987) 'Social policy under state socialism: market redistribution and social inequalities in Eastern European socialist societies', in Rein, M., Esping-Anderson, G. and Rainwater, L. (eds) (1987) *Stagnation and Renewal in Social Policy*, New York, Armonk.

Tausz, K. (1992) 'The Housing Situation in Hungary', *French Revue of Social Affairs*, no.1, pp.67–80.

Italy

Patrizia David and *Giovanna Vicarelli*

Health Policies and Private Medicine

The Market in the Development of the Health Service

The Italian welfare state at the end of the last century was concerned only with prevention and public hygiene, and there was no public provision for individual health care. This was dictated, on the one hand, by the powerful religious and charity organisations which directly controlled the hospitals, and, on the other, by the growing number of friendly societies which also provided social insurance for workers. Both of these strongly resisted public intervention for many years (Cosmacini, 1988).

At the same time, the weakness of the private health market encouraged the medical profession to promote a decentralised system of public health care. These doctors, lacking real ability, and relying on new bacteriological and pathological discoveries, attempted to control the public health system (Cherubini, 1963–4). A public system which had intervened directly in the field of environmental health, while at the same time reinforcing the traditional presence of public doctors in the urban and rural areas (Forti Messina, 1982), gave rise to a large medical class who were seeking economic and social status (Frascani, 1982; Betri, 1984).

The rapid expansion of the private health market in the early decades of the twentieth century, in conjunction with the tenacious and powerful religious-charity sector, succeeded in blocking proposals for compulsory health insurance made in the Giolitti period. In fact, the majority of doctors, concerned by the growing possibility of a limitation of their professional autonomy, joined both entrepreneurs and the Church in opposing proposals by liberal leaders to introduce a welfare scheme similar to those developing in the UK and Germany (Piperno, 1986; Cosmacini, 1989). Consequently, the liberal period ended with a welfare system which had only three of the four fundamental elements in place – accident, pension and unemployment insurance. Compulsory health insurance was not to be realised until 1943 (Ferrera, 1984).

In reality, the idea of compulsory medical insurance was not abandoned until the end of the 1920s. It was only in 1929 that a decree by the Higher Cabinet of National Economics sanctioned, for economic reasons, the creation of *casse mutue* or sickness benefit funds, which allowed the state to avoid direct responsibility in the matter. Although the *casse mutue* were public institutions, and directly controlled by the Fascist Party, they were based on the principle of private health care. The *casse mutue* belonged to companies and workers, who financed the health services with equal contributions. Ideologically, the *casse mutue* were to offer their services to 'as many citizens as possible who were not rich enough to pay for their own doctor and not poor enough to be listed as poor' (Cosmacini, 1989, p.222).

At this time, market weakness induced doctors to accept the sickness benefit compromise, about which they had always maintained certain reservations and ideological misgivings, and from which they had tried to distance themselves in order to maintain their professional autonomy. Having lost the unifying strength of the previous period, the medical profession then tried to fit into the Fascist system, while deriving as many benefits as possible (both in economic and political terms) from the *casse mutue* system and from the private market (specifically the developing market for pharmaceutical products). These developments involved not only the *casse mutue* doctor, who also worked in the private sector, but also the public doctor who worked for the social security sickness benefit system, and hospital doctors who obtained their initial entry into the system from the opening of private fee-paying wards. Moreover, all were potentially open to illegal payments.

After the fall of the Fascist regime, proposals for rationalising the health service were put forward by the Council of Venice in 1943 and by the Commission of Aragona in 1947. In the post-war period, however, Italy was economically exhausted, and the medical profession once again found itself accepting an accommodation between public and private which did no more than continue the health system created by the Fascist regime without any real modifications. This position was supported by both business interests and the Church, and was directly backed by governments during the years of reconstruction.

Although during the 1950s the number of services and beneficiaries grew due to the gradual extension of medical insurance to an increasing number of categories (Ferrera, 1984), doctors still attempted to maintain either legal or actual autonomy, not only on a clinical level but also, when possible, on an economic-organisational one. In other words, the medical profession largely sustained and directed the interweaving of public and private health services. During the 1960s and 1970s this led to the inclusion of the private service within the public (Paci, 1989).[1]

Despite this, the labour movement and a small number of doctors and hygienists started a process of reform, with the objective of first reorganising public health services, and later transforming health policies into a universal and institutional welfare system. The reform movement was, in time, to become an expression of the new social and health demands, with the workers being joined in the 1970s by youth, women's and anti-psychiatric movements, so that it eventually became an even greater instrument of democratic reform (Vicarelli, 1990). The majority of doctors, while maintaining strong reservations about the National Health Service, began to see new occupational possibilities in primary health services for the growing number of young doctors and medical students (Vicarelli, 1989a).

The National Health Service would never have been realised had its setting up not coincided with a serious economic crisis for the *casse mutue*, which were now on the brink of bankruptcy due to increasing hospital costs. Another factor was the changing political and social climate, which at the beginning of the 1970s saw the unions and the Communist Party becoming much stronger. Indeed, the whole of society seemed prepared for change.

The reform was passed in December 1978, completing the process of the inclusion of the health services within the public system. The stages of this process had been marked by the Hospital Law of 1968, and by the assigning of health service functions to the regions, as well as by the eventual financial recovery of the *casse mutue* with assistance from the state.

Medical Knowledge and Market Relations in the 1980s

The 1980s opened on a radically changed panorama. The country emerged from the political crisis of the 1970s and the economic crisis at the start of the decade (Ginsborg, 1990) with both its liberal principles and the power of the market apparently widely accepted. This fact is explained by the industrial restructuring and the flourishing economic situation which followed, strengthened by the union confederations and the Communist Party crisis, and finding fertile ground in the increased

1. As more recent data demonstrates, there is an extensive connection and mix between the public and private sectors, even after the establishment of the National Health Service. In 1985, for example, there were at least 170,000 doctors under contract in the general, specialist, private and hospital sectors and 541,641 employed in the National Health Service. In the same year 41,967,826 million lire was required to cover health service expenditure: 40.6 per cent to cover staff costs and 38.6 per cent to cover the costs of private contract work.

prosperity which propagated models of merit and individual action.

It was in this period that medical knowledge took a leap forward. The 1980s marked a crucial stage, not only for biology and genetics, but for all those areas which were stimulated by the application of new drugs and technology; they also saw the expansion of medical knowledge following discoveries which, for the first time, made it possible to hope for the defeat of the most serious diseases of the century. This involved a vast technological-scientific movement which, while creating great expectations, offered new methods of investigation, chemotherapies, and medical specialisations at a very high cost and an equally high rate of replacement of equipment.[2] This meant that the developing health market involved a high capital intensity, which tended to create areas of private intervention to compensate for the rigidity (both bureaucratic and financial) of the public health system.[3]

A similar medical-technological development, accompanied by the failure of the public system in the field of preventive and primary medicine, seemed to justify the use of alternative therapies.[4] Whatever the reason might be for turning to alternative medicine, it has led to the development of a 'parallel market' which has achieved growing importance within the community. This development has led to new lifestyles and forms of consumption (Donati, 1989), which in turn have supported new markets related to nutritional habits, personal care, psychophysical activities and even entertainment.

The more recent epidemiological discoveries, which led to the identification of the relationship between the onset of tumours or cardiovascular diseases and factors of exogenous origin (the working environment, lifestyle, diet, smoking, alcohol and drug abuse), have also become more important in creating profits for those offering compensatory services and commodities than for public health education (Ingrosso, 1990).

2. According to ANIE (National Association of Electrical Engineering and Electronic Industries) estimates, the market for electrical medical equipment, equal to 680 billion lire per year, has seen an expansion of 53 per cent in the last three years. The entire medical technology market, according to Assobiomedica data (association of companies working in the sector) is worth L2,000 billion.

3. In Milan, Naples and Rome recently, large private hospitals have been opened, while all over the country joint stock companies which offer services involving innovative technologies are increasing; a survey carried out between 1988 and 1989 by Censis, on private non-religious clinics shows that these are extremely well equipped. Nevertheless, standard biomedical treatment prevails over high-tech medicine. It should be noted that it is the clinics which are not related to the national health service that are relatively better equipped (Censis, 1990).

4. According to a study carried out by Parliament (Camera dei Deputati), by the end of the 1980s there were 4,000–5,000 people employed in this sector, with one million regular patients and five million patients attending for single treatments.

It is not easy to determine whether the power of the market or the gaps left by the National Health Service explain this situation. What is certain is that the absence of public structures in the areas recommended by the Health Reform Act of 1978 (primary medicine and community medicine) led to or encouraged market activity (official and parallel) which often offered services or commodities which the state was not in a position to provide.

The actual value of this market cannot be quantified because, in Italy, unlike other countries, there is little systematic information on the use of public and private health facilities, and also because national data does not reveal expenditure on health outside the National Health Service (National Health Council, 1989). However, we do know that there has been a marked increase in medical expenditure by families: this went from 16.7 per cent of the total in 1980 to 21.7 per cent in 1987, with an increase of 1 per cent per year (Salvemini, 1989). This expenditure resulted from restrictive policies introduced by the government, and included significant recourse to the private market.[5]

This was confirmed by the 1986 survey on Italian health (ISTAT, 1987), which showed that more than 40 per cent of those who had consulted a specialist had used (by choice or necessity) the private market. Over 11 per cent of Italians had diagnostic examinations carried out in private practices or clinics; about 10 per cent had used private hospitals with health insurance agreements, and 2 per cent had used private hospitals without such agreements. This recourse to private services involved all types of families, but is greatly affected by level of income and education; it is higher-income families and university degree holders who most regularly pay for medicines and admission to private facilities (Bariletti et al., 1990).

According to a survey by the Chamber Commission of Social Affairs, during 1987 families spent 4.307 billion lira on private medical care services and 3.691 billion lira on admissions to private hospitals; at the same time, according to some estimates, the use of non-official medicine is in the region of 300 billion lira. Also in 1987, health insurance collected premiums of 460 billion lira and supplementary health insurance collected contributions of about 600 billion lira (National Health Council, 1989).

During the 1980s, the success of technological medicine seemed to support a health market characterised by high capital intensity, which tended to reduce public intervention. A vast field of economic and production interests found ready allies in the medical profession, which

5. The effect on private consumption was an increase of 0.9 per cent in 1980 and 2.1 per cent in 1987.

saw its occupational and income potential increased thanks to much greater specialisation, and which realised a power previously boasted of but never actually achieved. On the other hand, the contradictions and the failures of technological medicine led to the expansion of parallel health markets.

These were the economic and cultural pressures surrounding the emergent public health system in the 1980s: a climate so unfavourable that the introduction of the National Health Service coincided with plans to transform it.

The Market and the Reform of the National Health Service

In the new liberal climate of the 1980s, and under pressure from the different health markets, Italian political parties develped unclear and contradictory policies. Nevertheless, in an outburst of statements and denials, of proposals and counter-proposals, the five-party government began a stop-go procedure of reform of the institutional law on the National Health Service.

Following a long series of Acts and many more failures and compromises, which resulted in the reduction of the financial resources and the institutional and organisational instruments necessary for growth, the public health service became progressively inactive (Vicarelli, 1990). At the same time, a 'reform of the reform' was started. This was begun in 1984 and is still incomplete.

It is paradoxical that, at the beginning of the 1980s, in the first phase of the National Health Service, the government and the Ministry of Health were led by two members of the very parties (Republican and Liberal) that had firmly opposed it. The Liberal Party Minister, for example, faced with a reduction of health expenditure which dated back to 1981, proposed a return to indirect forms of health care and the guarantee of total financial coverage only in the case of high-risk illnesses.

Disagreement was widespread, above all in the regions and municipalities, where there were complaints about reforming a law which had never been implemented. The National Federation of Medical Orders (FNOM) also backed this position, and, while admitting that it had raised no objections to Law 833 (which created the National Health Service) during its preparation, it now offered its co-operation to the 'government, Parliament and regions to translate the law into working reality' (Parodi, 1982). This co-operation was interpreted by the ministry as an attempt to stifle ideological pressure, and to try to 'form a service according to the number of existing physicians rather than in relation to the requirements of the citizens'. A survey carried out by the National Committee of Local Authorities in 1982 found that most sections of the medical profession lacked the conviction and commitment required for the implementation of the innovative aspects of the law. Only general practitioners, especially the younger ones and female doctors, seemed to approve of and effectively support the objectives of prevention, the development of primary medicine, and its integration within the field of specialist and hospital medicine.

During the early years of the 1980s, the willingness among these latter groups to co-operate clashed with the attempts of the five-party government to limit health expenditure, and to control medical activities by means of bureaucratic orders issued by the Ministry of Health. This alienated the general practitioners, who saw their hopes of an improvement in primary medicine disappear, to be replaced by increasing bureaucracy (Vicarelli, 1986).

From the beginning of the 1980s, the plan was to deregulate health management, giving responsibility to the regions, with the obligation on their part to impose additional contributions should resources not meet costs. At the same time, proposals were strengthened to remove large hospitals and inter-regional public preventative services, from the control of Local Health Units.

In 1984 the Socialist administration introduced proposals for rationalisation which, it was claimed, would revitalise the public system through an injection of market-style efficiency. The public system was to be based on selective principles and on a plurality of providers. It was during this period that a philosophy of intervention in health care, directed by financial laws and the Treasury and based on the three main principles of cuts, charges and expenditure limits, was introduced.

Therefore, as the left failed to find a line of opposition to counteract the economic arguments for welfare restrictions, a process of rationalisation was started. The objective was less concerned with freedom of action for the doctors than with dealing with the problems of party-related influence, together with the technical inability of those directing the Local Health Units. The co-operation of doctors was sought by offering them recognition of their professional role, and autonomous contracting (for which they had so keenly fought), as well as the opportunity to participate in the management of the public health system.

A change of government, with the return of the Christian Democrats, once again altered the situation. The clash with the medical profession was reopened and intensified by the impromptu methods of management introduced by the new Health Minister, and his repeated attempts to restrict professional power.

Several months after its election, the government presented a plan for the reform of the National Health Service which rejected all solutions based on privatisation; it thus jettisoned the tendencies of the previous

Socialist government, which had envisaged widespread recourse to voluntary social insurance. Instead, it planned a separation of health functions and institutions which destroyed the health system created by Law 833. New structures and boards, differentiated by competence and power, would now be introduced. The 'company-like' departmentalisation of Local Health Units therefore coincided with their loss of functions resulting from the contraction of primary health care; with the granting of autonomy to large hospitals; with the separation of hygiene and public health, and with the fragmentation of the organic relationship with the municipalities and the local population (Vicarelli, 1988).

It was in this setting that, in the autumn of 1989, the new Liberal Party Minister of Health presented yet another proposed law, which contained substantial modifications and was included in a law accompanying the financial law.

The dismemberment of the health service was not only put into effect, but in certain cases speeded up, from the moment when the Local Health Units became 'regional service companies' with their own legal status and autonomous organisation, thereby resolving any dispute about their legal nature and their dependence on the municipalities. Apart from urban areas, which can obtain administrative health functions, the municipalities' only relationship with the new Local Health Units is that of electing the board of directors whose task it is to formulate guidelines for management. These 'Regional Service Companies' are then under the directorship of a general manager, engaged under a private contract and selected on the basis of technical or administrative experience in public or private organisations.

Highly specialist hospitals were turned, by regional law, into 'company-like' hospitals with organisational and administrative autonomy, while non-specialised state hospitals remained under the direction of the Local Health Units, but with full functional and financial autonomy. The reorganisation of multi-zone prevention was assigned to those regions permitted to use their own directives, but whose point of reference is now the provincial territory.

The new management criteria for these regional 'service companies' aim to satisfy the need for more efficient services. To this end, many innovative steps are planned, from accounting directives to expenditure and profit analysis techniques, and even more importantly, experimentation with indirect methods of payment (where the patient initially pays and is then reimbursed).

Moreover, the overall financing of the service is being transformed. National funding is to cease and is to be replaced by a new inter-regional fund entrusted to a state-region commission. The changes here are substantial because, while the previous funding had come entirely from the state budget, the new fund is supported by sickness contributions with a supplement from the state. The regions, moreover, may impose additional charges or, if necessary, turn to indirect methods of finance. Recourse to indirect methods of finance is also planned for certain highly technological services offered by boards outside the health insurance scheme, in cases where the public service is unable to offer immediate coverage.

The foreclosure of the legislation prevented the completion of the parliamentary debate on the new health system, but the government managed to have a considerable number of directives approved with a law accompanying the financial law of 1992 (Law 412/91). These included the directive regarding management experimentation, taxation autonomy for the regions, as well as financial parameters determined by the resident population. Contributions towards health expenditure have also been increased on drugs and diagnosis: citizens now have to pay 50 per cent of the cost of these. Law 412 also states that doctors employed by the National Health Service must choose within a year either to work within or outside the public health system. They are, however, allowed to run a private practice outside working hours, both within the public system and in totally private institutions. This would seem to open up additional potential for private markets.

The year 1993 was crucial for Italian democracy, as it marked the disastrous fall of the five-party governments, under the pressure of the economic crisis and, more importantly, the accusations of corruption and dishonesty. The crisis directly affected the area of health, so much so that the Liberal Minister of Health (De Lorenzo) was shown to have been implicated, in person and through one of his personal staff, in the most serious scandal that had ever touched the health and pharmaceutical services of the country: a scandal that brought about changes at the top of the Ministry of Health, the Drugs Council and the Federation of the Pharmaceutical Industries, and in the Presidency of the National Body of Pensions for Doctors. This meant that many of the people who had been directly or indirectly in control of the sector over the previous twenty years had been found to be involved in illicit and self-serving management.

It is in the light of these radical changes, that in 1993, the problem arose of whether to transform or to implement the 502 Legislative Decree. This marked the end of an extremely lengthy legislative process by which the pentaparty governments had attempted to bring about substantial changes to the whole health organisation. The 'transitionary government', guided by Mr Ciampi, had made some partial but important decisions aimed at asserting the public character of the health system. It had also tried to bring about organisational changes to cut out the waste and abuse, and increase efficiency. This implied that the Ciampi government had intended abandoning the privatisation process planned by the previous governments. The aim was to create a minimal public health system with integrative forms of health services for the middle classes and selective forms for the less protected classes.

Nevertheless, the 1994 victory of the right-wing coalition orchestrated by Berlusconi, means that the 502 Decree may be re-directed once again towards privatisation. Although by August 1994, no proposals had been made by the new government with regard to the health sector, governmental documents seem to indicate the inclination to widely privatise the health system, at least in the long term. It appears the Prime Minister and the Liberal Health Minister do not want to add any further unpopular measures to those associated with the state pension sector. This means that the privatisation of the health service, that was strongly promised in the electoral campaign, will be left for a second phase.

Concluding Observations on Markets in Health Care

The impression one gains from the political direction of health care reform in the 1980s is that of two contrasting positions: the neo-liberal position, which aims at dismantling the universal welfare system created by Law 833, and the neo-conservative position, which tends to perpetuate a use of health services according to desert.

When Ciampi replaced Amato as Prime Minister in 1993, he initiated an austerity programme which involved cuts in health expenditure. A particular concern was the escalating pharmaceutical bill. The government divided drugs into three categories: those attracting full reimbursement of charges (a greatly reduced number); those attracting 50 per cent reimbursement, and those for which no reimbursement was available. This resulted in patients having to pay a greater proportion of the cost of medicines and a drastic reduction in the subsidies to the pharmaceutical industry.

In the general election at the end of March 1994, the right-wing parties were successful. Berlusconi, leader of Forza Italia, became the new Prime Minister. He had campaigned on the basis of cuts in expenditure on health, pensions and the buraucracy. However, as leader of an uneasy coalition of right-wing parties who are often in open disagreement, he has so far (September 1994) been too weak and indecisive to give effect to his policies.

This means that, once again, the future of the public health system will depend on the conflicts and compromises within and among the majority parties, which today, as never before, seem to be moving away from social provision towards involvement with private markets. While weak forms of association have been developing from the fragmentation of groups during the 1980s, and while a divided left has had problems in developing a strong programme of reform, the health market has channelled the interests of large economic units in the wake of both new medical discoveries and the return to alternative medicine. In this it has had the approval of consumers, who found themselves caught between the birth of new values, increasingly distorted information, and the obvious deterioration of some public health services.

This is the first time in the history of the Italian health system that the market has proved to have its own impetus; if in the future this is backed by legislation, it may lead to a welfare system in which the market and not the state has a dominant position, and in which public action and community networks have residual and compensatory functions. In other words, there could be a 'long-term oscillation' (Paci, 1989) leading to a different mix of resources in the Italian health system. The equality and fair distribution resulting from this mix, and the minimum level of health care it ensures, remain to be evaluated; but these concerns do not seem to be given any consideration by current Italian politicians and economists.

The Personal Social Services

State Social Care

In Italy the private sector has always been closely involved in the provision of social care. Although the informal network of families and kinship has always occupied a central position in meeting social needs, the Church and its welfare associations have played an almost equally important role. While the commercial market sector has never occupied a prominent position, because for many decades social care almost exclusively involved the poor, the same does not apply to the non-profit private sector, made up of Catholic institutions and associations which have existed for years and which are still important. Indeed, it was only recently that this sector experienced the secularisation which occurred in many other European countries several centuries ago. It has to be admitted that economic interests were amply represented in this sector, but they have always been manifested indirectly and covertly, since the historical and cultural implications of welfare are contrary to the explicit principles of profit (Ranci, 1990).

In Italy, the strong reluctance of public authorities to assume responsibility for caring for the poor resulted in a tendency to delegate this field to the traditional presence of the Church. So, despite the fact that charity organisations had become public,[6] the Church maintained a prominent position even after the unification of the country, creating a welfare system which was strongly characterised by public and private intervention. Neither the Fascist regime nor the first two decades of Republican rule brought many changes to a system in which the public sector had almost no part in designing services. It did, however, finance a private non-profit sector which guaranteed continuity and was inexpensive, thanks to the unpaid work carried out largely by the religious workers used by the welfare institutions.

In the 1970s, however, the cultural and legislative upheavals in Italian society heavily involved the welfare sector; social and health services were seen as a right by citizens, and therefore required the full responsibility of the state. At the same time, guidelines relating to participation, decentralisation and the integration of social and health care were issued. At the top of the list for reorganisation were the regional organisations (regions and municipalities). These started to build a network of personal social services which were highly innovative compared with the methods that had been used up to that time (economic subsidies together with institutionalisation).

The Church, seen as a supporter of conservative rather than innovative ideas, was consequently reduced to a role of secondary importance in the welfare policy of the country, and it was supplanted by the development of regional public services.

It is interesting that the strong reformist character typical of the introduction and development of these social services also slowed down the growth of the commercial sector, which, despite the socio-economic changes in the country, was still trying to find its own identity in the field of social security. The standard of services offered by the public sector, around which the interests and experience of the most highly qualified social workers and researchers revolved, and which attracted the largest number of clients, was in fact so high that neither the market nor the traditional non-profit private sectors could compete against them. One need only consider the public day nurseries, which were undoubtedly one of the most advanced services offered in terms of education for children from one to three years of age. Another example was the public counselling services, which also became important centres in the field of maternity and women's health.

At the end of the 1970s, however, as the spirit of innovation began to diminish, a new cultural-political profile began to emerge; its objective was to control and reduce public expenditure, and its

6. Religious welfare institutes, which in 1890 were transformed into IPABs, namely welfare organisations.

support was widespread. During the 1980s, social policy tended increasingly towards privatisation. Public services became the main target of those who accused the state of inefficiency in allocating resources and called for the intervention of the market. The increased interest in the voluntary sector – seen as a way of resolving the problem of excessive public expenditure without having to rely immediately and directly on a commercial sector (which, in terms of social services, lacked legitimisation) – proved to be particularly important for social care policy.

The measures adopted for reducing public expenditure on personal social services included: an increase in fees for consumers; a reduction in the services offered; a freeze on staff taken on by local authorities, and the limitation of expenditure on staff training and renewing equipment. All of these changes led to the a growing inability of the public sector to meet expanding and changing social needs.

Consequently, Italy is experiencing what may be described as a tendency to informal privatisation, as compared with the more formalised experiences in other countries. In the case of personal social services in particular, this involves a modification of the organisation of services, which have passed from direct management by the local authorities to a system of contracting out to an external agent whereby the local authorities limit themselves to paying private companies for their services (Comandini, 1991). This method of provision continues to increase: the majority of contracts are awarded to co-operatives.

Co-operatives

Even though the exponential growth of social co-operatives, which in 1988 were estimated to number more than a thousand, has occurred only in the last ten years, the earliest co-operatives in health and personal social services date back to the end of the 1960s. Their increase at the end of the 1970s occurred not so much because of a desire to reaffirm the place of the private sector alongside the public sector, but more from the occupational needs of certain segments of the labour market (women, disabled people, and professional workers in the personal social services sector unable to find employment because of the cutbacks). This tendency was encouraged by the new local authority policy of contracting out (Bianchi et al., 1988). The fields of intervention where these co-operatives most frequently operate are home services, services for children at risk, drug abuse, disabled people, and elderly people in residential care.

Today, there are three main types of co-operative in the personal social services; all have the same legal status. The first consists of integrated co-operatives which aim at providing work for those who cannot easily find a place in the labour market. Periodically, they also provide services to people with physical or mental disabilities. These are the oldest co-operatives. Their development has been affected both by the limitation of the law on the obligatory employment of disabled people and by the de-institutionalisation of patients in psychiatric hospitals and the consequent need to include them in the labour force.

The second group involves social service co-operatives consisting of professionally qualified workers who offer the consumer or local authorities their services directly, in order to guarantee work and economic benefits to participants. Their development is essentially the result of the reorganisation of the personal social services, coupled with the employment problems encountered by some social service professionals.

Finally, the third distinctive type of co-operative is specifically concerned with providing social services as an act of solidarity; the scope and nature of these co-operatives make them very similar to the voluntary groups from which they often originate. Their development, just like that of voluntary groups, has been encouraged by an increasing tendency in society towards self-management and personal involvement (Borzaga, 1988).

It has, however, been observed that the development of co-operatives in the personal social services is also due to certain peculiarities of the co-operative formula, which means that often it is preferred both by those directly involved and by public administrators. Above all, there are several juridical advantages. Among the most important of these are: the absence of private speculation (guaranteed by the obligation to invest registered capital, after the reimbursement from shares, in services of public utility); the legal limitation on the amount of income derived from company shares which may be distributed to member employees to augment salaries, and the impossibility of redistributing profits to members beyond the maximum terms established by the law. All of these have the effect of redirecting the profit-making policy of what is, after all, a commercial venture (Borzaga, 1988). Moreover, the openness and accountability of economic management, very difficult to attain in the traditional non-profit sector, is achieved because the co-operative, as a company, is obliged to keep audited books. Co-operatives seem to ensure an entrepreneurial management of services, required today more than ever, which encourages desirable efficiency in the field of public expenditure, without totally abandoning values of solidarity and help in favour of pure market interests.

Another very important feature of the co-operative formula should not, however, be neglected. This involves the many possibilities for management flexibility, both within the services provided and the labour force. The contracting out arrangements of local authorities are based substantially on the principle of the lowest cost, and it should not be forgotten that the very high economic competitiveness of social co-operatives is often attained by integrating voluntary and paid employment; by offering part-time work, and by the predominant use of workers who have few guarantees in terms of employment and salaries (cf. Bianchi et al., 1988).

The use by local authorities of these co-operatives is not only made more attractive by regional laws implemented by the Local Health Offices and by laws on the reorganisation of the personal social services system, but also encouraged by the enactment of the national law governing social co-operatives (Law 381 of November 1991). This directive acknowledges their role in the social services system, and assigns specific aims to the co-operatives, such as the employment of disabled people and the management of social and health care and educational services.[7] According to this law, co-operatives may utilise not only professional social workers, but also voluntary workers, who must not, however, make up more than half of the total number of members, and who must not be used as replacements for professional workers. Disadvantaged workers must constitute at least 30 per cent of the labour force of the co-operative.[8] These companies, who must be registered regionally, receive a direct subsidy from the state in that they do not have to pay social contributions on the salaries of disabled employees; they pay only a quarter of rateable and mortgage taxes, and they can draw up agreements with local authorities for the supply of goods and services even in derogation of laws on public administration contracts (Ferrario, 1991).

Church Related Services

Resumed interest in the private non-profit sector, which in Italy has always been largely represented by Catholic organisations, has focused attention once more on the role of the Church in the provision of welfare services. The publication of the results of the second piece of research on Christian charity and welfare organisations in Italy reveals the number, type, and juridical-organisational status of the majority of voluntary organisations

7. For a complete analysis of the new institutional and legislative situation, including the recent laws on voluntary care, which has been delineated in the Italian welfare system, see the dossier 'Solidarity, voluntary work, welfare state' 1992.

8. The condition of 'disadvantage' must be documented; this term refers to physically and mentally disabled people; de-institutionalised psychiatric patients; those requiring psychiatric care; alcohol and drug abusers; children at risk, and convicts serving alternative non-custodial sentences.

which currently operate in the personal social services sector. The survey examined in the region of 4,600–4,700 services, and reported that a third of them were founded after 1977. This confirms the earlier comment that the recovery of this private service parallels the crisis in the public sector. The services continue to favour the clients they have traditionally helped, such as elderly people (42 per cent), children (34 per cent), and disabled people (24 per cent), but from 1977 there was an increase in the number of agencies dealing with new social problems, such as drug and alcohol abuse and AIDS (12 per cent), ethnic minorities (14 per cent), families at risk and unmarried mothers (15 per cent). The fact that the major concentration of these is in the north serves to exacerbate rather than to reduce the significant regional inequalities which already exist in the public sector (National Council of Charity and Welfare Organisations, 1990).

Although many of the personal social services run by the Church retain their traditional form, an increasing number are associations or co-operatives, with a juridical form recognised and supported by the public sector. There are estimated to be over 76,000 workers, meaning that each service employs at least eighteen people, half of whom work on a full-time basis. Even though 50 per cent of these services have given refresher training to their permanent staff, the survey demonstrated that the overall professional level is rather low: only 26 per cent of these agencies have at least one university degree holder, and 43 per cent use staff defined as 'occasional voluntary workers' who are mainly religious carers. The use of occasional voluntary workers is sometimes criticised as providing an additional labour force with very little professional training, and which is used only for subordinate work.

The income comes mainly from the fees paid by local authorities (in 18 per cent of cases these contributions are more than 50 per cent of income); fees paid by clients; private donations, and contributions from public authorities. About 43 per cent of the services have agreements with local authorities, and are therefore undoubtedly subsidised. It follows, therefore, that a large part of the social services run by the Church depend very largely on public financing.

By comparing the situation of services prior to 1977 with today's services, the survey also underlines a number of structural changes which have occurred within this sector. The first of these is the multiplication of agencies with very specific and somewhat limited objectives (such as care centres, social or first aid centres), which undoubtedly meet many of today's needs, but which may also conceal a reduced ability on the part of workers to provide professional care. The second is the growth, as previously mentioned, of new juridical forms more suited to the socio-cultural changes which have occurred in the last decade in the social care system, and which seek to move away from traditional forms which too often involved institutional services. In only a minority of cases has the quality of services improved through a more favourable consumer/worker ratio and more highly qualified staff.

On the whole, in recent years the social services provided by the Church appear to have encountered the same difficulties experienced by the public sector in meeting the growing needs of a radically altered society. The development of initiatives has been characterised by a lack of planning and co-ordination, and there has been very little clarity in terms of choices and methods.

Old Mix or New Collaboration?

The beginning of the 1990s in Italy has seen a concealed privatisation in the social care sector, involving not so much the commercial agencies – which are increasing but whose ability, experience and knowledge is, to say the least, insufficient, and whose existence comes to light only when the most significant cases of oppression and abuse of power against clients is reported in the press – but more the vast range of agencies positioned generically in the private sector, characterised by very different legal and economic circumstances.

This phenomenon conceals the necessity for the public sector to overcome operative obstacles caused by local authority cutbacks, poor flexibility, and the very typical tendency to make operations heavily bureaucratic.

It is necessary to fully understand both the risks and the potential of the present situation. There is significant evidence to suggest that privatisation has developed very extensively in recent years because it allows local authorities to limit their involvement in particularly volatile areas of social care, such as areas of exponential growth (like services for elderly people), or those which raise particularly difficult politico-social problems.

The gradual withdrawal from involvement and responsibility for certain services on the part of the public sector means there is a risk that this same sector may reduce its involvement in the setting up of guidelines and the co-ordination of local social care (Pasquinelli, 1991). Even though the present debate surrounding the problems of the public welfare system tends increasingly to favour the private sector, it is evident that the public sector must act as guarantor by co-ordinating and promoting both strategies and resources in order to safeguard the citizen. At the same time, the private sector must participate in planning services in order to avoid becoming an instrument of low-quality management, providing unprofessional services and inadequate staff.

The real situation, however, is becoming more complicated. A national survey of groups of voluntary workers in the social care sector, carried out by the Institute of Social Research in 1988/9, revealed that public administration is not only using private organisations to meet its obligations, but it often sets them up, both within and outside its own institutions (De Ambrogio and Ranci, 1989). What is happening, in fact, is the reintroduction in a different way of the old polarisation between the public and private sector, based on the traditional separation between the financing source (public organisation) and the producer (private agency) of social care services. The novelty today lies in the fact, as shown by the experience of social co-operatives in Milan, that, rather than the dependence of the private sector on state finance, there is a relationship of reversed dependency of the public sector on private agencies:

> When a service is supplied for years by the same organisation, there is not only an increase in the qualification and ability of the same, but also an increase in the level of integration between public and private sectors; the same organisation becomes indispensable for the public subject which is increasingly less prepared to support the costs of a change of the private organization and still less to interrupt the relationship; a symbiosis is consolidated between the two subjects, in the sense that a relationship is created which produces important reciprocal benefits; more so that control and verification of services are extremely limited and purely formal. (Pasquinelli, 1991)

The law provides for the formation of autonomous instrumental organisations, which will be subject to controls relating to their efficiency and expenditure, and which will be responsible to the local authorities for the management of personal social services. If the intention of the legislation is to reinforce the central role of the public sector in planning the lines of intervention in social care, it is just as true that there is also a desire to constitute new forms of relationship, founded on collaboration rather than division, between public and private organisations in managing personal social services (Ascoli, 1992). The question is whether the opportunity this presents will be seized.

In point of fact, the present government's economic strategy is not clear and it does not include specific measures in the field of personal social services. The fact, however, that local boards have seen their budgets cut, without having in exchange more autonomy, makes it reasonable to expect further curbing of local expenditure on social protection. In this field the key words again relate to the introduction of selective measures aimed at those categories where need, disadvantage and marginalisation are concentrated. The emphasis is on the development of economic participation by beneficiaries as well as the search for private management solutions. These selective measures are associated with a new and more vital role for the family and for the community infrastructure in the field of social protection.

References

Ardigò, A. (1980) 'Towards a reorganisation of the state's health and welfare service?', *La Ricerca Sociale*, no.23.

—— (1991) 'Welfare in the post-communist society', *Argomenti*.

Ascoli, U. (1992) 'New settings for the social politics of the 1990s: a stable period for voluntary work?', *Polis*, no.2.

Bariletti, A., Gabriele, S., Marè, M. and Piacentino, D. (1990) 'Distributive aspects of the use of health services in Italy', *Economia Pubblica*, no. 20, pp.193–200.

Betri, M. L. (1984) 'Doctor and patient: the changes in the relationship and the premises for an elevation fo the profession' in *Storia d'Italia*, Annals no.7, Turin, Einaudi.

Bianchi, M., La Rosa, M., Minardi, E. and Zurla, P. (1988) 'Cooperation between services in Emilia-Romagna', *Sociologia del Lavoro*, no. 30–1.

Borzaga, C. (1988) 'The cooperation of joint social responsibility: first reflections on an emergent sector', *Sociologia del Lavoro*, no.30–1.

Censis (1982, 1986) *Report XVI and XX on the State of the country's welfare services*, Rome.

—— (1990) *Growth through competition. The combination of public and private sectors and the role of nursing homes*, Rome.

Chamber Commission of Social Affairs (1988) *Family Spending on Health Services*, Rome.

Cherubini, A. (1963–4) 'On a history of public services in Italy', *Previdenza Sociale*, 1 April 1963 and 3 June 1964.

Cosmacini, G. (1988) *The history of medicine and Health in Italy*, Bari, Laterza.

—— (1989) *Medicine and health in Italy in the twentieth century*, Bari, Laterza.

Donati, P. (ed.) (1980) *Health and Social Involvement*, Milan, F. Angeli.

—— (1989) 'From politics to the consumer. The ecological question and the movements of the 1970s', *Rassegna Italiana di Sociologia*, no.3.

Ferrario, P. (1991) 'The role of cooperation in the services system', *Prospettive Sociali e Sanitarie*, no.22.

Ferrera, M. (1984) *The welfare state in Italy*, Bologna, Il Mulino.

Forti Messina, A. (1982) 'Local doctors following unification', in Betri, M.L. and Marchetti, G.A. (eds) (1982) *Health and the working classes in Italy from unification to fascism*, Milan, F. Angeli.

Frascani, P. (1982) 'The doctor in the nineteenth century', *Studi Storici*, no.3.

Ginsborg, P. (1990) *The history of Italy from the postwar Period to the present day*, Turin, Einaudi.

Ingrosso, M. (1990) 'Social ecology and health', *Animazione Sociale*, no.27.

Institute of Social Research (1990) *National Survey of Voluntary Workers*, Rome.

ISTAT, (1987) 'Investigation into the health of the population and recourse to the health services', *Notizario*, VIII, 17.

National Committee of Local Authorities (1982) *Survey of Medical Attitudes to the National Health Service*, Rome.

National Council of Charity and Welfare Organisations (1990) *The Church and Marginalisation in Italy*, Rome.

National Health Council (1989) 'An Account of the Country's Health Services', Rome, *Graphical Institue and National Mint*.

Paci, M. (1989) *Public and Private in Modern Welfare Systems*, Naples, Liguori Publishers.

Parodi, E. (1982) 'Decentralization or subdivision?', *Il Medico d'Italia*, XI, 21.

Pasquinelli, S. (1991) 'The handicap of the archipelago', *Prospettive Sociali e Sanitarie*, no.2.

Petri, D. (1982) 'On a social history of fascist Italy: the protection of heath in the organization of the corporate state', in Betri, M.L. and Marchetti, G.A. (eds) (1982), *Health and the Working Classes in Italy from Unification to Fascism*, Milan, F. Angeli.

—— (1984) 'The hospital problem in fascist Italy: one aspect of corporate modernization', *Storia d'Italia*, Annal 7, Turin, Einaudi.

Piperno, A. (1986) (ed.) *The politics of health in Italy. Between continuity and change*, Milan, F. Angeli.

Ranci, O. E. (1990) 'Welfare politics' in Dente, B. (ed.) (1990) *Public Politics in Italy*, Bologna, Il Mulino.

—— (1992) 'Solidarity, voluntary help, welfare state', *White and Red*, no.25.

Salvemini, G. (1989) 'Complementarity and overlap between the public and private sectors in Italy', *Economia Pubblica*, no.7–8.

Vicarelli, G. (1986) 'Professions and the welfare state: general practitioners in the national health service', *Stato e Mercato*, no.16.

—— (1988) 'Health service personnel, in AIS-ISTAT' (1988) *Images of the community in Italy*, Rome.

—— (1989a) 'The doctor in the feminine gender: Women in the development in the medical profession in Italy', *Polis* 2.

—— (1989b) *Castles of Sand*, Ancona, Clua.

—— (1990) 'The national health service between politics and the community', *Democrazia e Diritto*, 1.

Visco, C. V. (1991) 'Local and public benefits of privatization: Italy's case in relation to the experience of the United Kingdom and the United States', in Santagata, W. (ed.) (1991) *The Private Donation of Public Benefits*, Bologna, Il Mulino.

–7–

Poland

Stanislawa Golinowska and *Katarzyna Tymowska*

The Debate on the Future of the Welfare State, Role of the Market and Privatisation

The process of transforming the economic system which started in Poland in the late 1980s was preceded by several attempts at introducing economic reforms which would still maintain the omnipresence of a central planning mechanism. After 1956, efforts were made to reduce the degree of centralisation in managing the economy, by devolving some of the powers to state-owned enterprises, allowing them to draw up short-term plans on their own. In 1972 a further attempt was made to bolster the position of managers in large companies and organisations. But it was not until 1980–2 that more far-reaching plans were put into effect to reform the economic system. The first result was the much wider autonomy of state-owned enterprises in the area of self-financing, self-management and self-reliance. These reforms were meant to improve the efficiency of operations in the state sector.

In the latter half of the 1980s, proposals were advanced, and analytical studies appeared concerning the fundamental importance of private ownership and of switching the Polish economy onto a market-based track.

An important step in the process of economic reform was the adoption in 1989 of the Law on Economic Activity (dubbed 'the Business Bill of Rights'), which enabled the rapid expansion of the private sector to take place. Until that time, setting up a private firm had entailed the need to obtain a licence, and the number of these was strictly controlled. The 1989 law reduced this business licensing requirement. It was in 1989 that the private sector in Poland really took off, following radical and extensive changes to aid its development. In that year the private sector – including private farms as well as industrial and business companies – generated some 19.2 per cent of the net material product, with half of that being accounted for by private businesses outside agriculture.

In 1990, private non-agricultural business was already generating approximately 18 per cent of the net material product. More recently, 1991 estimates put this share at approximately 30 per cent. Non-farming private businesses continue to be small, however, and are concentrated mainly in the field of commerce. Their economic potential seems to be limited, and they employ, on average, only two or three people. Only the foreign equity companies are generally larger.

In parallel with efforts to improve the economic environment for investment in new private ventures, another policy thrust has concerned the privatisation of state-owned enterprises. The Privatisation Act, which was pivotal if progress was to be made, was adopted in July 1990.

Privatisation of state-owned enterprises is brought about by one of two methods. The first is the so-called 'liquidation path', which means that when an enterprise is on the brink of insolvency it is liquidated, with the assets being sold off to private investors. An enterprise can also apply for liquidation in order to privatise. The second method is known as the 'equity path'. Here an enterprise is first transformed into a wholly-owned stock company of the Treasury under the terms of the Commercial Code of 1934, and then the company stock or shares are offered to a third party. The procedure for share offerings is determined by the Minister for Privatisation, representing the Treasury. The equity path is used for large and medium-sized enterprises.

By the end of 1991 the privatisation record looked as follows: the liquidation path was applied in 417 cases, with 90 per cent of these enterprises transformed into employee-owned stock companies; the equity path was applied to 20 large and sound state-owned enterprises. In effect, transformation mechanisms were applied to some 11 per cent of the total number of registered state-owned companies.

The focus on reforms in general, and on problems linked to the consequent functioning of businesses, is essential to an understanding of the ownership changes which have taken place since 1989 in the area of social policy, which were primarily the consequence of changes occurring in the economy at large. This meant that state enterprises in the field of social care and cultural provision were, or could be, subject to the same processes which affected industrial ventures. In this way, privatisation processes extended to publishing houses, book shops, holiday hotels and health recuperation centres, as well as to pharmacies.

Along with that, completely new private firms appeared, offering social services to the general public. This process of growth of a private sector in the social policy field was fuelled by two elements. First of these was a sense of freedom – Polish intellectuals active in the area of culture and education were able to set up private publishing ventures, schools, art galleries or theatres, all without censorship and without being tied by state-allocated funds. Furthermore, after 1989, Polish doctors with the right to practise their profession no longer had to apply for administrative permission to set up private practices.

The second factor which prompted the growth of private services was the myriad scarcities in the area of social provision. The scarcities in this field were as marked as those troubling the economy, both in Poland and wherever 'real socialism' (as the system used to be called) had been practised. Such new provisions appeared as private health insurance for the better-off; private kindergartens, and also private educational ventures in under-supplied areas of knowledge: business management, banking, marketing and foreign languages.

It is important to note, however, that the process of forming new private companies, along with the process of transforming state-owned services into private businesses in the area of social care, was not preceded by any significant debate about how social policy was to be administered in a state undergoing far-reaching transformations. Changes in the social services area have been, and continue to be, to some extent spontaneous, although some aspects of development have been necessitated by economic pressures. Reforms are accompanied by high social cost and a large increase in welfare clientele such as the unemployed and others qualifying for welfare assistance. These people are lining up at state welfare assistance institutions which now have only a limited capacity to handle the burden.

Poland now represents a model which could be termed the 'drifting social policy of real socialism'. There is still only a marginal proportion of market-type institutions, and the field serviced by voluntary, non-profit organisations is only expanding slowly. The growth of these two sectors will obviously be determined in the immediate future by both the scope and the quality of state social security guarantees. At present, the ineffective performance and the limited capacity of state welfare institutions has not met expectations, and has eroded the sense of social protection resulting from so-called 'state guarantees' of social security which were seriously entertained by the government in 1991.

Political Determinants of Private Sector Development

It must be emphasised that opposition to the totalitarian state and to the inefficiency of central planning in Poland, represented by the Solidarity political and union movement, was not directed against the system of state social policy. In this area, problems were seen primarily in the context of improving the efficiency of the Welfare State's operation, rather than reducing its scope. There was little accent on individual responsibility for social affairs, individual care and protection, and there were few calls for developing market-based social service institutions.

In the struggle for political and union liberties during the early 1980s, the independent trade unions even called for the extension of the scope of state welfare provision, entering into negotiations with the government to secure a higher share of spending on health, education and culture. This culminated in the signing of the Gdansk Accords in the autumn of 1981. As the 1980s drew to an end, the calls continued for higher spending to meet social policy ends. In the Round Table Agreement (the agreements reached between the last Communist government and Solidarity in early 1989), the Solidarity position reflected a claimant attitude *vis-à-vis* the government. Demands centred on guarantees of public funding for social welfare, while at the same time a reduction in the role of the state in controlling economic activity was called for.

System changes in the area of social policy still depend on the position taken by the Solidarity trade union, which continues with a social policy thesis coined when the union was in opposition to the Communists. Such persistence is also connected with the presence of a competing trade union formed during the 1980s by the Communist rulers to take the place of the then outlawed Solidarity. The post-communist trade unions, known as the OPZZ (the All-Poland Alliance of Trade Unions) still enjoy the support of employees in state-owned enterprises, and still continue with their stand of pressing claims on the government in relation to social questions.

The trade unions take it for granted that the state still has obligations to the people throughout the entire area of social policy. Every attempt to reduce the scope of social benefits, due to the crisis in public finances which is inescapable at a time of change and economic recession, comes up against a wall of staunch union opposition. In the autumn of 1991, following adamant union criticism, the government backed out of a plan to reduce child support benefits, despite the ineffectiveness of such dispersion of funds as a policy tool.

Poland has yet to develop a model of tripartite bargaining over wages and social benefits. Currently, disputes are still debated along a dividing line running between society (represented by the trade unions) and the authorities (represented by the government).

However, there is now one voice to be heard speaking out in favour of the commercial provision of welfare. The liberal party, the Liberal-Democratic Congress (KLD), has been applying political pressure to develop the market and private ownership in all areas. This party ruled the country for one year (1991), and one of its founders, Jan Krzysztof Bielecki, headed the government. During that year there was an evident speeding up of privatisation processes, and very clear approval for the promotion of private sector development in the area of social services, particularly in the field of health. Indeed, private health insurance was advertised on state television. Private developments in the field of culture, however, caused more controversy. The lease of a prestigious Warsaw theatre to a private businessman dominated the culture columns in Polish newspapers throughout the latter half of the year.

These developments demonstrated the effect of the 'new thinking'; they were the public articulation of market-centred values in areas such as private health insurance, which were earlier considered 'off-limits' for ethical reasons. During the 1980s, social scientists advanced a theory of the need to 'denationalise' social policy (Piekara and Supinska, 1985). However, political programmes and practical actions focused on decentralising the Welfare State rather than denationalising it, and on the devolution of social policy institutions to local government level.

In March 1990 a law on local self-government was passed, and local elections were held two months later. The primary social policy institutions were transferred to the local authorities. These were politically immature bodies, lacking the required social and organisational experience and, even more significantly, constrained by regulations relating to the collection of local taxes. The main part of local government funding still continues to come from the central budget. The record of local authorities in the area of social policy following the May 1990 elections has yet to be studied in depth. The fragmentary information so far available is insufficient for a full-scale diagnosis, especially considering the exceptionally fluid economic and political situation which pertained all through 1990 and 1991.

Selected Areas of Private Sector Development in Social Services

Health Care

Under the regime of 'real socialism' the margin left to private provision in the health services was very limited. This was true of both primary care (diagnostics, treatment, rehabilitation, terminal care), auxiliary services and supplies.

The main instrument used to limit the development of commercial health services was the requirement that private medical practice be combined with a job in the public sector, and the necessity of obtaining permission from local health administrators to set up a private medical practice. Another constraint was the shortage of sufficient funds to launch a practice, and the absence of insurance companies which would refund the medical care expenses incurred by private patients. Budget resources could not be made available to the private sector (except on a very limited scale, for specifically commissioned projects). Until 1991 the main source of revenue for the private health care sector was the fee paid directly by the patient. In 1991 the first medical insurance was offered by Westa-Medical, but for the time being its scope is marginal.

Until the early 1970s, when free medical care was extended to the rural population, there were a few rural health co-operatives operating in the countryside. Their revenues were in the form of member shares, budget subsidies, and fees paid by local patients. There are also some out-patient diagnostic and rehabilitation wards in co-operatives for disabled people, financed with rehabilitation funds obtained from tax relief available to these co-operatives. Nevertheless, their share of the entire health market remains quite limited.

Private health services in Poland are still not widespread, being restricted mainly to out-patient treatment. In the last two years, however, several very small private clinics have been organised, specialising to a large extent in plastic surgery. Yet it is doubtful how successful these will be in the present economic climate.

The fees for private health services were previously anything but exorbitant, yet these services were mostly used by the better-off; those who did not use private services claimed that high cost was the main obstacle (Korzystanie, 1990). A second element, equally important in characterising the patients who decided on private treatment, was their higher educational standing, and hence greater sophistication in the area of health culture; their greater mobility, and the ease with which they obtained information about the existence of private practices.

In 1986 the share of private health services in the total number of officially registered medical visits was low, at 2.5 per cent (Tymowska, 1987). Such services are available mainly in the larger cities, and are offered generally through private practices and medical co-operatives.

The above statistics, however, underestimate the real share of private treatment, as they take no account of the 'grey' sector of private services offered in public health service facilities. Nor do they include the unreported services by private practices. Such 'reporting inaccuracies' reflect both the previous and the present practice of assessing lump-sum taxes, without taking full account of private practice revenues, costs and spending.

The first private group practices operating under the regulation of the Commercial Code, with regular book-keeping, were formed in 1989, following the introduction of the right to operate private practices as businesses, subject only to court registration. There is no longer any necessity to obtain formal permits, nor any requirement to hold an additional job in the public sector. Even though, in the latter half of the 1980s, such administrative permission was granted (albeit reluctantly), the elimination of this requirement under the new Business Act speeded up the process of forming new private practices. This is true both of single-doctor and multi-speciality practices, including diagnostic practices. The trend was encouraged by the deteriorating quality and the increasing difficulty of access to public health services – longer queues, shortage of funds, equipment and personnel – and by the increasing differentiation of income levels, with more people having higher disposable incomes.

There are are other important elements conducive to the formation of private medical practices, the foremost among them being the low pay levels in the public health sector. The quest for additional income always was, and continues to be, an important factor behind decisions to enter the private sector. This is true of both 'official' and 'unofficial' earnings. It is possible to obtain the latter in the private sector for two reasons. First, a weak fiscal policing system leaves a part of the income untaxed. At the same time, private practice is still being combined with a job in the public health service (except for dentists). This, together with the shortcomings of the public health service, is conducive to the co-existence within the public sector of a private 'grey' sector. The lack of proper controls over entry into the public system; lack of a link between the level of engaged resources and the range of service; lack of cost accounting at cost source, or clearly assigned responsibility for spending incurred – all these factors encourage the operation of a 'parallel health service' within the public sector.

There is unspoken acceptance of such a state of affairs by the general public. Unfortunately, however, no reliable data are available concerning the current scale of either official or unofficial private practice.

In addition to the elements already discussed, another factor leading to the development of a formal and informal private sector must be particularly noted. In Poland, although nearly 100 per cent of the population is entitled to receive free medical care, the right to choose the treating physician or clinic is severely restricted. A patient is assigned to a given region, and only some of the clinics in cities offer the right to choose a doctor. The private sector is better at guaranteeing the right of choice, and leaving the patient with complete freedom of decision.

Since 1991 private emergency services have been available in the bigger cities. They charge lump-sum fees payable in advance, offering in exchange the right to prompt and complex medical care, often including basic diagnostic services. These services are not funded through insurance policies, as they do not operate according to insurance company rules. Since the range of services offered is incomplete, these private emergency services have, of necessity, had to pass a proportion of the medical care costs (such as the cost of complicated therapy) on to the state. They take the patient by private ambulance to the chosen hospital, which is often not the local hospital assigned for state-funded patients, but they do not cover the cost of treatment.

The financial rewards for health service personnel, and the patient's right to choose a doctor and bypass the long waiting lists, are the main reasons behind the development of the private health sector in Poland. It is claimed at times that the rationale for encouraging this sector should take into account the fiscal consequences for the state budget: freeing the state of some financial commitments and shifting the burden onto the shoulders of individual wage earners. It is, however, somewhat difficult to accept this argument, firstly because supply induces demand for health services: expanding the scope of the private sector on the supply side does not necessarily entail reductions in public spending on health. Secondly, private ownership of health service facilities has not been matched so far by the development of a private capital market in the insurance sector. The sustained expansion of the private sector in Poland will be possible only when it is able to obtain third-party payment through insurance policies or the state budget (Tymowska, 1991).

One cannot, however, expect any dynamic growth of private insurance, as companies continue to come up against a barrier of a lack of demand for insurance services. Employers in Poland do not have a statutory obligation to pay for health insurance cover, as there is no legally binding national insurance scheme. In effect, the cost of insurance cannot be split between the employees and the employers. This is the main reason behind the very high charges for a private insurance policy offered by the commercial Medical-Westa insurance company. In addition, as well as the cost of the policy, which relates to a guaranteed specified amount of cover or to a maximum treatment cost, the patient has to pay 10 per cent of the cost of treatment him or herself. Moreover, the range of medical services covered is not fully comprehensive.

Neverthless, Medical-Westa does have a great deal of capital accumulated from the other forms of insurance which it offers. Some of these funds are now being deployed for the construction of its own health care facilities, or for co-funding public sector investment, in exchange for the future right to use a part of the jointly created infrastructure. Therefore it will not be a shortage of supply which will limit the future growth of Medical-Westa: it will be their failure to secure a sufficient policy portfolio from health insurance due to the small number of people willing to take out a personal health insurance policy to compensate for the lack of employment-related schemes.

The future development of the private sector may be helped along significantly, however, by the adoption of provisions which came into force on 14 January 1992 (the Law on Establishments of 1991), allowing the state – currently the main source of health service financing – to allocate a portion of funds to that sector. The supplier of public funds will have the right to sign a contract with bodies, regardless of ownership status, for the provision of health services to the general public. This provision should be conducive to the allocation of funds to the private sector once it has become accepted by those who hold the purse strings as being more efficient in administering such funds, and more effective in securing health policy objectives. We have written elsewhere of our support for such allocation criteria in a proposal for health sector reform (Golinowska et al., 1991).

We believe that the development of the private sector may be promoted by the state in order to further the rationalisation of public spending. It is difficult to predict whether this is in fact going to happen; whether the private sector will indeed grow thanks to government contracts, and whether the private sector will prove to be the more effective supplier of health care. One measure of support is the projected tax changes, which stipulate that all health service institutions should be exempt from VAT.

Obviously there may be dangers in reducing state spending on health care. One example occurred in 1990 and 1991, when pharmacies, originally part of the state pharmaceutical chain, were privatised through sale. Now 80 per cent of pharmacies are in private hands, and we have seen a resulting lack of control over the prescription of medicines; poor control over sales; the stockpiling of supplies in the expectation of changes in the regulations governing payment for medicines, and a growing turnover of pharmacies geared towards profit-making. Moreover, the state budget has actually had to increase its outlay on subsidising medicines. This experience with privatising pharmacies has led to a general slowing down of the move towards privatisation, and to the introducion of stricter controls on privatising those state enterprises which supply medical equipment. Nevertheless, numerous private companies have been formed in this field, making the state monopoly of medical equipment supply a thing of the past. Regulation is planned for this market by requiring certification for capital equipment purchases financed from public funds. Control over distribution of medicines is to be achieved by limiting price refunds, licensing pharmacies, and by the introduction of wholesale distribution centres.

Next in line will be the privatisation of auxiliary health services, such as laundries, cleaning, kitchens and technical maintenance. The law on state and non-commercial establishments introduces motivation instruments to assure rational operation. It is possible that these will promote a more dynamic progress towards privatising auxiliary operations.

There are no expectations, however, of private sector development through the privatisation of current primary health care institutions, either at a national or a municipal level. Nevertheless, the practice of renting out empty premises and unused equipment to private bodies will continue. During the period of the severe budget deficit in the second half of 1991, many health centres resorted to this device in order to procure additional funds for primary care. This became possible through a special regulation which permitted state-funded institutions to retain such revenues within their accounts.

Education

The many declarations of system changes in Poland, backed up by legislation offering the freedom to form new institutions, has set in motion the process of decentralising and, to some extent, denationalising educational institutions. This process has not as yet gained much momentum, but it has captured the public imagination.

The process of denationalising education generally means the formation of so-called 'social schools' – schools organised through local community efforts, usually by parents' organisations. They receive some 50 per cent financing from the public purse. Truly private schools are a rarity in Poland: in the 1990/1 school year there were only three private primary schools and six private secondary schools in the country. In contrast, there were eighty social primary schools and twenty-four social secondary schools. In the 1991/2 school year there were already 450 non-state schools at each level, equivalent to approximately 2 per cent of all schools operating in Poland; but the share of private schools among these is negligible.

There are also considerable developments in the area of non-public post-secondary schools, and their number now exceeds a thousand. These vary from institutions offering a motley assortment of courses, to organisations operating as fully-fledged colleges. More than 60 per cent of all these schools are in Warsaw. The non-public schools formed spontaneously, under provisions of the Law on Associations of 1989. However, official sanction was eventually given to the process of forming social and private schools by the Law on the System of Education of September 1991. This law spelled out the rules for financing such schools, and listed curriculum requirements qualifying them for official recognition of their diplomas. Under this law, non-public schools (social, private and church-sponsored schools) have the right to a subsidy equivalent to 50 per cent of the operating costs per pupil in public schools of the same level. Decisions on whether to operate such schools are taken by the local authority. Non-public schools, on a par with public schools, are exempt from real estate tax. The right to a state subsidy also applies to those non-public schools whose curricula have not been accepted as equivalent to public schools. In such cases the subsidy is awarded by the Minister for National Education.

At present one notes a levelling-off of the trend to set up new non-public primary and secondary schools. The reasons are connected with the economy at large: a declining living standard, limited opportunities for securing properly equipped school premises, waning chances for obtaining the state subsidy due to the crisis in public financing, and the shortage of private sponsors.

This waning enthusiasm concerns both denationalising and decentralising education. In fact, the 1991 budget deficit resulted in increased pressure on the government to guarantee public funds for the wages of state employees in the education sector, and for the maintenance of state schools.

Cultural and Recreational Institutions

In some ways, leisure, recreation and recuperation facilities were part of the total health and education care package offered by the state. The current process of reorientation towards the commercial market was most marked in the field of culture and recreation from the very onset of reforms in 1989 and 1990. Private book shops, art galleries, publishing houses and recreation centres mushroomed everywhere. This was followed, somewhat later, by the process of privatising large cultural and recreational organisations, both those functioning autonomously and those tied to businesses.

In the case of business-linked social and cultural facilities, the change was more intensive, as additional factors came into play. State-owned enterprises forced to make financial cuts in the wake of the stabilisation programme (dubbed the 'Balcerowicz Plan') started by ridding themselves of the ballast of social and cultural facilities. Industry-operated cultural centres and holiday estates were offered to local authorities and housing co-operatives, put up for sale, leased out, or reorganised as commercial ventures yielding revenue for the industrial owners.

The resultant fate of these facilities varied. In many cases the formerly member-only centres were opened to entire local communities, and came under the administration of local authorities. These also became more active in securing revenue, and took a more prominent part in the social life of the communities associated with them. In most cases, however, the centres completely changed the profile of their activities, and now operate on a fully commercial basis. Something that was taken for granted under 'real socialism' – the access of employees to free or very low-cost social and cultural services – was changed radically. The number of people on state/employer-organised holidays in 1990 declined by approximately 40 per cent compared with 1980.

The Culture Institute conducted a study in the autumn of 1991 (Golinowska and Ilczuk, 1992) on the formation of private firms in the area of culture. This study pointed to several characteristic features of emergent businesses in this field. First, this is a clearly polarised sector.

At one extreme are the specialised cultural institutions, catering to a public with elevated cultural tastes. The object of the owner is not so much profit as an opportunity for pursuing his or her personal cultural interests through the independent operation of a firm offering cultural services. At the other extreme are the highly commercial operations, catering to a public seeking popular and low-brow entertainment.

In the area of culture there is also a continuing process of privatising state enterprises engaged in the production and sale of cultural objects and in rendering cultural services. This is the path of privatisation through liquidation, already mentioned, initiated by the employees along with the management. Since 1991 this path has been used for transforming several large publishing houses, two printing houses and a number of large book-selling houses into companies with employee-held stock. So far, this is the only form of positive ownership transformations applied to cultural institutions.

Liquidation of enterprises due to bankruptcy and their sale to private investors leads to a complete change of the product profile. New owners rarely want to have anything to do with cultural services.

No privatisation of cultural enterprises has been attempted by the equity path, also previously mentioned. The Minister for Privatisation has rejected initiatives in this field, fearing the public's limited propensity to invest in the stock of cultural institutions.

A new development in the operating of state cultural institutions in 1991 was the emergence of financing sources other than a state subsidy from the Ministry of Culture. Two factors combined to produce this. On the one hand, there was a severe cutback of public funds and the liquidation of a special extra-budgetary fund, which up to that time provided a steady and secure source of financing for cultural institutions; on the other hand, legislation offered complete freedom to cultural institutions to tap extra funds on their own – a possibility which was earlier quite restricted. This question was resolved in a parliamentary bill concerning the organisation and conduct of cultural activities (October 1991). Hence it became essential to try to procure additional sources of funding, given the budgetary constraints, and legal possibilities were made available for an organisation to seek funds from sponsors other than the Ministry of Culture.

The first study of the situation of sponsored culture, carried out in November 1991 (Golinowska and Wieczorek, 1992), has shown that this phenomenon arose from the initiative of managers of the increasingly impoverished cultural institutions, who started 'ringing doorbells' for funds. They scored successes mainly with the public sector from outside the cultural field, from administrative authorities, industrial ventures, banks and insurance companies.

Much more modest funds were received from private sponsors, both individual and institutional. Significant help was secured through sharing premises or some facilities. Frequently, significant aid-in-kind was obtained from grateful audiences, such as decorating materials or detergents. In effect, those actively vying for support managed to procure it, and their institutions did not founder, but still, an immense group of people actively involved with culture found themselves helpless once state funding was withdrawn, and Poland as yet has no professional consultants who could help out in this specific field.

Such processes of change have, on the whole, resulted in reduced access to cultural services, recreational facilities and holidays for members of the general public.

Housing

In the years of 'real socialism' in Poland, housing was practically a social commodity, even though policy in this field changed with time to a more economy-based model. During the 1950s, housing was obtained from the state, and rents were nominal. During the 1960s, people were asked to save up for housing, and housing co-operatives were organised, conceived from the outset as state-subsidised institutions. Special savings booklets for housing were issued by the PKO Bank, with the value of deposits guaranteed against changes in housing construction costs. Despite increasing savings for housing purposes, the occupiers' share in financing housing construction was quite modest, and amounted only to some 4 per cent (Golinowska, 1990), while rents continued to be little more than peppercorn.

In the latter half of the 1970s a decision was made to allow the private purchase of state housing, with the intention of engaging a higher share of personal funds in housing costs. The state subsidised people wishing to buy their flats, by writing off 40 per cent of the standard cost of the accommodation. This was a policy favouring the wealthier sections of the population.

In 1981 the authorities declared a policy of equal treatment for all housing investors, but the constraints imposed by scarcities in all areas of the economy did little to bring this about, even though there was a slow but steady expansion of private house construction.

Rationing of housing resources still continued within the state and co-operative sectors, and it was this factor – all the difficulties notwithstanding – that frequently led people to decide to build their own houses by 'do-it-yourself' methods.

During the Round Table negotiations of 1989, mentioned earlier, declarations were made with the intention of putting the housing sector on an economic footing, and of providing a social umbrella to shield people from excessive outlay on housing investment and from high rents. Demands were also pressed for legislative guarantees of house ownership rights and the freedom of housing acquisition.

Before the launch of market reforms, private housing accounted for 42 per cent of the total housing stock, 23 per cent being in urban areas. Co-operative housing represented 24 per cent, council housing 19 per cent, and employer-built housing 12 per cent.

Currently, this means that nearly a quarter of all housing in cities and towns is in the hands of private owners. The people who (in earlier years) bought the flats which they occupied (with the aid of massive state subsidies) now stand, in theory, to realise major capital gains from their property; however, it is highly unlikely that they will realise such gains. The supply of housing during the 1980s was low, and the housing industry continues to stagnate today, leading to a very inactive housing market. Meanwhile, Poland has one of Europe's fastest-growing populations, and hence the housing needs of the country are considerable. In reality, people continue to be tied to their house, though now to a considerably more costly one.

Setting rents at levels reflecting full costs could bring about a situation where, for many families, the houses in which they live could become too expensive to maintain. Already the formerly unheard of phenomenon of non-payment of rent and service charges is appearing (in some co-operatives up to 30 per cent of people fail to pay their rent).

The government response to this developing crisis is the proposal of a guaranteed subsidy on house expenses such as loan repayments, interest and rent where these exceed 25 per cent of the household budget.

Social Welfare Institutions

In the age of 'real socialism' the existence of people requiring social assistance was not considered a problem worthy of an institutional solution. This was an 'unmentionable' problem, approached as simple gap-filling in a system of social welfare linked closely to employment. Social welfare institutions were nationalised, and for thirty to forty years functioned as state institutions or state-social institutions. During the 1980s – under agreements concluded with the Ministry of Health, which until 1990 was responsible for social assistance – the list of institutions eligible to supply autonomous welfare services was extended to include many social organisations and Church-sponsored groups. At present, the largest organisations of this type, with a considerable tradition of welfare assistance, are the Polish Red Cross, the Polish Committee for Social Assistance, and CARITAS, closely associated with the Catholic Church.

Comprehensive regulation of the field of social assistance was still required to define the criteria for eligibility for assistance; the form and scope of assistance; the rights of various bodies, and the duties of the state in this respect.

Under the terms of the Round Table Accords of 1989, a team was set up to draft a policy outline for the organisation of social assistance. This culminated in the Law on Social Assistance which came into effect in January 1991. Under these provisions, the system of welfare assistance institutions may include non-governmental bodies, which must, however, come under an administrative umbrella – the Voivodship (provincial) Team for Social Assistance, which will provide information about the needy; advice, personnel training, and supplementary funding.

Recent years have brought several newcomers into the social assistance field. These include self-help (voluntary) institutions and new social organisations, among which one of the most popular is the Youth Movement Against Drug Addiction (MONAR). However, there are still no private for-profit institutions.

Social assistance services, particularly nursing of elderly, infirm and ill people, are rendered primarily by the families themselves. Polish society still retains close cross-generation bonds and a sense of family duty. Indeed, it must be remembered that Poland is a country with a relatively high proportion of family-owned farms, and a comparatively recent industrial base (large-scale industrialisation dates back no more than twenty to forty years). The country is also very dynamic demographically. The economic crisis which continued, apart from a brief interlude, all through the 1980s, and which moved into a recession stage in 1990 and 1991, only perpetuates the traditional model.

There is, however, a market system of home-based nursing services. The high number of working women in Poland is the main factor behind this. These services have to be classified along with other services in the 'grey' sector. Those who render such services pay no taxes on their earnings and are not subject to any external controls. The market prices of nursing services are very high, and those rendering such services have no interest in having this market regulated, while the patients and families benefiting from such services are still insufficiently organised to demand the introduction of necessary regulation into this market.

Conclusion

Private profit-orientated institutions are a complete novelty in the field of social policy in Poland. Such institutions do exist in certain sections of the health services, and the process of general transformation has started some movement in the direction of developing non-governmental organisations. As a rule, these are organised by local communities as private initiatives, and on a non-profit basis.

The emergence of such institutions was helped by regulations adopted during the 1980s as part of the process of economic reform, and above all by the latest regulations adopted during the 1980s and 1990s. These include the following legislation: the Law on Foundations (1984), the Law on Associations (1989), the Business Act (1989) and also numerous specific laws governing defined types of social, educational and cultural activities in non-governmental forms, such as the Law on Social Assistance (1990), the Law on Health Service Establishments (1991), the Law on the Educational System (1991) and the Law on Organising and Conducting Cultural Activities (1991).

Foundations have played a fundamental role in the process of forming the non-governmental sector in the area of social policy. They have served the function of amassing the capital required to establish specific social service institutions. Tax relief offered on donations to foundations resulted, however, in such institutions being used as an expedient for the 'cold storage' of capital, without there being any intention of using it for the statutory ends of the foundation. This has given such foundations a bad name in Poland. Yet, alongside such abuses of foundation status, there were many really positive initiatives which have contributed significantly to the establishment of social service institutions funded outside the state budget.

Reforms in Poland have reached the stage of denationalising social policy institutions, but there has been no corresponding movement towards putting them onto a market-driven basis.

Early experience with privatisation and the immense social cost of reforms, with unemployment growing from zero to around 20 per cent in a matter of two years, is behind the ambivalent feelings expressed by Poles on the subject of further privatisation, even though the existing private sector has found full acceptance (CBOS, 1992). In the future a slowing-down of ownership transfers may be expected.

References

Golinowska, S. (1990) *Central Role in the Shaping of Consumer Structure*, Warsaw, State Economic Publication.

—— (1992) *The Market in Culture*, Warsaw, Institute of Culture.

Golinowska, S., Tymowska, K. and WÆodarczyk, C. (1991) 'In the Interest of Health Care' project of the reform of Health Care, no.3 and no.4.

Gains from Health Care in 1989 (1990) Central Statistical Office.

Piekara, A. and Supinska, J. (eds) (1985) *Politics in Times of Change*, Warsaw, PWN.

Tymowska K. (1991a) 'Privatisation: A panacea for all ills', *Gazeta*

Bankowa, no.43.
—— (1991b) 'Health Care in Times of Transformation: Hopes and Reality', Economy Conference.

–8–

Slovenia

Majda Černič Istenič

The transformation of economic structures in Slovenia is directly linked with changes in the structure of social services. The present severe crisis in the social services and in other spheres of social life is the cumulative inheritance of previous decades. Therefore the evaluation and understanding of recent changes in this field is conditioned by a description of the former system. This chapter will look at the effects of privatisation in relation to health care, housing, and the care of elderly and disabled people.

The Position of Social Services During the Period of Self-Management

Until the end of the 1950s, institutions such as schools, hospitals and social institutes operated under the patronage of the state. They had the status of state institutions; decisions about their financing, development, standards and extent of their activities were controlled by the state. Professionals in social institutions were merely performers of functions determined by the state and its bureaucracy. In the late 1960s it was decided that the existing system should be replaced with something more democratic and effective, where the creative and professional initiatives of all employees and community members could be expressed directly and put into practice. This was the main idea behind a new project for social management, so-called 'self-management'.

With the introduction of self-management in all spheres of social life – which implied the reduction or even abolition of the state and some of its functions – the position of the social services changed. The new constitution of 1974 gave such institutions the status of autonomous labour organisations: 'Basic Organisations of Associated Labour' (BOALs). Their position in the social structure became the same as those of economic enterprises based on social property. Every BOAL in the sphere of non-material production – such establishments as kindergartens, homes for elderly and disabled people, and hospitals, for example – became

– 155 –

autonomous organisations, complete with all management functions.

Another aspect of self-management was to be seen in the establishment of 'Self-managing Communities of Interests' (SMCIs). These have been described as places where producers of social provision and their consumers meet to bargain for individual programmes and activities, to arrange their development, and to oversee their standards and financing.

Despite many legislative changes, the financing of health care during the period of self-management remained largely unaffected. The funds for health care came from a percentage of the BOAL's income and a percentage of the employee's income. The percentages varied from year to year, as indicated in Table 8.1. In principle, the insured person was entitled to most health care services. For the following services, however, cost sharing was required:

	1976	1980	1981	1986	1987	1988	1989	1990	1991
Percentage of BOAL's income	7.5	7.3	1.2	0.4	0.4	8.7	11.5	10.9	7.2
Percentage of employee's gross income	1.8	1.6	8.7	10.2	10.4	0.5	0.8	0.6	6.6

Table 8.1 Financing Health Care During the Period of Self-management, Slovenia, 1976–91

1 from 1952, for prosthetics, dental prosthetics, spa treatments and some medicines;
2 from 1981, for basic health services and hospital in-patient treatment (war veterans, handicapped people, pensioners and children were exempt);
3 from 1987, for basic health services and hospital in-patient treatment, with no exemptions.

Agreements on the distribution of Gross National Product (GNP) among different social sectors, such as health care, education, science and culture, were endorsed in assemblies of SMCIs attended by representatives of producers and consumers without the presence of the state. This procedure was named 'the Free Exchange of Labour' (FEL). Through FEL the role of the state and its bureaucracy as a mediator and decision-maker was to be replaced by representatives of direct interests. The state reserved the right to arbitrate in cases when agreement between different interest groups could not be achieved. Therefore SMCIs should have been distinctly anti-bureaucratic institutions: they should only have been places for bargaining. However, the result of these innovations was just the opposite.

The Disadvantages of Self-Management in the Social Services

Before the introduction of self-management, each institution was formed only of practitioners, with almost no administration. But, after their financing and management became independent, every institution had to employ a fixed number of administrators, accountants and managers which in many cases even exceeded the number of practitioners. The practitioners had to take part in self-management activities, to the detriment of their social service work. Responsibility gradually shifted from the individual to the collective, and resulted in general irresponsibility.

The SMIs also employed a great number of administrative and managerial personnel. These communities could not remain simply meetings of producers and consumers of social provision, since the general intention was the replacement of the state and its functions. The SMCIs had to adopt a wide range of expert tasks earlier performed by the state, and thus they themselves became bureaucratic centres.

The introduction of new areas of self-management required completely new legislation. Thus the sphere of social services, with the corresponding SMCIs, became the most intense area of legislation in the period following 1974. In spite of intentions to reduce administration and bureaucracy, three parallel, autonomous management structures had been created. Instead of the state's three-level management structure (political, executive and administrative), six identical management levels were added to the whole system – three new levels for the SMCIs and three for the BOALs (Smidovnik, 1989). This apparatus was characterised by inefficiency, due to lack of co-operation and information, and the cost of administrative and professional staff employed in social services tripled.

The overall result of the implementation of self-management in social services was its financial collapse in the transitional period. The collapse occurred not because of the cost of the social service itself, but because of its hugely oversized, unproductive and parasitic administrative infrastructure and the general lack of clear responsibility.

Legislative Actions to Establish a New Structure of Social Services

The Parliament of Slovenia, elected in April 1990 in the first free elections since the Second World War, charged the government to solve the critical situation of the social services. The general intention is to form a system of social services which reflects the European pattern. The government's first task was to ensure permanent and lasting financial resources by establishing a system of public funding. To achieve this task the following steps were taken:

1 The professional services of the SMCIs were integrated within the structure of corresponding regulatory government bodies.
2 A special law was passed to cover one year's financing of plans from the earlier period.

The second, even more important, task was to prepare and implement procedures for drawing up new laws regulating the social services. Those drafting the bills were required to take into consideration the following guidelines:

1 the position of social services should not be identified with the position of the economy;
2 the principle of total solidarity must be exchanged for the principle of insurance (mandatory and voluntary);
3 social services need financing from the budget;
4 social services should not be exclusively state services;
5 a national programme and responsibility for every area of social services should be defined;
6 the basis for the bills shall reflect a modern and professional approach.

The new bills mean the affirmation of the state's role in public finances, public regulatory bodies, and political responsibility for the control of public functions. This, to a certain extent, means a return to the Slovenian system of thirty years ago. On the other hand, they mean the introduction of the pluralistic model of welfare familiar in many other European countries. In the following section the pluralist model of health care will be explained, paying special attention to the private sector.

Health Care

Health care in Slovenia is in a very critical situation in comparison with other social services. For decades there was no clear national programme and no national health care policy. The main problems are: a severe shortage of foreign currency to import medicines and basic materials; low wages and low motivation among health care employees, and limited acquisition of urgently needed medical equipment and spare parts.

Extremely economical use of the resources still being collected under the former system, and the re-structuring of health care into a financially stable system, will be necessary. Among corrective actions indicated by the Health and Health Insurance Act of 1992, the most benefit is expected from the introduction of private practice, and of an obligatory/voluntary health care insurance system.

Since 1992 the employer has contributed 9.4 per cent of the basic employee's gross salary to the obligatory health insurance fund and the employee has contributed 8.7 per cent. This fund covers the complete costs for such items as preventive health care and rehabilitation of children; health care of pregnant women; compulsory vaccination; AIDS prevention, and urgent medical help. Costs of some health care services – such as transplants, treatment of infertility, prosthetics and dental care – have to be shared by the patient or by his/her voluntary insurance fund. The usual share is between 5 per cent and 50 per cent of the total service cost.

Private practice in Slovenia as an official institution was abolished in the late 1950s, but still persisted as a 'grey' activity during the self-management period. According to data from the Survey on the Quality of Life in Slovenia (1984), the share of unofficial private practice within general practice was 1.1 per cent, gynaecology was 0.6 per cent and dental care was 5.5 per cent. Most probably the actual shares were even larger. Some special forms of 'shadow' private practice, such as bribery and the buying of special treatment in hospitals, were also known but difficult to identify.

The basic question concerning the introduction of private practice into the health care system was how extensive it should be. In addressing this question, consideration had to be given to both the advantages (greater economic efficiency, more humane relationships and an integrated approach towards patients) and the disadvantages (inequality of opportunity for poorer patients, and the scant interest of private practitioners in the health care of the general population). Even before the changes in health care legislation began, there was a general consensus among professionals such as physicians, sociologists and economists that health care should be an appropriate combination of the public and private sector (Boh, 1989; Brus, 1990; Keber, 1990; Svetlik, 1989). The shares of the public and of the private sectors respectively are indicated in the Health Care Act.

The Act provides for the operation of private practice, both within and outside the framework of the public health care service network. In both cases, permission of the regulatory body (the Ministry for Health) will be required. The performance of a public service additionally requires a concession.[1] This concession may be given by a consensus from among

1. By definition, a public service in Slovenia is performed by a public institution. Founders of public institutions are the republic, local communities and towns.

representatives of the county government, the republic's government, the republic's health insurance agency and the Chamber of Physicians. Moreover, it may go to the lowest bidder as a result of a public tender process. In 1994, 328 health care practitioners received concessions to engage in private practice: 82 general practitioners, 143 dentists, 53 specialists, 29 pharmacists and 21 others. This is approximately 6 per cent of all health care practitioners employed in Slovenia (Health Insurance Institute of Slovenia, 1994 – personal communication).

Citizens of Slovenia and foreign citizens who fulfil all the conditions determined by law are permitted to run a private health care practice.[2] Private work is possible in all branches of medicine, except in some explicitly defined cases: blood supply, storage and transplantation of human organs, hygienics, epidemiology and pathology.

The Act assumes, in principle, equal basic rights for health care workers in the public sector and in the private sector. But, in the opinion of many, especially physicians, the actual conditions will not be equal due to the existence of the so-called 'paragraph on competition', which prevents employees from having a regular job in the public sector and in a private practice at the same time.

The opponents of the paragraph on competition argued that the Health Care Act requires physicians starting private practices to immediately quit their regular jobs in the state institutions. That means starting from zero in a situation where they may not have accumulated any initial capital due to low wages, but where they are nevertheless forced to comply with the provisions of the Act regarding working standards.[3]

Most physicians support the idea of a transitional period during which a regular job in a state institution and in a private practice would be allowed. This arrangement would permit the gradual acquisition of private patients, equipment and premises. It would also prevent the abrupt departure of top specialists, full professors and associate professors from state clinics to private practices which would adversely affect the training of a new generation of physicians.

The Ministry for Health supported the Act, arguing that the paragraph on competition makes a distinction between regular and 'afternoon' jobs;

2. Health Care Bill, October 1991, Paragraph 38: a private person shall fulfil the following conditions for performance of a private health care activity: possess the appropriate professional education and the ability for autonomous work; agree not to perform any other regular job; no legal bar to the performance of health care activity or profession; suitable workplace, equipment and co-workers if necessary; have the necessary approval.

3. Under the Health Care Bill, the founder of the public institution (the state) is responsible for equipment, accommodation and funding, while the private practitioner has to be self-financing and self-providing, or hire at a market price.

reduces unemployment among health care workers and promotes competition; decreases the load on health care workers and increases their professionalism; in addition, that the combination of a regular job and a private practice is not recommended by the World Health Organisation, and is usually an exception, and that the Act includes the provision that a professional may treat private patients in his or her domiciliary public health centre.

Thus most disagreements about the Act are centred on the paragraph on competition, which has also been given extensive coverage in the mass media. The paragraphs on the status of private work or private health institutions in the health system have attracted less attention.

By some accounts (Rus, 1992), the Law on Public Institutions, as a basis for other laws in the area of social services, does not give enough internal autonomy to the private institutions. The law requires both internal and external supervision of the institutions by the state regardless of their ownership status (state or private). Private institutions with concessions have to comply with the requirements of the state or the county (local community), not only regarding quality standards and fees, but also by allowing the state or county to nominate the director and define the internal structure of the institution. Such a relationship will, in Rus's opinion, lead to unresolvable conflicts between ownership and management, and it does not conform with the main trends of de-institutionalisation and re-privatisation in Western countries.

Restrictions on the internal autonomy of private practice in health care is also indicated by the wording of the Health Care Act, which refers to private health care workers but not to private health care institutions. The summary of the Act defines health care as a public service guaranteed by the state, county or town. The restrictions imply that private practice will be relatively successful when the needs of the population cannot be satisfied by the public health care system, but there is little chance for private practice when competing with the public sector. Private practice is envisaged as being primarily for specialists, since, under the rules of the Act, the state health centre remains the provider of basic health care. Because of the use of advanced technology, and expensive equipment, the private physicians will have to link organisationally with the public health centres, and this will indirectly expose them even more to the supervision of the state.

The autonomy of pharmacists will be restricted even more than the autonomy of physicians and dentists, because, according to the Act, their work must be performed exclusively as a concession. Whether the service is offered by a public institution or a private pharmacist will be decided by the local communities themselves, depending on their requirements. Only one concession in a certain area can be given to an individual pharmacist.

The critics of the Act argue that such rules render the opening of new pharmaceutical shops impossible; preserve monopolies of existing pharmaceutical institutions, and prevent competition. Some critics argue that pharmaceutical shops should be run exclusively by private pharmacists. This is countered by pointing out that other European countries only allow pharmacies to operate as a state service performed by a pharmacist with a concession. The neighbouring countries of Italy, Austria and Switzerland serve as a model: they do not allow the formation of pharmaceutical companies, and give only one concession per pharmacist.

As was mentioned earlier, it was decided that health care insurance to finance services in both the public and private sectors will be a combination of mandatory and voluntary health care insurance. In some countries, for example the United States, a commercial health insurance system is widely used. This system is not acceptable in Slovenia because of economic conditions, and because it introduces too much discrimination. It would also be contrary to tradition and to the practice of neighbouring countries.[4]

An analysis of the text of the Health Care Act, and comparison with the former system of social services, leads to the conclusion that the legitimisation of private practice signifies a major breakthrough; at the same time it is evident that the introduction of private practice is not strongly encouraged. Nevertheless, physicians have shown keen interest in this kind of work. Parliament should consider the resourcefulness, but also the difficult financial position, of physicians and pharmacists, by introducing some concessions during the transitional period. This would provide the means for the evolution of such private practice in Slovenia as would contribute to improving the quality of the health care services.

Housing

Contrary to the position in the health care system, the housing system has always allowed private forms of housing provision, though there were several important changes during the post-war period. Until the 1950s there was no limit on the number of houses or apartments a person could own. Then the state nationalised all private houses, allowing the owners to keep

4. The latest public opinion survey in Slovenia indicates that almost half of the population still favours the old system of health insurance, where the health insurance premium in the form of a fixed share of gross income was deducted from pay. Under the Health Care Law, all citizens of Slovenia are entitled to mandatory health care insurance; at present 1.45 million people, out of a total population of approximately 2 million, make additional voluuntary contributions. Only 4,000 people are insured for medical services of a higher quality (Health Insurance Institute of Slovenia, 1994 – personal communication).

one apartment in a multiple-apartment house, or an entire single-apartment house.

During the self-management period, the predominant type of private provision was autonomous, self-help housing construction. This also represented a method of securing a long-term investment and the accumulation of private property. This mode of housing provision was not subject to such severe restriction as other areas under socialism: it was regarded as a marginal, more or less self-sustaining sector.

The only institutional form in this period was represented by 'self-managing housing communities' (SHCs), in which the predominant responsibility for social housing provision was given to companies. They provided houses for rent, and housing loans; access to social housing provision and corresponding benefits was strongly dependent on employment status.

The SHCs endeavoured to provide all the basic necessities of housing, but they never fulfilled expectations. In the late 1970s a housing crisis began, which intensified in the 1980s. Although it was partly due to the economic recession, with very high inflation leading to a decrease in housing investment and to the shrinking of enterprise housing funds, the main cause was the unsuitable institutional structure, which did not provide either enough incentives for investment, or an economic, efficient and socially just use of resources. The quantity of social housing construction eventually started to drop.

This led to an increase in private, mainly self-help housing construction, which in turn sparked off some minor responses in housing policy: existing state housing funds were used more and more for the provision of housing loans to individuals. The general objective of these changes was to shift the responsibility for housing provision from the state to the individual (Mandič, 1992). This rise of private, self-help housing construction was mostly sustained by the high direct labour involvement of households and kinship networks. While some of the population could adjust to these changes – through a greater reliance on the family, in the form of both money and help, to compensate for the lack of available resources in the SHCs and other enterprises – a substantial proportion of the population (mainly sections of the younger urban population) could not.

As a result of this development, by 1989, 67 per cent of the national housing fund was in private ownership (almost synonymous with home-ownership) and the remaining 33 per cent was in the social rental sector (Mandič, 1993). More specifically, the Quality of Life research data indicates that, in 1987, the structure of the housing sector in Slovenia was as follows: corporate housing 15.2 per cent; self-help house construction 16.6 per cent; buying 7.3 per cent; living with parents 32 per cent; inheriting 17.7 per cent; roomers (subtenants) 1.7 per cent and social solidarity housing 3.5 per cent. At the same time, more than one-third of the Slovene population was living in unsuitable apartments (Mandič, 1989).

Thus housing policy during the self-management period could not satisfy the demand for new housing, either quantitatively or qualitatively. The goal of the National Housing Programme is to ensure a satisfactory amount and quality of housing for all residents of Slovenia. These goals are expressed in the Housing Law, passed in October 1991, as follows:

1 the development of a market economy in the housing sector;
2 abolition of monopolies;
3 new organisation of the enterprise, co-operative and public sectors;
4 establishment of the non-profit housing sector.

The Law of De-nationalisation and Re-expropriation, which returns property to the former owners or their heirs, was passed at about the same time.

The most profound and far-reaching change proposed by the Housing Law is the reform of the allocation of housing resources. It is expected that this will lead to entirely new institutions reflecting a general shift to the further institutional promotion of private home-ownership. Some already operate, following the conversion of the existing social rental fund and the creation of the National Housing Fund, while others, such as the non-profit organisations, are still in the initial stages.

The Housing Law makes possible the purchase of previously-rented social housing. The tenants or their close family were not only given the right to buy, but were also offered very favourable terms. The initial sale price of each apartment was lower than the real value if sold on the open market, and, additionally, a 30 per cent discount was guaranteed. Purchase could be made immediately, with an extra 30 per cent discount, or by means of long-term repayment over a maximum of twenty years. If the instalments are paid in less than twenty years, a special discount is guaranteed as well. The resources collected from sales are split between the previous owners (the enterprises and municipalities that took over the property of the SHCs) and the newly-established National Housing Fund, which receives 20 per cent of the resources.

In the case of the restitution of former private housing to families or their heirs, a conflict between the right to buy and the right to be restituted emerged. To solve this contradiction, some instruments for a compromise solution are applied. The Housing Law allows for the new owner to be partially compensated upon agreement to sell the unit to the tenant. If the tenant is leaving the restituted apartment, the new owner is obliged to give him or her compensation.

As previously mentioned, the major newly-created institution is the National Housing Fund. Its purpose is the reconstruction of badly-maintained houses; promoting the construction of new houses by advancing favourable loans to private individuals (income dependent loans); providing loans to the non-profit sector; the abolition of monopoly in the housing market, and to influence pricing policy.

Under the new law, home ownership becomes an even more predominant type of housing provision. In the six months immediately following the Housing Act, almost half of the social rented accommodation had been transferred into private ownership. By 1993, home ownership accounted for 85 per cent of the National Housing Fund. However, this is one aspect only of privatisation in housing provision in Slovenia. One of the main features of this development – the establishment of a non-profit sector – has yet to materialise.

Social Care for Elderly and Disabled People, and Handicapped Children

A private sector of social care for elderly, disabled people and handicapped children did not exist under the previous system. Formally organised social services had the monopoly over this sphere of welfare, but their expansion was strongly dependent on the unpaid network of kinship, neighbourhood and friends. Even the voluntary organisations and charities were supported only as much as was necessary for regulation. Although the non-formal sector was not promoted through prevailing social policy, it was tolerated since it mitigated the shortcomings of formal organisations and professional social services.

The economic crisis that emerged in the 1980s forced the state to restrict resources for social services. The number of programmes remained the same, but each of them received significantly reduced resources. Three strategies emerged (Kolarič, 1991):

1 rationalisation: organisations and services tried to find ways of making more effective use of the resources available to them, or provide unchanged programmes with decreased resources.
2 commercialisation: social services tried to change their provision and sell their services to different users.
3 externalisation: social services began to interact with informal and semi-formal service providers.

New forms of social care provision for elderly and disabled people and handicapped children emerged and are still emerging. These new forms represent a mix between the formal and informal sectors. This development is due to a 'normative vacuum' – the previous legislation is no longer supported but the new order does not yet exist (Kolarič, 1991). This normative vacuum allows social workers to search for additional financial resources and to determine services that can be paid for directly by the users.

These new forms of social care are provided by private individuals or corporations, which provide social care services in conjunction with state institutions and/or voluntary organisations. The latter are generally the founders of such services; they provide resources, premises, equipment and staff. Quality control of services is performed by users themselves, the founders and the state regulatory bodies.

Quasi-privatisation is therefore taking place through these new forms of social care service. Part of a research project entitled *De-institutionalisation and Privatisation of the Educational System and Social Care* (Kolarič, 1991) indicated that at least five types of quasi-private forms of social care services for elderly and disabled people and handicapped children could be distinguished:

1 Those in which the initiators are state social institutions, for example homes for elderly people, educational establishments for children and young people, institutions for mentally and physically handicapped people, and centres for social work. A typical case is the contracting out of services such as cooking, home help, laundry and daily care for elderly people in their own homes.

2 Voluntary organisations and associations – lay or religious.

3 Those where at least two founders act jointly: these might include public social institutions, the state, private individuals and/or corporations, and voluntary organisations.

4 Corporations where the social worker is a private individual who makes a contract with the corporation. The services are paid for directly by the users.

5 Those where the private person is both founder and performer of the service.

The last two groups represent purely private forms of social care. The privatisation of social care services had therefore already been taking place – as is evident from this short review – even before the legislation was passed in its entirety. In the mean time, individuals and groups of citizens with an interest in providing different sorts of social care could acquire the status of an association, which encouraged the development of private services of this type.

The evolution of the private sector in the era of the 'normative vacuum' was strongly dependent on the needs and financial capabilities of the users, and on the inventiveness and initiative of the private social workers. The Social Care Bill highlights the following trends:

1 The public network, which is in the jurisdiction of the state, should be gradually taken over by non-public social workers by means of concessions. The Social Care Bill provides some advantages for the voluntary and charity organisations compared with private individuals and private groups. Present employers in the public sector strongly oppose this development; they also have to obey the paragraph on competition.
2 Social care should no longer be financed exclusively by the state, but also by charity and voluntary organisations, donors, enterprises and the users. The state should finance public programmes: social prevention, primary social care, institutional care for elderly and disabled people, handicapped children, and young people.

Conclusion

The privatisation of social services in Slovenia is not a uniform process. Private initiative in some areas, such as housing, was already quite strong in the past, while in other areas, such as health care, it is only now in the initial phase. These differences are reflected in the new legislation. It is therefore expected that the levels of privatisation in social services will be variable.

References

Boh, K. (1989) 'Prispevek k poskusom za prestrukturiranje zdravstva' (A contribution to the attempts to reconstruct health), in Svetlik, I. et al. (eds) (1989) *Prestrukturiranje Druzbenih Dejavnosti* (Restructuring of Social Services), Ljubljana, Raziskavalno Porocilo ISU.

Brus, A. (1990) 'Odprta vprasanja novega zakona o zdravstvenem varstvu' (Open questions for the new Health Care Law), *Zdravtsveni Vestrik*, no.6, pp.301–8.

Keber, K. (1990) 'Zdravje, posameznik in drzava' (Health, individual and the State), *Nova Revija*, no.95, pp.533–43.

Kolarič, Z. (1991) *Poblike Zagotavljanja Storitev za Ostarele, Prizadete Otroke in Invalide* (Quasi-private forms of care for the elderly, handicapped children and disabled people), Ljubljana, Raziskovalno Porocilo IDV.

Mandič, S. (1989) 'Stanovanjska preskrba: Opis njene sektorske strukture, dosedanji trendi in mozne razvojne strategije' (Housing provision: Structures of sections, current trends and possible development strategies), in Svetlik, I. et al. (eds) (1989) *Prestrukturiranje Druzbenih Dejavnosti* (Restructuring of Social Services), Ljubljana, Raziskovalno porocilo ISU.

—— (1993) *Restructuring of the Housing System in Slovenia: Its Logic and Anticipated Effects.*

Ministrstvo za Zdravsto (Ministry for Health, Family and Social Care), (1991) *Druzino in Socialno Varstvo* (Bill of Social Care), *Osnutek Zakona o Socialnem Varstvu*, 14 November.

Porocevalec (1991a) *Osnutek Zakona o Zdravstvenem Varstvu in Zdravstvenem Zavarovanju* (Bill of Health Care and Health Insurance), 23 May.

—— (1991b) *Osnutek Zakona o Zdravstvenem Varstvu in Zdravstvenem Zavarovanju* (Bill of Health Care and Health Insurance), 1 October.

Rus, V. (1992) *Med Antikomunizmom in Postsocializmom* (Between Anticommunism and Post-socialism), Ljubljana, Knjizna ZbirkaTeorija in Praska.

Smidovnik, J. (1989) 'Problemi upravljanja na podrocju druzbenih dejavnosti' (Management problems in social services), in Svetlik, I. et al. (eds) (1989) *Prestrukturiranje Druzbenih Dejavnosti* (Restructuring of Social Services), Ljubljana, Raziskavalno Porocilo ISU.

Svetlik, I. (1989) 'Od Segmentiranih Druzbenih Dejavnosti k Pluralnemu Sistemu Blaginje' (Transition from segmented social services to a plural system of welfare), in Svetlik, I. et al. (eds) (1989) *Prestrukturiranje Druzbenih Dejavnosti* (Restructuring of Social Services), Ljubljana, Raziskavalno Porocilo ISU.

Uradni List Republike Slovenije (1992) *Stanovanjski Zakon* (The Health Insurance Law), 11 November.

–9–

Sweden

Sven E. Olsson Hort and *Daniel Cohn*

Introduction

The Swedish public sector is regularly acknowledged as being the largest in the Western world. This situation is a product of only the last thirty or so years. Between 1960 and 1980 the amount of Sweden's Gross National Product (GNP) which was absorbed by the public sector leapt from an unremarkable 30 per cent to more than 60 per cent. During the 1980s, approximately one-fifth of an average OECD nation's workforce were public sector employees, while in Sweden the figure was in excess of one-third, and this is still the case in the early 1990s.

The economic problems faced by all Western nations during the 1976–84 recession were just as destabilising in Sweden as elsewhere. During this period of economic turbulence a sea change in attitude towards the public sector began to take place in Swedish society. Increasingly large proportions of the population began to see the size of Sweden's public sector not as a solution to the country's problems, but rather as a problem (Premfors, 1991, pp.85–6; Korpi 1989, pp.305–6). This was due not only to economic factors, but also to changing social conditions and values. A new generation of Swedes emerged who had benefited from the democratic empowerment which had occurred during the long unbroken rule of the Swedish Social Democratic Party (1932–76). A generation which was disturbed by the apparent arbitrariness, and 'one size fits all' social services available from the Swedish Welfare State (Rothstein, 1992, p.24).

These people wanted more say in the nature of the social services which they consumed, and in choosing who should provide them. The agencies of capitalism in Sweden, especially the powerful employers' associations, latched on to this discontent and began to promote their privatisation agenda as a way of providing such choices. An example of this can be found in the works of the Swedish Federation of Industries' economist, Per-Martin Meyerson (1985, p.109; 1991, pp.180–2). This dove-tailed nicely into the propaganda war which the employers' associations have been conducting over the last decade against what they see as the excesses of the Welfare State and the attempted socialisation of production (Olsson, 1988, p.71; Micheleti, 1991, pp.151–3).

During the 1980s, the four largest political parties in Sweden, from the left-of-centre Socialdemokraterna (Social Democratic Party) to the neo-liberal Moderata Samlingsparti (Conservative Party), were more or less won over to the view that public expenditures had to decline, and that the growth in the public sector which had occurred in the previous twenty to thirty years had been overdone.

As is common in politics, however, even though the various parties agreed on what the problem was, they disagreed on how best to solve it. Throughout the 1980s the Social Democrats advocated enhancing the public sector's efficiency and productivity. This would theoretically allow more public services to be produced for less money, and consequently decrease the size of the public sector (Premfors, 1991, p.87). Meanwhile, the Conservative Party, while fully endorsing plans to make the public sector more efficient, was concentrating its intellectual energies on producing plans which would bring about a shrinking of the public sector. In their view, this should principally come about not through enhancing public sector efficiency, but rather through decreasing its scope (Premfors, 1984, p.282).

As a result, two very distinct forms of privatisation began to be promoted during the 1980s. In the view of the Social Democrats and the labour movement with which it was allied, privatisation was a method for making the delivery of publicly-planned and financed services less costly. In this case, privatisation was only acceptable in some areas, and only when it could be shown to be a more economical form of provision, and where it could be integrated into the broader public plans for welfare and health provision.

In the second case, promoted by the Conservative Party and its allies in the employers' associations, it was argued that both the financing and provision of a wide variety of services should be removed from the public sector and placed in private hands. Taxes on individuals and firms should be substantially reduced, leaving those Swedes with the financial ability to do so free to contract for more of their own welfare needs in either the private market or from the public sector providers.

Meanwhile the other two major political parties, Folkpartiet (the Liberal Party) and Centrepartiet (the Centre Party) tried to differentiate themselves from the two larger parties to their left and right by offering privatisation programmes which were either more aggressive than the Social Democratic version or less aggressive than the Conservative version. Even when these two parties entered a coalition government headed by the Conservatives in 1991 this reluctance to fully endorse the Conservative programme remained.[1]

Given the dominance which the Social Democrats exercised over Swedish politics during the 1980s, it should not be suprising that up until 1991, when they lost power at the national level and in most counties and municipalities, it was their view on the uses of private provision of health and welfare services which prevailed.

In this chapter we will present evidence which suggests that the private provision of health and social services increased during the 1980s. While most of the growth has been through private commercial providers acting as contractors to the public sector, there has also been growth in the purely private sector, where services are both privately financed and delivered.

The causes behind this growth seem to have been problems occurring in the public system itself, as well as an increase in recent years in the overall disposable incomes of Swedish families. These have increased by about 11 per cent during the 1980s (Ministry of Finance, 1992a, p.43).[2] This increase in household wealth, combined with the desire for more choice noted previously, has made the private purchase of additional or alternative health and welfare services a possibility for an increasing number of Swedes.

Most of the evidence presented in this chapter is related to health care in Sweden. This area was selected because the public health care system is one of the most widely supported programmes of state welfare in Sweden (Svallfors, 1991, pp.612–15). If Swedes are willing to tolerate a large amount of private commercial provision of health care, it would be logical to assume that they would accept private commercial provision of other welfare services which are less treasured.

Another reason for selecting this particular area is that there has been considerable international interest in Swedish health care and the public policies which govern it: 'Sweden has set a standard and a model that others have aspired to, and has been the teacher more than the learner' (Evans, 1991, p.119). From Andersen (1968) to Hollingsworth et al. (1990) authors

1. This government also included another centre-right party, Kristdemokratiska Samhällspartiet (the Christian Democratic Party), which in 1991 gained seats in Parliament as an independent party for the first time. Their only previous seat in Parliament was won in 1985, via an electoral alliance with the Centre Party.

2. There have been a great number of short-term and long-term factors which have led to this rise in disposable income. Among the short-term factors were an overheated labour market during the second half of the 1980s, and tax reforms which increased take-home pay. Most notable among the long-term factors appears to be an increase in the amount of paid employment Swedish women engage in (Ministry of Finance 1990a, pp.45–6).

of comparative studies of health care have felt the need to examine how Sweden has addressed the issues which are of concern to them.

Social Democratic Universalism and the Nature of the Swedish Welfare State

One of the key factors in explaining the current shape of welfare provision in Sweden is the political dominance over the last sixty years of the Social Democratic Party. From 1932 until 1976 the Social Democrats governed Sweden, either as the lead party in coalitions with the Farmers' Party (now known as the Centre Party), or independently.[3] The Social Democrats returned to power nationally in 1982, and remained in power until September 1991. After only three years in opposition, they were again returned to power in September 1994. As a result of this long political dominance, social democratic values, as opposed to liberal capitalist ones, helped shape the Swedish Welfare State. One of these values is the concept of universalism which underpins the Swedish Welfare State. Sweden and the other Social Democrat dominated countries have taken the concept of universalism further than most other countries, in an attempt to build broad popular legitimacy for the Welfare State (Esping-Andersen, 1990, pp.68–9).

Indeed the depth, breadth of coverage and high quality of the services provided by the Swedish Welfare State are among the first things that one notices when looking at the system.[4] However, even the Swedish Welfare State can not satisfy every citizen's needs for welfare services completely. As a result, private commercial welfare provision and financing, although comparatively small, has continued to exist, and exist robustly.

Examples of this are the occupational welfare benefits negotiated between unions and employers. These have a history almost as long as the Welfare State's, and form an integral part of the retirement savings accumulated by most Swedes. Beyond this, one in every ten Swedes has contracted individually for a private pension savings scheme with a bank or insurance company. However, even in these private schemes the state is a major participant, providing favourable tax treatment to participants (Olsson, 1988, pp.72–3).

Furthermore, something must be said about unemployment insurance

---

3. During the Second World War there was also an all-party (meaning all parties except the Communists) 'unity' government.

4. Ironically, the claim that the Swedish Welfare State provides cradle-to-grave coverage is not quite true. In fact, the Welfare State ceases to protect the individual immediately after death. Burial is still by and large a free-market matter, except for the indigent.

in Sweden. Until July, 1994 unemployment insurance was the one major form of social insurance which was voluntary in Sweden. Before that time one joined an unemployment insurance fund by joining a union. The country's trade, salaried employees' and professional unions run unemployment insurance funds on a non-profit basis, albeit with heavy subsidies from the state. Alternately one could apply only to join the unemployment fund run by a union but in 1986 less than 1 per cent of workers chose this option (Rothstein, 1990, p.335). Since July 1994, employed people not enrolled in union unemployment funds are automatically enlisted in a public sector scheme (*Svenska Dagbladet*, 1 July 1994, N2).

The Structure of Swedish Health Care

In Sweden the regional authorities, known as county councils, have for the last two decades been both the principal financiers and providers of health care.[5] In fact, providing health care is the prime reason for the existence of the Swedish county councils. In 1989, health care comprised on average 77 per cent of each county's expenditure (Landstingsförbundet, 1990, p.18). Recently, however, there have been moves by many councils to open up a secondary role for private providers by means of contracting out – increasingly hiring private organisations to provide services to their residents.

There are no firm figures about the proportion of Sweden's health care which is supplied by commercial for-profit providers; this is because no official statistics are kept on what is spent outside the publicly-financed care systems. However, Statistics Sweden (SCB) publishes figures for the amount of money paid every year to private-practice physicians, dentists and other professional providers who are working as contractors to the public system. In 1985, 5.9 per cent of public health expenditures were paid to private-practice dentists and physicians. By 1988 this figure had increased to 7.3 per cent, which represents a growth of 19 per cent for the entire three- year period (SCB, 1988, p.113; 1990, p.181; 1991, p.196).

While the public sector continued to make increasing use of privately-provided professional services until the end of the 1980s, the rate of increase clearly slowed down. The growth of private medical practice has generally been a large-city phenomenon. As can be seen from Table 9.1, even after a period of considerable growth, visits to private medical

5. Three Swedish municipalities – Gotland, an island off the Baltic coast, and the major cities of Gothenburg and Malmö – do not belong to counties. These provide their own health care services. However, they will be included in the discussion as if they were county councils.

County	1984 Private %	Public %	1988 Private %	Public %
Major Urban Areas				
Malmö	36	64	40	60
Stockholm	26	74	29	71
Gothenburg	24	76	26	74
Southern Counties				
Malmöhus	16	84	20	80
Kristianstad	15	85	14	86
Halland	13	87	15	85
Blekinge	11	89	8	92
Gotland	9	91	10	90
Kronoberg	9	91	13	87
Älvsborg	8	92	8	92
Jönköping	6	94	11	89
Mid-Sweden Counties				
Uppsala	15	85	18	82
Södermanland	12	88	12	88
Värmland	10	90	9	91
Bohus	10	90	9	91
Örebro	9	91	8	92
Östergötland	8	92	9	91
Skaraborg	8	92	8	92
Kalmar	7	93	6	94
Västmanland	5	93	4	96
Northern Counties				
Kopparberg	9	91	7	93
Gävleborg	6	94	8	92
Västerbotten	4	96	7	93
Västernorrland	3	97	4	96
Jämtland	3	97	5	95
Norrbotten	3	97	5	95
All Sweden	15	85	17	83

Note: Includes visits paid for under contracts with counties and those paid for by billing the National Insurance Funds.

Source: National Audit Bureau (1991, p.86).

Table 9.1 Publicly-financed Physician Visits: Percentage to Publicly and Privately Practising Physicians, Sweden, 1984 and 1988

practitioners were still rare in smaller communities, and especially in northern Sweden.

The Swedish county councils, with the help of the municipalities and the Swedish national government, provide a public health care system which is available to all and which covers everything from medical to dental care, as well as prescription drugs, and home care for elderly people. Although health care in Sweden has been socialised, in the sense that it is overwhelmingly provided by the public sector, it is not free of charge to the patient. Health services are provided subject to the payment of user fees which have been steadily rising (see Table 9.2).

Voluntary groups, non-profit organisations and charitable agencies are virtually non-existent in the modern Swedish health care system, with a few exceptions. Most notable among these are the Swedish Red Cross and the grass-roots movements which have sprung up in response to the spread of HIV and this virus's related tragic symptoms. Private commercial care is scarce by the standards of other countries.

Public health care and publicly-salaried physicians have a long tradition in Sweden. Among the initial promoters of the idea were the physicians themselves. Practising in an impoverished nineteenth-century country, many physicians saw a public salary as the best way to secure a stable livelihood (Berg, 1980, p.35). Public ownership of hospitals is also well entrenched. Since the 1890s over 90 per cent of all hospital beds in Sweden have been found in publicly-run hospitals (Hollingsworth et al. 1990, p.35).

In the post-war era, the national government, through Socialstyrelsen (the National Board of Health and Welfare) and in co-operation with Landstingsförbundet (the County Council Federation), tried to plan the provision of health in Sweden rationally. Over the years the national government's role has decreased sharply, culminating in the 1982 reforms of the Health and Health Care Law, which saw the counties take control of virtually all service delivery and local planning in the health field. This reduced central government's input to providing support (such as drug testing, information gathering, education, and publishing statistics) and partial financing (Swedish Parliament, 1982; Ham, 1988, p.396).

Beginning in the 1960s the country was divided into six regions, each having one or two central regional hospitals. The regional hospitals teach medical students and provide the most complex care and procedures to the residents of the counties they serve. The central government also funds the regional hospitals to offset the costs that they incur in providing medical education (National Audit Bureau, 1991, pp.19–22). Under these are the county hospitals which provide fewer procedures, and district hospitals which are even less broadly equipped. This system was designed to avoid over-capitalising the hospital system, and to ensure that resources are spread evenly among all the geographic areas of the country (Calltorp,

1990, p.32). However, as early as the 1970s there were indications that the policy was not working as successfully as anticipated (Navarro, 1974, p.84).

Physicians working in the public hospitals are employees of the counties and are paid on a salary basis. As of the autumn of 1991 there were six

Service	User Fee (SEK) 1981	1984	1986	1989	1991/2
Treatment by a public physician[a,b]	20	40	50	60	100[c]
Each treatment by a medical care professional other than a physician	15	20	25	35	0–140[d]
Maximum per prescription[e]	40	50	50	65	90
Each day of hospital care (deducted directly from patients' National Insurance Fund sick pay)	40	45	55	55	70[f]
Dental care					
% insured below	2,500	2,500	2,500	3,000	3,000
	50	50	40	40	40
% insured above	2,500	2,500	2,500	3,000	3,000
	75	75	75	75	50
% insured above					7,000
					75

Notes:
a. If a treatment requires more than one visit the patient only pays once.
b. User fees for visits to private practitioners affiliated to the National Insurance Funds or under contract to their county were SEK 5–10 higher until 1989. They are now 40 per cent higher.
c. In 1991, counties were given the power to set charges for visits to physicians and other medical professionals themselves. The fees listed here are for Stockholm county.
d. Fees now vary in Stockholm depending on the type of non-physician professional.
e. If more than one drug is prescribed as part of the same treatment they are counted as one prescription.
f. Unemployed and pensioners are only charged SEK 65. As well, a wide variety of schemes exist to offset costs of those in danger of accumulating large bills. For example, if a person uses medical care services fifteen times in a year, all subsequent care is free. Parents are allowed to register all of their children on one card.

Sources: Landstingsförbundet (1987, p.120), Ministry of Finance (1982, pp.85–8; 1988, pp.80–1; 1989, pp.82–3; 1990, pp.50–1; 1991, pp.54–5), Mosten.

Table 9.2 User Fees for Health Care in Sweden, 1981–92

private general hospitals in the country.[6] Much of their space was used on contract by the county systems. As counties shed assets the number of privately-owned general hospitals is likely to rise.

Most Swedish general practitioners are also county employees. Since the early 1980s, many have conducted their practices in multiple-service primary care clinics called *vårdcentraler*, which are owned by the counties. Like their hospital-based colleagues, they are paid on a salary basis. The same rational planning which applied to organising the hospital system was also used in the apportionment of district medical officers, and their later amalgamation into clinics. Each county was broken up into districts, and the inhabitants were assigned to a specific clinic in their area of residence (Twaddle, 1986).

The current system of county employment of physicians dates back to the so-called 'Seven Crowns Reforms' which took effect in 1970 (Serner, 1980, pp.103–4). In 1975 a law was enacted allowing those physicians completely opposed to the new scheme to practise privately and charge Försäkringskassan (the National Insurance Funds) for their services. The only penalty the patients of these publicly-funded private physicians faced was the payment of a slightly higher user fee than would be encountered at a public clinic (Ministry of Health and Social Affairs, 1978, pp.8–9). Due to the limited number of private hospital beds, until recently private practice almost always implied providing only ambulatory care.

In dentistry, private practice has continued alongside public practice. Children and teenagers receive free dental care through dentists employed by the counties. Coverage for adult dental care from the National Insurance Funds was instituted in 1974. A standard user fee of 50 per cent of the cost of care was initially set (see Table 9.2 for how fees have changed since), regardless of whether one is treated by a publicly-salaried or privately-employed dentist. The rest of the fee is paid to the dentist, or the county which employs the dentist, by the National Insurance Funds.

In 1968 the government took action to limit the costs to patients of prescription drugs (see Table 9.2), establishing a programme to partially compensate Swedes for the costs of these (Ministry of Health and Social Affairs, 1978, p.8). Eventually Sweden's pharmacies were brought under public ownership and consolidated into one agency, Apoteksbolaget (the National Pharmacy Company). The money to subsidise patient prescriptions comes from the National Insurance Funds. Pharmaceutical products used by patients while being treated in hospitals are completely paid for by the hospitals, while non-prescription over-the-counter drug

6. Two in Stockholm, and one each in Gothenburg, Uppsala Linköping and Örebro, although this final institution is not all that private, since Örebro county is one of the hospital's owners and its largest customer (*Dagens Nyheter*, 28 October 1991, S2).

purchases are wholly paid for by the consumer (Jönsson, 1989, pp.14–15).

The National Pharmacy Company is the part of the Swedish public health system most in peril. As sole retailer for both prescription and non-prescription drugs (even common household remedies such as aspirin must be purchased from the National Pharmacy Company's stores), negotiations between it and suppliers regulate the prices at which pharmaceuticals are sold. Now that Sweden has reached an accession agreement with the European Union and is expecting membership in 1995 (following the results of the national referendum), it will have to give some thought to creating alternative arrangements, since the current system is probably not compatible with the European Union's competition policies (Von der Schulenburg, 1991, pp.95–6).

The 1980s and the Changing Emphasis from Accessibility to Cost Control

At the end of the 1970s, Swedish health care was poised at a crucial point. The main goal of all the reforms of the 1970s had been achieved: there were no longer any financial barriers to health care for Swedes (Serner, 1980, p.104; Kjellström and Lundberg, 1987, p.74). However, in solving this problem, others had either been left unaddressed or inadvertently created as the effects of the reforms of the 1970s were compounded by other social and economic changes. These problems included:

1 the high cost to society of providing such a broad health coverage;
2 the lack of personal choice such a rationally planned system gave individual patients;
3 and later on, the effects which the plans implemented to address the cost problems had on the quality of care in the public system.

It was these problems more than anything else, occurring at a time when Swedes were becoming less willing to defer to bureaucratic decisions, which gave private health care in Sweden a new lease of life and led to its significant growth in the second half of the 1980s.

The combination of rising health care costs and slow economic growth made the high cost of Swedish health care a prime political issue in the late 1970s and early 1980s. As a result, cost-cutting came to be a top priority in Swedish health policy (Ministry of Health and Social Affairs, 1982, p.3).

The rise in health care costs experienced in the late 1970s was not unique to Sweden. Extraordinary recent advances in medical technology, and increased demand from the public for medical care, drove health care costs upwards in all Western nations (Hollingsworth et al., 1990, p.175). However, there have also been uniquely Swedish causes behind cost increases. Paramount in these are the changes which occurred in Swedish labour laws, and advances made by health care workers and professionals in their collective bargaining on pay. The key problem in this regard has been time-off allowances. In the early 1980s the Swedish Ministry of Health and Social Affairs estimated that the health sector requires 1.4 people for every nursing position within the public system, due to contractual and statutory time-off allowances (Ministry of Health and Social Affairs, 1982, p.70). Similar problems exist with other health care professions, most notably physicians, about which more will be said later.

Even though cost-cutting has been at the top of the political agenda for nearly a decade now, the crisis in medical care financing has continued to grow. It appears that the counties have not been able to restrain spending as rapidly as the percentage of Sweden's GDP available for the health care sector has shrunk (see Table 9.3). As Table 9.4 indicates, one cause of this imbalance is undoubtedly the fact that national government subsidies to the counties have not kept pace with inflation (National Audit Bureau, 1991, Introduction, pp.6–7).

| | Percentage of GDP | | | |
	1975	1980	1985	1987
FRG	6.2	6.2	6.4	6.3
France	5.0	5.1	5.7	5.8
Italy	5.0	5.6	5.4	5.4
Sweden	7.2	8.7	8.6	8.2
UK	5.0	5.2	5.2	5.3

Source: OECD (1990, p.10).

Table 9.3 Public Expenditures on Health Care in the Federal Republic of Germany, France, Italy, Sweden and the United Kingdom 1975–85

In September 1990 it was reported that since 1987 the county councils had collectively accumulated a SEK 4 billion shortfall between income and running expenses (*Svenska Dagbladet*, 26 September 1990, D1). Even more disturbing is the fact that, at the start of the 1980s, the county councils were collectively in surplus and had extensive reserve funds. However, to meet the shortfall in their budgets, the counties started to draw on these to pay their bills (Slunge, 1991, p.12). By the end of the decade these reserves had been completely exhausted and the councils were collectively

	1984	1985	1986	1987	1988
Total in (SEK m)	15,611.3	15,563.8	14,341.5	13,782.3	13,189.1
Total in (SEK per Capital)	1,874	1,866	1,716	1,644	1,568

Note: Does not include transfers to pay for medical education.

Source: National Audit Bureau (1991, Appendix 7–8)

Table 9.4 Health Care Subsidies to Counties from the Swedish National Government, Adjusted for Inflation (1984 Prices) Using the County Council Index

in debt (Ministry of Finance, 1990c, pp.63–4). In the 1980s the central government also imposed restraints on the tax raising powers of the counties (Ministry of Finance, 1990a, pp.130–1). In 1990 an absolute freeze was imposed on county taxation rates.

The counties have partly passed this shortfall on to patients through steep increases in user fees. While there has been a fourfold increase in the consumer price index since 1970 (SCB, 1980, p.225; 1992, p.45), the SEK 7 fee for a trip to the doctor, introduced in that same year, has increased more than fourteenfold (see Table 9.2).

During the 1980s an increasing amount of evidence was emerging that Swedish health care's overemphasis on hospital-based curative medicine was not the best possible arrangement. Sweden expends more of its health budget on secondary care and less on primary care than any other OECD country (Van de Ven, 1991, p.59). It was becoming common to hear arguments that the system's lack of emphasis on primary and preventive health care was costly and possibly detrimental to overall health in Sweden (Ministry of Health and Social Affairs, 1979; 1982, pp.75–94).

It is not suprising, therefore, that the official policies of the national government and most counties began to place more emphasis on disease prevention and shifting resources more towards less expensive ambulatory care. This led to a series of attempts to increase the level of funding to the primary care system and to heighten the prominence of the primary sector in the overall health plans of the county councils.

One of the most commonly used strategies by the counties was the restructuring of how their health systems were administered. Instead of having one standing committee on health care administering the whole county system, many counties chose to decentralise decision-making – in the case of primary care, sometimes right down to the neighbourhood level

	Public Expenditure for In-patient Care		Public Expenditure for Ambulatory Care	
	SEK (m)	GDP (%)	SEK (m)	GDP (%)
1977	22,800	6.16	2,755	0.74
1978	25,581	6.20	3,212	0.78
1979	28,502	6.17	3,450	0.75
1980	34,111	6.50	4,159	0.79
1981	37,447	6.50	4,865	0.85
1982	40,792	6.50	5,772	0.92
1983	45,237	6.41	6,356	0.90
1984	49,335	6.25	7,353	0.93
1985	53,091	6.17	8,703	1.01
1986	54,920	5.89	9,744	1.05
1987	63,212	6.23	12,637	1.26

Source: OECD (1990, pp.132,134,198).

Table 9.5 Swedish Public Expenditure for In-patient Care and Ambulatory Care, 1977–87

– by creating committees to supervise every primary care clinic (Lawson, 1984, p.2).

This reorientation of funding towards the primary care sector may have helped to reduce queues, which were being experienced in that sector. In the long run this reorientation will also probably reduce the incidence of serious diseases, and consequently costs. However, placing more emphasis on preventive and primary care did little in the short run to rectify the problem of increasing waiting periods for some forms of elective surgery. Queues, sometimes long ones, exist for some forms of elective care in some parts of the country.

It should also be noted that hospital committees are finding it difficult to provide all the care which is requested of them and still keep within their budgets. For example, Stockholm county's southern hospital district found it necessary to cancel all elective surgery at Söder Hospital, one of the county's major hospitals, from mid-October 1990 until the end of the year, so that the district could stay within its budget (*Dagens Nyheter*, 18 October 1990, D2).

Another major change which increased the availability of primary care in Sweden's major cities was forced on the counties by the private sector. Over the years, changes in the collective agreements signed by the Swedish Medical Association (SMA) and the counties gave public doctors increasing amounts of time off in lieu of pay for work at nights, on weekends, etc. In return for weekend and night work, Swedish physicians receive two hours of paid leave for every hour worked. During the 1979–85 period this gave the average public physician an extra twenty-five days of paid vacation on top of the seven weeks which he or she would have normally received (Rosenthal, 1989, pp.170–1).

As inflation ate away at the value of physicians' salaries in the early 1980s, many began to see patients privately in their increasingly plentiful free hours, billing the National Insurance Funds for their work on a fee-for-service basis (Rosenthal, 1986, p.602).[7]

At first this trend did not pose any great challenge to the public systems. Then in 1983 Praktikertjänst, a nationwide company owned by the privately-practising doctors and dentists who are its employees, took on the task of organising and systematising these part-time private practices.[8] This was accomplished by the opening of City Akuten (the City Clinic) in Stockholm's city centre. The City Clinic was successful because it harnessed an abundant resource – physicians with plenty of spare time – to a need consumers felt to be unfulfilled by the public system.

As noted previously, Swedish health care is planned on an area basis, and clinics and hospitals at the time were all fed patients based on the patient's area of residence. However, in a large city such as Stockholm, where residential areas are often separated from work areas by many kilometres, this can be problematic. An afternoon appointment with a doctor could mean a half-day off work if you had to travel back to your neighbourhood health clinic. By being located right in the city centre and seeing patients on a walk-in basis, the City Clinic solved this problem for many people. In return for this added convenience, patients only had to pay the slightly higher user fee charged to those visiting a private rather than a public doctor (Olsson, 1988, pp.76–7).

The City Clinic showed that the private sector providers could produce healthy financial returns not only by competing with the public sector, but

7. It is perhaps important to explain why physicians find it so attractive to practise privately in their free hours instead of simply collecting extra pay for working at nights, on holidays, etc. This is due to the vagaries of Swedish taxation laws, which tax income earned through labour much more severely than income derived from profits (Ministry of Finance, 1990a, p.84). Consequently, physicians who incorporate their part-time private practices and at the end of the year declare a dividend can save substantially on their tax bills.

8. The company is essentially a producer co-operative. Physicians, dentists and physiotherapists who are employed by the company and who work on average ten hours a week or more for the company are entitled to vote at annual meetings, stand for election to the board, etc. However, each individual practitioner's work is a separate profit centre, and he or she is the sole beneficiary of the profits that are created in his or her practice (Mosten, March 1990). In 1989 the company employed 1,087 physicians and 1,903 dentists (Praktikertjänst, 1990, p.2). The company's revenues that year stood at SEK 2,700 million (Praktikertjänst, 1990, pp.10–12). In 1991, company revenues were up over SEK 500 million to SEK 3,283 million (Praktikertjänst, 1992, p.21).

also by complementing the services provided by local counties.[9] The facility could be seen as an extra primary care clinic (albeit one with less than complete services; for example, no psychiatric care is provided by the City Clinic) which Stockholm county did not have to pay the capital costs to create.

A strong case can also be made that many of the patients seen there were not 'stolen' from the public clinics. It could be argued that if it were not for the convenience of the private clinic they likely would not have bothered to see a physician about their conditions. Even worse perhaps, they might have gone to the already over-used hospital emergency wards after work hours.

Praktikertjänst, which initially wanted to compete directly with public medical care providers for patients (as it does with dentists) ended up moving into a partnership with the public medical care system through offering complementary services such as the City Clinic. It was forced into an even deeper partnership with the counties by the so-called 'Dagmar Reforms' of 1984. Up until the introduction of this legislation, publicly-funded private practice was paid for on a fee-for-service basis. The doctor submitted a bill to the National Insurance Funds for the work done, based on the Insurance Funds' fee chart, and patients paid a user fee slightly higher than those charged by publicly-run clinics. The Dagmar Reforms instead substituted a national grant to each county to pay for the purchase of such services from part-time private physicians. Full-time private physicians were allowed to continue billing the funds. However, all new full-time private physicians required the approval of their county council before they could be granted billing privileges with the National Insurance Funds (National Audit Bureau, 1991, Section I, pp.9–10).

The grants to the counties were relatively free of restrictions. Therefore, if a county wished to channel parts of its grant into the public system, leaving less to pay private physicians, it was allowed to do so. Of course, counties could also do the reverse and spend more than their allotted grants on privately-provided care.

With the publicly-funded, part-time private practitioners now being paid from county coffers, they were effectively made into contractors to the counties. Having said this, it should be noted that the last six years have seen considerable growth in private medicine in most counties. What started out as a minor revival of private practice has become a boom.

Instead of squeezing out private practices and services, the counties seem to be calling on the private sector to provide more and more of the

---

9. 'Complementary' is the word Praktikertjänst uses in its annual report to describe the relationship between the services that it provides and those provided by the county-run systems (Praktikertjänst, 1990, p.12).

services which the counties are compelled to make available to their residents by national legislation. However, this has increasingly been done on terms established by the individual counties. Instead of allowing the part-time and full-time private physicians to open up shop and bill as they like, the counties have been granting contracts for specific tasks, which they themselves define (Rosenthal, 1992, p.157). Some counties have even privatised whole areas of their medical care systems, or are experimenting with systems where the public sector and private sector bid competitively for the right to provide services to the county and its neighbourhood primary care councils.

In 1987, Halland county (in the south-west of Sweden) contracted with a private group of physicians to run a whole area of its primary care health system. In the same year, Stockholm began a similar experiment, leasing the operation of an entirely new primary care clinic to a private operator (Saltman, 1990, pp.606–7). In September 1990, Stockholm county agreed to study a plan which would involve selling one of its hospitals, Sabbatsberg, to a co-operative consisting of the hospital's 1,800 employees (*Dagens Nyheter*, 9 December 1990, D2). To put the above examples into a broader perspective, we should perhaps note that, as recently as 1986, none of Sweden's 784 publicly-owned primary care clinics were under private for-profit management. At the beginning of 1992 the running of eleven clinics had been contracted out, and one expert predicted that the number would likely exceed thirty by the end of 1992 (Mosten, 1992).

Also of interest is the case of Kopparberg county (Dala), which lies north-west of Stockholm, extending from the centre of the country to the border with Norway in the west. In 1991 this county began implementing a plan to decentralise spending on health care to the county's local primary health councils. Under the plan, neighbourhood health councils control a budget based on the number of residents in their region. It is then up to them to decide which services to provide in their own primary care clinics, which to buy from county hospitals, and which to buy from outside suppliers – such as another county's health system – or private commercial providers (Heinsoo, 1991, pp.84–8; *Dagens Nyheter*, 24 September 1990, A5).

Previous attempts to place more emphasis on primary care in Sweden have met with mixed success. The so-called 'Dalamodel', will theoretically help in this regard by placing most spending decisions in the hands of the administrators of primary care. Furthermore, by allowing the committees to select from competing providers, they should, according to the plan, be able to bargain prices down. The combined effect should be higher-quality care at reduced costs, and, more importantly for this chapter, a further opportunity for private sector health care providers to act as contractors to the public sector (Larsson, 1990).

The reader will undoubtedly have noticed the large number of conditional statements in the above passage. This is because two key questions have yet to be answered about the Dalamodel. The first is whether or not there will be large enough savings to make the process of tendering worth while. If prices do not fall substantially, the extra cost of administering the bidding process may actually create higher costs for the county. This will partly depend on there being enough competition, and partly on the neighbourhood councils acting aggressively to break up any attempts at price-fixing by suppliers. The second question is whether Kopparberg's politicians are willing to take the system to its logical conclusion. If major public facilities cannot provide the lowest price, and lose business – especially to organisations outside the county – will the politicians let their local public facilities close (Saltman and Von Otter, 1992a, pp. 149–50)?

The Dalamodel may have helped Kopparberg county to reduce queues and to boost the quality of care; however, it has not proved to be as successful as its inventors hoped it would be at cutting health care costs. Hardly any of the SEK 200 million in savings the plan was supposed to generate have emerged. Further, the reorganisations involved in establishing the new system have provoked some serious dissatisfaction among residents in the county (Landstingsvärlden, 13 August 1992). Even so, Kopparberg has done better than Stockholm county. When Stockholm introduced its own experimental quasi-market system, which involves a group of primary care clinics 'buying' secondary care from hospitals on the basis of Diagnostic Related Groups (DRGs), a study of the scheme predicted it would increase health care costs by SEK 50 million a month if the plan were implemented county-wide! The officials in Stockholm claim to have identified the problem as over-generous initial specialist compensation levels, which have now been reduced to prevent a recurrence in the future (Landstingsvärlden, 18 June 1992).

Despite these setbacks, separating purchasers and providers to create internal markets and private competition for the public sector is now the accepted wisdom in Sweden. This is symbolised by the selection of Toivo Heinsoo, one of the creators of the Dalamodel, to be the new director of the health and health care section at the County Council Federation (Landstingsvärlden, 13 February 1992, p.12). This appointment was part of a larger reorganisation of the federation.

Along with these experiments in private provision on a basis of contracts and internal markets, many counties have been responding to their residents' feelings of discontent over the arbitrary nature of the health care system by creating greater freedom for patients to chose their own health care providers, both within the public system and increasingly from for-profit providers. Patient freedom to change clinics and physicians is now available in most counties.

Since 1989, Stockholm has allowed patients wide freedom to select which clinic they will be treated in, and also which specialist and hospital clinics their general practitioner refers them to (*Sting*, 1991, p.25). By 1989, ten of the twenty-six county health care systems allowed patients to choose which clinic they were enrolled with, and twelve others allowed patients a choice 'under certain circumstances' (Saltman, 1990, p.609). In 1993, Stockholm planned to take this system one step further and allow residents to choose to see privately-practising physicians, who agree to abide by the county-approved fee schedule, at public expense (Haas, 1992).

British experience seems to indicate that the right to choose which provider you will be seen by and in which facilities you will be treated are often not meaningful rights outside of large urban areas (*Business*, 1991, p.92). If there is only one clinic for several kilometres, and one hospital capable of providing the care required within hundreds, as is very likely in many areas of Sweden, then choice within the county health care system really becomes a moot point, except for the one in three Swedes who live in major urban areas.

Nor is privatisation likely to improve this matter. Choice is a function of having a number of providers within a reasonable proximity. It is very unlikely that rural areas will be magically inundated with physicians and other health care professionals due to increased opportunities for private practice.

A few thousand Swedes each year pay for private health insurance.[10] Most of the plans are run in a manner similar to what have become known as Health Maintenance Organisations (HMOs) in the United States. For an annual fee the insuree gains access to the insurer's treatment network of physicians, other health professionals and facilities. The main benefit that private insurers offer their customers is not higher-quality care – many of the Swedish physicians who are involved in these plans hold full-time appointments in their county's public system and only see private patients in their time off (Rosenthal, 1989, p.175) – but rather, speedier care.

Queues are common and occasionally long for some procedures in the Swedish public health system, and this has provided a business opportunity for insurers.[11] By purchasing space for their clients in the small number

10. Not discussed in detail here, but also useful to remember, is that those who visit or plan to reside in Sweden for under one year are not covered by the public system, and often buy private insurance to reimburse themselves if they need to pay for medical care.

11. How long someone must wait for care before a queue is said to exist varies from country to country. It seems that in Sweden the answer to this question is that when people wait more than three months for care there is said to be a queue.

of private Swedish facilities and in foreign hospitals, as one insurer has done, or by buying control of one of Sweden's private hospitals, as another has, the HMOs can offer queueless access to facilities. These plans were originally marketed as a form of 'executive protection' for large corporations, who could ill afford to have a key employee incapacitated for a lengthy period. However, the main purchasers have tended to be small businesses and the self-employed.

By June 1986 the two largest Swedish insurance companies, Skandia and Trygg Hansa, had between them signed up 5,500 individuals for their HMO plans (Rosenthal, 1986, pp.603–4). Initially the plans were tax-deductible business expenses for the corporate bodies which purchased them for their employees (Olsson, 1988, p.76). However, since 1988 the plans have ceased to be tax-deductible (Saltman, 1990, p.603).

The insurance companies are unlikely to meet their initial market forecasts of between 6 and 12 per cent of the Swedish population. A reversal of the above-mentioned tax decision, or a large enough deterioration in the quality of the care provided in the county run systems, which would make the cost of private insurance worth while, could change this prediction. Current estimates place the number of policyholders at around 15,000 individuals (Calltorp, 1990, p.32).

Even among the patients of some purely private medical practitioners, the use of private health insurance is a relative rarity. Dr Kurt Haas estimates that only around 15 per cent of the patients he saw in 1991 in his private orthopedic clinic and surgery had third-party coverage, the rest paid for their care through their own resources (Haas, 1992).

In care for the elderly there is a slowly increasing trend across the country to publicly-financed private provision of serviced apartments for the elderly. In 1991, 5,000 senior citizens were housed in serviced apartment buildings operated by private and co-operative firms, and within a few years this number is likely to increase to 9,000. All of Sweden's major private and co-operative building firms are interested in providing such units (*Dagens Nyheter*, 15 September 1991).

This should not come as too big a surprise. Sweden is currently in economic recession. With other portions of the construction market stagnating, builders are looking to the one market with potential for rapid growth – accommodation for the elderly. The fact that this accommodation is paid for, in part or in whole, by public funds, and is built more in accordance with need than the economic climate, should constitute a useful buffer against recession in the asset portfolios of the large property and building concerns.

How deeply the urge to co-operate with the counties has replaced the urge to compete with them among private care providers can be seen by the ideas Carl Evert Mosten, Praktikertjänst's Medical Services Director, has developed to run joint public/private hospitals. In his theory, a hospital is really five separate sets of services:

1 a hotel and office complex;
2 a set of diagnostic services;
3 a set of services for ambulatory patients;
4 an emergency infirmary;
5 a set of services for non-ambulatory patients.

Why not, Mosten argues, have a hotel operator and property managing firm look after the hotel and offices, hire an office management firm to run the administrative end, while someone like Praktikertjänst handles the diagnostic and ambulatory patient services. This would leave the counties to concentrate on what he claims they do best – emergency care and major surgical care (Mosten, 1990). The fact that these two areas are also the most difficult to run on a for-profit basis is never mentioned by Mosten, but it probably crossed his mind.

This is probably what raises the greatest concern among those who are opposed to greater use being made of outside contractors in the provision of health and social services. The possibility that the private sector will attempt to cream off the most lucrative sections of the system cannot be dismissed lightly. If the public system became too dependent on for-profit providers, would those who suffer from conditions deemed difficult to treat profitably receive care of lower quality than they do presently?

The 1991 Election and Beyond

On 15 September 1991 Sweden held its three-yearly elections for all three levels of government (national, county, and municipal). The result at the national level was the defeat of the Social Democratic government. The party also lost control of many of the county and municipal councils which it had previously led.

Seven parties managed to gain seats in the Riksdag (Swedish Parliament). Along with the Social Democrats, the leftist Vänster Partiet (literally 'the Left Party') was also present.[12] The five other parties were to the right of centre, including the three traditional right-of-centre parties – the Conservative Party, the Liberal Party and the Centre Party – and two newer parties – the Christian Democrats (Kristdemokratiska

12. Until the summer of 1990 this party referred to itself as the Vänsterparti Kommunisterna (the Left Party Communists), and before 1967 as simply Kommunisterna (the Communists). For more on this party's periodic facelifts and the ideological and historical causes behind them, see Olsson (1986).

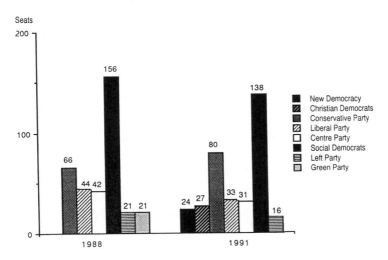

Source: Aftonbladet, 16 September 1991.

Figure 9.1 Party Representation in the Swedish Riksdag, 1988 and 1991 Elections

Samhällspartiet) and New Democracy (Ny Demokrati).

The five right-of-centre parties together had enough seats to command an absolute majority in Parliament; however, such a coalition proved impossible to create. The Liberal Party refused to participate in any coalition containing the New Democrats, who are seen as exceptionally far to the right in some circles, and as Le Pen-style extremists in others. As a result the four other parties formed a coalition government which was five votes short of a majority, commanding 170 of the Parliament's 349 seats.

In the past when right-of-centre coalitions governed Sweden (1976–82), they were hesitant to break with the long-standing policies and trends in social welfare provision and financing which had been established during the Social Democrats' forty-four years in office (Heclo and Madsen, 1987, p.65). The election propaganda of the right-of-centre parties led many to believe that things would be different this time around, and that, on taking office, the new government would launch a vigorous assault on many of the cornerstones of Swedish social policy and practice.

As part of their election campaign, the Conservatives and Liberals (who held 113 of the coalition's 170 seats) issued a joint platform document called *Ny Start För Sverige* ('A New Start for Sweden'). In it they promised to allow Swedes more choice concerning the type of social services they receive and who provides them (Conservative and Liberal Parties, 1991, p.24).

In fact, the leader of the Liberal Party, and Sweden's new Social Affairs Minister, Bengt Westerberg, was involved in creating a private company for the provision of child day care, Pysslingen AB (Olsson, 1988, p.75). When the company began operations, the then Social Democratic government introduced a law prohibiting private child care organisations from receiving public funds (in the Swedish scheme of things the official Swedish Church is considered a public organisation, and so was not affected by the ban). Over time the Social Democrats relaxed this ban so that, when they left office, it only applied to private for-profit providers (Rothstein, 1992, p.20). As Social Affairs Minister, Westerberg promised to clear away all central government regulations that prevent parents from receiving public subsidies when they place their children in private centres, or which prevent municipalities from contracting out for such services. However, a condition was that any private centres receiving public money would have to operate in a truly public manner. This means that such centres have to co-operate with municipal planners, such as by accepting children from the day care centre queues previously created by municipalities where shortages exist, and by accepting applications from families on a first come, first served basis. (*Dagens Nyheter*, 5 November 1991, A8). The law implementing these changes is scheduled to take effect on 1 January 1995 (Ministry of Health and Social Affairs, 1994, p.6). However, these reforms may not survive the return to power of the Social Democrats in September 1994.

Many of the newly-elected municipal and county authorities seemed to be eager to follow the new Minister's view, that the private sector should be allowed to act in the public interest. Following the September 1991 elections, the major Swedish newspapers were full of articles about the plans that the newly-elected local authorities were considering in anticipation of the national government's actions to reform the laws regarding day care and education.

At the end of October, Malmö City Council proposed going further than the government's proposed minimum standard by offering parents a subsidised free market in day care. Families would be issued day care vouchers. Parents would be able to enroll their children in public centres or private centres of their choosing (*Dagens Nyheter*, 31 October 1991, D8). In November, the new leader of Stockholm City Council announced a similar voucher system would be introduced for that city's schoolchildren by the autumn of 1993 (*Dagens Nyheter*, 27 November 1991, D4). In the same month the Stockholm suburb of Solna announced similar plans (*Dagens Nyheter*, 7 November 1991, D2), while another suburb of Stockholm, Nacka, was laying plans to go even further. Here the city council planned to contract out the running of the city's largest primary school to a private provider (*Svenska Dagbladet*, 19 November 1991, A8).

There have been some implementation troubles with these plans to introduce competition into the running of schools: for example Nacka was unable to find a suitable outside contractor to run one of its schools. In the cities planning voucher schemes, some of the details of these plans have yet to be worked out, so it is too early to comment on their prospects.

The government's election propaganda also committed it to cutting public spending so as to afford a reduction in taxation. To this end the government planned a reduction in transfer payments to the municipalities of SEK 5 to 10 billion during 1993 (*Dagens Nyheter*, 6 November 1991, A6).

This posed serious problems for some municipalities, not least because their responsibility for elderly people has been increased. Formerly the municipalities were only responsible for providing serviced apartments and visiting home service helpers to elderly people. Their role has now been enlarged to include long-term care facilities, as well as home nursing visits, which were formerly the responsibility of the counties. To help pay for these new duties some tax revenue is also being transferred from the counties to the municipalities. However, the transfers will not meet the full costs of the services involved, since one of the reasons behind the move is to relieve the financial strain on the counties. Some municipalities, caught between financial restraint and the cost involved in taking on these new legal responsibilities, may try to contract out these services in the hope that such actions will cut costs. The city of Stockholm has already begun to take this step. Starting in 1992 it contracted with Svensk Hemservice for the operation of a serviced apartment building for senior citizens (*Dagens Nyheter*, 26 November 1991, D1).

Ironically, the company involved in this privatisation is owned by Procordia, an investment vehicle partly owned by the national government. On a more ominous note, this episode may provide ammunition for those who claim that privatisation cannot occur without 'creaming' occurring. It is the serviced apartment buildings – those in which older people live independently while receiving light support services from residential staff – in which Svensk Hemservice is interested, not the more intensive- care nursing homes.

Another irony of this decision by Stockholm to contract out in order to 'save money' is that the company involved in the plan does not have a very good record in this regard. One of Svensk Hemservice's first clients, the city of Danderyd (a suburb north of Stockholm), conducted a study on the cost savings which the city had realised as a result of contracting out part of their services for elderly people from 1989 to 1991. In the end the city discovered that, rather than saving money, contracting out had cost the city more than if they had provided the services themselves (*Dagens Nyheter*, 25 September 1991).

Evidence seems to indicate that these two goals – increasing choice for consumers and providers and lowering cost to the public – are not compatible, at least in health care (Hollingsworth et al., 1990, p.201), and possibly in other social services as well. If this is indeed the case, one wonders which goal the government will eventually discard.

Potentially far more revolutionary, however, was the government's anticipated attitude towards the private financing of services. Private financing of services has grown much more slowly and – true to Sweden's universalist social welfare creed – has not previously been actively encouraged to any large extent. It is the Swedish Welfare State's provision of universal benefits at a level which is meaningful to the expectations of most individuals which is considered to be the main source of its broad legitimacy (Esping-Andersen, 1990, p.69).[13]

The Conservatives and the Liberals claimed during the 1991 election that they wanted to change this and force the better-off in Swedish society to take more personal responsibility for their own welfare, especially in the area of pensions (Conservative and Liberal Parties, 1991, p.16).

Unfortunately for the handful of right-wing ideologues in the ranks of the Conservative Party, the government trimmed its sails back towards a more pragmatic political course. The examples given above seem to suggest that the Social Affairs Minister wanted to integrate the private providers into a publicly-financed system, operating in the public interest. He did not seem to want to promote the creation of a separate, privately-financed private health and social service sector, a view he still seemed to hold going into the 1994 general election (Ministry of Health and Social Affairs, 1994, pp.2–3).

There were undoubtedly several reasons for such a decision: among the most important was probably the number of parties that were required to form a working coalition (but one that was still, nevertheless, short of a majority). Although its two largest constituent parties may have campaigned on a joint platform, their commitment to this compromise platform is open to debate. Many Conservatives probably feel that the platform was too moderate, and many Liberals that it was too extreme. The other two partners in the government, the traditionalist Christian Democrats and rural-rooted Centre Party, were even less committed to the coalition and its platform.

---

13. Even within the Welfare State, the few programmes involving means tests – programmes available only to those deemed needy, or those in certain circumstances such as unemployment – are not as broadly supported as the universal programmes (Marklund, 1988, p.80).

This was demonstrated at the 1992 congress of the Swedish County Council Federation. During the debate on health care policy – usually a highly partisan affair – one of the leaders of the Centre Party delegation to the congress (the newly-elected chairman of the federation's health care committee, no less) refused to support the government's position that all patients should have total freedom to select their health care providers. (Landstingsvärlden, 4 June 1992, p.43).

One must also not forget that the government could also expect opposition to its plans from groups outside Parliament and local government. The Swedish labour movement is the best-organised and most professionally run in the world as is the Swedish Farmers' movement. Beyond its core in the major trade unions and their central confederation there are also numerous co-operative and member-owned organisations allied to it.[14] All of these organisations, which command a large sector of the Swedish economy and the cultural landscape, have large membership bases and a certain level of interest in maintaining the Welfare State. They can be expected to act if they feel threatened. Similarly, the white-collar Salaried Employees' Central Organisation (TCO) and SACO/SR, which represents professionals, voiced concern over the government's plans at the very start of its term in office. In fact, the government might have found it too difficult to act until its efforts to weaken the labour movement, both legally and financially, had taken effect. The government wished to amend the various labour statutes to allow local and county governments greater ability to lay off workers and contract work out. An investigatory commission was charged to recommend ways of implementing such amendments. In addition, the government cut educational subsidies to the unions (*TCO Tidningen*, 17 January 1992, p.4). It wanted to nationalise their role in providing unemployment insurance (Viklund, 1992, p.12) but instead settled for only providing a purely public sector competitor for the trade union unemployment insurance funds. Since July 1994 those who do not join a trade union unemployment insurance fund are automatically enrolled in a state fund (*Svenska Dagbladet*, 1 July 1994, N2). This may indeed weaken the unions financially and remove one of the most common reasons why Swedes join trade unions, but it has also with one stroke massively increased the role of the state in providing

14. Included are Sweden's largest retailer, Kooperativa förbudet (KF), the over half a million members of the National Association of Tenants' Savings and Building Societies (HSB); Fonus, Sweden's single largest director of funerals; the 700 People's Hall Associations (Folkets Hus Föreningar), which manage cultural centres ranging in size from small halls to major international venues all across Sweden, and the A Press, which publishes the 425,000 circulation *Aftonbladet* (the world's largest social democratic daily) and other titles and many more organisations (International Centre of the Swedish Labour Movement, 1989, pp.20–2).

welfare services.

It would have required far more time than the three years allotted to a Swedish government to pass the government's entire labour law reform agenda, and the government understood all of this at the outset. This is a situation which one would expect to produce compromise rather than decisive action. Bengt Westerberg, speaking to a Canadian journalist, recognised that a right-of-centre coalition government, would preclude any enormous changes. He stated that the new government's goal would be to reorganise the Swedish social model, not to destroy it (*Globe and Mail*, 14 September, 1991, D2). This would involve producing a privatisation policy which the four government parties could agree upon, and which the Social Democrats, still the largest party in the Parliament, could live with.

Such an agenda can already be seen to be taking place within the confines of the existing health care system, principally at the local level. Along with the initiatives already mentioned in this chapter, two important innovations being applied at the local level are important to note.

One of the major planks in the platform of the right-of-centre parties since the end of the 1980s has been what they refer to as a *vårdgaranti* (treatment guarantee). Basically, they promised to introduce regulations to establish maximum waiting periods for treatment. If the county makes a patient wait longer for treatment, the patient has the freedom to go to a private provider and send the bills to the county (*Dagens Nyheter*, 15 September 1990, D4). The party that thinks up ideas is not necessarily the party that implements them. In Stockholm, the Social Democrat-led council adopted the *vårdgaranti* itself (*Dagens Nyheter*, 9 October 1990, D2).

The guarantee has created a whole new catagory of publicly-subsidised patients for private commercial providers. In order to deliver their promises, some counties began extending their already existing arrangements with for-profit providers. In a sense, what the counties have done is to establish arrangements for leasing extra capacity and professional staff for handling backlogs of patients when they occur, and before they have waited long enough to qualify for the *vårdgaranti* (Haas, 1992). Since the 1991 election more counties have adopted the scheme.

Another change which has occurred at the local level is a direct result of the 1991 election. Right-of-centre-led county councils and autonomous municipalities have been more generous in granting permission to full-time private practitioners to affiliate with the National Insurance Funds than their Social Democratic predesessors were (Haas, 1992).

The purely private health care market (where both financing and provisions are private) grew during the 1980s. One factor in its rise was that physicians and other health care professionals wanting to work outside the county-administered systems, either part-time or full-time, could not get contracts from the counties to do so, or get their county's permission to affiliate with the National Insurance Funds (Rosenthal, 1989, p.175; Haas, 1992).

Meanwhile, at the national level, the County Council Federation and the government were until recently co-operating on a scheme known as Husläkarsystemet ('the Family Doctor System'). Every Swede would enrol with a general practitioner, or group of general practitioners, who would receive a capitation fee for managing the patient's health care, as well as some fee-for-service income for extra services. The general practitioners would therefore have to decide which services to provide themselves and which to 'purchase' for their patients from other providers, such as hospitals, prenatal clinics, etc. Patients would be free to change general practitioners (Ministry of Finance, 1992b, pp.19–20). This scheme is similar in many respects to the budget-holding general practices being instituted in the UK National Health Service (Saltman and Von Otter, 1992b, pp.32–3).

Not everyone is completely satisfied with the proposed family doctor system. Inger Ohlsson, Chairperson of SHSTF, the union which represents nurses, midwives and other health care professionals, has expressed concern about the planned changes (*Dagens Nyheter*, 26 June 1992, A4). Her main concern is that the new system will increase the dominant position of physicians in the health care system. If patients are required to visit a physician before gaining access to other points in the health care system, the independent practices of nurses and midwives will be placed more firmly under physician control.

As Ohlsson dryly notes, 'All patients will first visit the doctor, who will later send them off to the district nurse. What do we [society] gain by this unnecessary stop along the way?' (*Dagens Nyheter*, 26 June 1992, A4). Admittedly, it is quite ridiculous for a woman who thinks that she is pregnant to go to the doctor to announce this, if afterwards the doctor is just going to send the woman to a midwife for a pregnancy test.

More surprisingly, the group of professionals expected to gain most from the system, the district general practitioners, now officially oppose the plan. They seem to be concerned that the plan will create both over-serviced and under-serviced areas, and add to the amount of bureaucratic work each physician will have to carry out. The district general practitioners also have serious concerns about the effects that the plan will have on patient care. The plan rewards physicians for treating patients in their clinics and penalises them for referring them to hospitals. According to economists, this will encourage physicians to keep their patients healthy. According to the district general practitioners, it will only encourage physicians to seek out healthy patients and to try to keep those likely to experience serious chronic illnesses off their patient lists (*Dagens Nyheter*, 22 August 1992, A14). Many counties seem to agree with these criticisms and are now having second thoughts about an idea of which they initially approved (Landstingsvärlden, 13 August 1992, p.9).

The main problem identified by both the district general practitioners and the counties seemed to be the government's decision to couple the planned reorganisation of how health care is paid for with a blanket right for physicians to set up in practice wherever they wish. In other words, the plan would scrap the rules which currently ensure that publicly-employed and publicly-financed private physicians are spread equally around the country, and which apportion each physician a cross-section of the population from within the area which they serve.

Beyond this important reorganisation of primary care, the 1991–94 government and the County Council Federation seemed to be more interested in pursuing the reshaping of health care provision in the long run. Even basic principles of the health care system are now open for debate. This process began in the years before the centre-right government took power (Landstingsförbundet, 1991). However, the change in political leadership at both the national level and within the County Council Federation has possibly given the following questions a new importance. Who should be responsible for ensuring that health and medical services are available when needed? Who should be responsible for financing health and medical care, care of the elderly, sick leave compensation, early retirement, etc.? Who should be responsible for producing health services? And who should be responsible for monitoring the quality of care? All of these questions were asked in a County Council Federation study on the future of Swedish health care (Landstingsförbundet, 1991). The answers that will be given to most of these questions are at present unknown.

Undoubtedly plans will emerge in the future, but it is far too early to make any concrete predictions regarding this topic. Whatever happens, it is clear that in the near future the public providers of health and welfare services are going to have more competition for the public funds that support their activities, and that the private for-profit providers of health and welfare services will be taking a growing slice of the pie.

However, any further ideas as to how to reform health and welfare in Sweden will have a decidedly social democratic tint, following the defeat of the right-of-centre coalition. The county councils will continue to be the dominant financiers and providers of health care in Sweden (*Dagens Nyheter*, 2 September 1993). The parliamentary defeat of the legislation needed to create the Family Doctor System on a nationwide scale has also left the individual counties free as before to make up their own minds on how to structure primary care, though many seem intent on pursuing the

Family Doctor scheme on their own. The Swedish model is always *and* never changing.

References

Andersen, Odin W. (1968) *Health Care: Can there be Equity? The United States, Sweden and England*, New York, John Wiley & Sons.

Berg, Ole (1980) 'The modernisation of medical care in Sweden and Norway', in Heidenheimer, Arnold J. and Nils Elvander (eds) (1980) *The Shaping of the Swedish Health System*, London, Croom Helm.

Calltorp, Johan (1990) 'Physician manpower politics in Sweden', *Health Policy*, vol.15, nos.2–3.

Conservative and Liberal Parties (Moderaterna och Folkpartiet) (1991) *Ny Start För Sverige* (A New Start for Sweden), Stockholm.

Esping-Andersen, Gösta (1990) *The Three Worlds of Welfare Capitalism*, Cambridge, Polity Press.

Evans, Robert G. (1991) 'Reflections on the revolution in Sweden', in Culyer, A.J., et al. (1991) *International Review of the Swedish Health Care System*, SNS Occasional Paper no.34, Stockholm, SNS, pp.118–57.

Haas, Kurt, M D (1992) 'Interview with Kurt Haas, M D', *Orthopediska Hus*, Stockholm, March.

Ham, Christopher (1988) 'Governing the health sector: Power and policy making in the English and Swedish health services', *Milbank Quarterly Review*, vol.66, no.2, pp.388–415.

Heclo, Hugh and Madsen, Henrik (1987) *Policy and Politics in Sweden: Principled Pragmatism*, Philadelphia, Temple University Press.

Heinsoo, Toivo (1991) 'Dalamodelllen – Et första steg mot en ny hälso- och sjukvårdsstruktur' (The Dala Model – A First Step Towards a New Health and Health Care Structure), in Arvidsson, Göran and Jönsson, Bengt (eds) (1991) *Valfrihet och konkurrens i sjukvården* (Choice and Competition in Health Care), Stockholm, SNS, pp.78–91.

Hollingsworth, J., Rogers, Hage, Jerold and Hanneman, Robert A. (1990) *State Intervention in Medical Care: Consequences for Britain, France, Sweden and the United States, 1870–1910*, Ithaca, New York, Cornell University Press.

International Centre of the Swedish Labour Movement (AIC) (1989) *The Swedish Labour Movement*, Stockholm.

Jönsson, Bengt (1989) 'Market power and consumer welfare: The Swedish pharmaceutical market', *The Study of Power and Democracy in Sweden: English Series*, Report no.33, Uppsala, Sweden, Maktu-tredningen.

Kjellström, Sven-Åke and Lundberg, Olle (1987) 'Health and health care utilization', in Erikson, Robert and Åberg, Rune (eds) (1987) *Welfare in Transition: A Survey of Living Conditions in Sweden, 1968–1981*, Oxford, Clarendon Press.

Korpi, Walter (1989) 'Can we afford to work?', in Bulmer, Martin, Lewis, Jane and Piachaud, David (eds) (1989) *The Goals of Social Policy*, London, Unwin Hyman.

Landstingsförbundet (Swedish County Council Federation) (1987) *Statistisk årsbok 1986/87* (Statistical Yearbook 1986/87), Stockholm.

—— (1990) *Statistisk årsbok 1990/91* (Statistical Yearbook 1990/91), Stockholm.

—— (1991) *Cross Roads: The Future of Swedish Health Care*, Stockholm.

Larsson, Bengt (1990) 'Interview with Bengt Larsson of the Swedish National Board of Health and Welfare', *Socialstyrelsen*, Stockholm, April.

Lawson, Robin (1984) *European Collaborative Health Service Study: Profile of Health Care in Skäreborg County, Sweden*, Sundbyberg, Sweden, Karolinska Institute for Social Medicine.

Marklund, Steffan (1988) *Paradise Lost? The Nordic Welfare States and the Recession 1975–1985*, Lund Studies in Social Welfare no.2, Lund, Sweden, Arkiv Förlag.

Meyerson, Per-Martin (1985) *Eurosclerosis: The Case of Sweden* (trans. Victor J. Kayfetz), Stockholm, The Federation of Swedish Industries (Sveriges Industriförbundet).

—— (1991) *Den Svenska modellens uppgång och fall* (The Swedish Model's Rise and Fall), Stockholm, SNS.

Micheleti, Michele (1991) 'Swedish corporatism at a crossroads: The impact of new politics and new social movements', *West European Politics*, vol.14, no.3, pp.144–65.

Ministry of Finance (Finansdepartment) (1980) *The Swedish Budget 1980/81: A Summary*, Stockholm.

—— (1981) *The Swedish Budget 1981/82: A Summary*, Stockholm.

—— (1986) *The Swedish Budget 1986/87: A Summary*, Stockholm.

—— (1988) *The Swedish Budget 1988/89: A Summary*, Stockholm.

—— (1989) *The Swedish Budget 1989/90: A Summary*, Stockholm.

—— (1990a) *The Medium Term Survey of the Swedish Economy* (trans. Patrick Hort), Stockholm.

—— (1990b) *The Swedish Budget 1990/91: A Summary*, Stockholm.

—— (1990c) *Landsting för välfärd, Bilaga 14 till Långtidsutredningen* (Landstings in Transition, Appendix 13 of the Medium-term Survey of the Swedish Economy), Stockholm.

—— (1991) *The Swedish Budget 1991/92: A Summary*, Stockholm.

—— (1992a) *The Medium Term Survey of the Swedish Economy* (trans. Patrick Hort), Stockholm.

—— (1992b) *Landsting i förändring, Bilaga 13 till Långtisdsutredningen*, Stockholm.

Ministry of Health and Social Affairs (Socialdepartment) (1978) *The Evolution of Swedish Health Insurance*, Stockholm.

—— (1979) *Mål och medel för hälso- och sjukvården: Förslag till hälso- och sjukvårdslag: Betänkande av Hälso- och Sjukvårdsutredningen SOU 1979:78* (Goals and Means for Health and Health Care: Recommendations for Health and Health Care Law: Report of the Health and Health Care Inquiry, National Investigatory Commission 1979: 78), Stockholm.

—— (1982) *HS 90, The Swedish Health Services in the 1990s: Health in Sweden – Facts From The Basic Studies Under The HS 90 Programme*, Stockholm.

—— (1994) *Social Welfare in Transition: A Presentation of Swedish Welfare Policies*, Stockholm.

Mosten, Carl Evert (1990) 'Presentation to Participants in Stockholm University's International Graduate School Social Welfare Seminar by Carl Evert Mosten, Director for Medical Services', *Praktikertjänst*, Stockholm, March.

—— (1992) 'Presentation to Participants in Stockholm University's International Graduate School Social Welfare Seminar by Carl Evert Mosten, Director for Medical Services', *Praktikertjänst*, Stockholm.

National Audit Bureau (Riksrevisionsverket) (1991) *Statsbidragen till sjukvården – En analys av Dagmarreformen m.m.: Förvaltnings-revisionen Utreder FU 1991:3* (National Subsidies to Health Care – An Analysis of the Dagmar Reforms and Other Matters: Performance Auditing Investigation FU 1991:3), Stockholm.

Navarro, Vicente (1974) *National and Regional Health Planning in Sweden*, Washington, DC, US Department of Health, Education and Welfare.

OECD (1990) *Health Care Systems in Transition: The Search For Efficiency*, Paris.

Olsson, Sven E. (1986) 'Swedish communism poised between old reds and new greens', *Journal of Communist Studies*, vol.2, no.4, pp.359–79.

—— (1988) 'Decentralization and privatization: Strategies against a welfare backlash in Sweden', in Morris, Robert (ed.) (1988) *Testing the Limits of Social Welfare: International Perspectives on Policy Changes in Nine Countries,* Hanover, New Hampshire, Brandeis University Press, pp.60–95.

Praktikertjänst (1990) *Annual Report*, Stockholm.

—— (1992) *Annual Report*, Stockholm.

Premfors, Rune (1984) 'Coping with budget deficits in Sweden',

Scandinavian Political Studies, vol.7, no.4, pp.261–84.

—— (1991) 'The "Swedish Model" and public sector reform', *West European Politics*, vol.14, no.3, pp.83–95.

Rosenthal, Marilynn M. (1986) 'Beyond equity: Swedish health policy and the private sector', *Milbank Quarterly Review*, vol.64, no.4, pp.592–621.

—— (1989) 'Physician surplus and the growth of private practice: The case of Sweden', *Scandinavian Studies*, vol.61, nos 2–3, pp.169–84.

—— (1992) 'The growth of private medicine in Sweden: the new diversity and the new challenge', *Health Policy*, vol.21, no.2, pp.155–66.

Rothstein, Bo (1990) 'Marxism, institutional analysis, and working-class power: The Swedish case', *Politics and Society*, vol.18, no.3, pp.317–45.

—— (1992) 'The Crisis of the Swedish Social Democrats and the Future of the Universal Welfare State', Paper Delivered to The International Conference of Europeanists, Chicago, March 1992.

Saltman, Richard B. (1990) 'Competition and reform in the Swedish health system', *Milbank Quarterly Review*, vol.68, no.4, pp.597–618.

Saltman, Richard B. and Von Otter, Casten (1992a) 'Reforming Swedish health care in the 1990s: The emerging role of public firms', *Health Policy*, vol.21, no.2, pp.143–54.

—— (1992b) *Planned Markets and Public Competition: Strategic Reform in Northern European Health Systems*, Buckingham, UK, Open University Press.

SCB (Statistics Sweden) (1980) *Statistisk årsbok 1980* (Statistical Yearbook 1980), Stockholm.

—— (1988) *Hälso- och sjukvårds årsbok 1987/88* (Health and Health Care Yearbook 1987/88), Stockholm.

—— (1989) *Hälso- och sjukvårds årsbok 1989*, Stockholm.

—— (1990) *Hälso- och sjukvårds årsbok 1990*, Stockholm.

—— (1991) *Hälso- och sjukvårds årsbok 1991/92*, Stockholm.

—— (1992) *Allmän månads statistik 1992:6* (General Monthly Statistics, June 1992), Stockholm.

Serner, Uncas (1980) 'Swedish health legislation: Milestones in reorganization since 1945', in Heidenheimer, Arnold, J. and Elvander, Nils (eds) (1980) *The Shaping of the Swedish Health System*, London, Croom Helm.

Slunge, Walter (1991) 'New approaches to managing health services', *World Hospitals*, vol.27, no.1, pp.11–20.

Sting (Stockholm County Council Magazine) (1991 no.9), Stockholm.

Svallfors, Stefan (1991) 'The politics of welfare policy in Sweden: Structural determinants and attitudinal cleavages', *British Journal of Sociology*, vol.42, no.4, pp.609–34.

Swedish Parliament (1982) 'Proposition 1981/82:97', *Årsriksmote 1981/82* (Parliamentary Sitting 1981/82), Stockholm: Riksdagen.

Twaddle, Andrew (1986) 'Swedish Physicians' Perspectives on Work and the Medical Care System, Part 1: The Case of District General Practitioners', *Social Science and Medicine*, vol.23, no.8, pp.763–71.

Van de Ven, Wynand P.M.M. (1991) 'Towards more efficiency, responsiveness and coordination in the Swedish health care system', in Culyer, A.J., et al. (1991) *International Review of the Swedish Health Care System*, SNS Occasional Paper no.34, Stockholm, SNS, pp.51–82.

Viklund, Birger (1992) 'Sweden: Labour law changes', *European Industrial Relations Review*, January, no.216, p.12.

Von der Schulenburg, J-Matthias Graf (1991) 'The Swedish health care system: Being efficient, having cost control and meeting the solidarity goal at the same time', in Culyer, A.J., et al.(1991) *International Review of the Swedish Health Care System*, SNS Occasional Paper no.34, Stockholm, SNS, pp.83–117.

–10–

The United States

Neil Gilbert and *Kwong Leung Tang*

Introduction

The social welfare system in the United States has a long history of using public, voluntary, and privately owned for-profit agencies to deliver social services. Often referred to as a 'mixed economy of welfare', these diverse arrangements can be traced back to colonial times, when public authorities 'contracted out' with private parties to provide housing, food and medical care for the poor. Indeed, in the early part of the twentieth century, most hospitals began as small doctor-owned private enterprises; more recently nursing homes, typically, have been started as small-scale family businesses.

Public sector activities in the mixed economy of welfare expanded dramatically from the New Deal in 1935 to the War on Poverty in the mid-1960s, as government played an increasing role in the finance and delivery of social services. During the last twenty years, however, the structure of this mixed economy has undergone notable changes, with responsibility for the delivery of social services steadily being transferred to units in the private sector.

The trend toward privatisation of social welfare in the United States follows two approaches to the allocation of social provisions. First is a preference for the allocation of benefits, where possible, in the form of cash rather than in-kind provisions. Cash benefits are allocated through direct monetary grants and through indirect transfers via fiscal mechanisms such as tax expenditures and credit subsidies. Over the last two decades, tax expenditures for child care, financial aid to low-income workers, pensions, and employee health benefits have accounted for the largest expansion of publicly-subsidised cash benefits outside of direct social security grants (Gilbert and Gilbert, 1989). The emphasis on cash benefits restricts the role of government to writing cheques for grants and tax refunds at the same time that it allows recipients to purchase welfare provisions from private sources. When social welfare benefits are allocated not in cash, but in kind, the second approach to privatisation involves purchase-of-service arrangements, through which the public sector finances goods and services produced and delivered by private agencies.

Scope of Privatisation

In light of the approaches noted above, the movement toward privatisation of social welfare in the United States may be gauged by examining the growth of indirect cash transfers and the extent of service delivery by profit-making agencies. With regard to indirect transfers, the costs of tax expenditures and credit subsidies for health, housing, personal social services, education, and income maintenance, are not typically counted in the conventional audit of social welfare spending. Although exact figures are thus unavailable, it is estimated that in 1988 indirect social transfers amounted to 25–40 per cent of the $US866 billion consumed by social welfare through direct public expenditures (Gilbert and Gilbert, 1989).

The growth of indirect transfers is reflected by the fact that between 1970 and 1982 there were 33 new tax expenditure items introduced, an increase of more than three times the rate of new items introduced between 1940 and 1970. The largest category of welfare-related tax expenditures for individuals encompasses provisions for income maintenance, such as the Earned Income Tax Credit and tax exclusions on retirement plans. Growing from $US42.5 billion in 1978 to $US93 billion in 1986, the costs of these indirect benefits related to income maintenance rose from 16 per cent to 32 per cent of the direct federal outlays for income maintenance. The second largest category of tax expenditure involves deductions and exclusions for housing, which came to $US37 billion in 1985, an amount considerably in excess of direct federal grants for housing.

Credit subsidies, another indirect method of providing cash transfers, are poorly understood and even harder to trace than tax expenditures. These subsidies to individuals derive from the difference between interest rates charged by government and market rates for similar loans, the costs of loan defaults, reduction of loan fees, and other financial benefits of public guarantees. Government loans are available mostly for housing and education. In the area of housing, for example, federal loan guarantees netted benefits of $US6.1 billion to borrowers in 1986, a sum amounting to about 50 per cent of direct federal expenditures on housing assistance.

The move toward privatisation has been fuelled not only by increasing use of benefits in the form of cash (which permits the purchase of goods and services on the private market), but by the growing use of public funds to purchase services produced and delivered by private for-profit agencies. By the 1990s, proprietary agencies have become firmly established in the delivery of services involving home-makers, employment training, transportation for eldery and disabled people, and meals-on-wheels. The areas in which private for-profit operations are most prominently represented include: nursing home care, day care, child welfare, health care, and housing.

Nursing Home Care

Since 1970, nursing home services increased from 6.3 per cent to 8.3 per cent of national health care expenditures, rising to a cost of $US35.2 billion by 1985. About half of these costs are paid for with public funds, mainly under Medicaid payments. Approximately 80 per cent of nursing homes and related residential care facilities are operated for profit (US Bureau of the Census, 1990). Although many of the private nursing homes have a limited number of beds, in recent years large-scale corporate chains have penetrated this market.

Day Care

This is a large and rapidly expanding market due to the massive shift of female labour from the household to the market economy. Between 1960 and 1985 the rate of participation in the labour force by married women with children under six years jumped from 19 per cent to 53 per cent, and most of them held full-time jobs. About 2 million pre-school-aged children are served by organised day care programmes. Estimates of the number of organised day care facilities vary according to the size and functions included in the definition of day care centres. In 1977, for-profit firms had enrolled 37 per cent of all children attending day care centres that served thirteen or more children, and were open at least 25 hours a week. These for-profit facilities accounted for about 41 per cent of all such day care centres (US Bureau of the Census, 1981). By 1987 there were at least 27,000 for-profit day care facilities with a combined revenue of about $US3 billion (US Bureau of the Census, 1990). Some portion of these private day care costs was subsidised by indirect government transfers through the child care tax credit, which totalled $US3.4 billion (Meyers, 1990). This tax expenditure applied to many different types of child care arrangements, including pre-school day care.

Child Welfare

Public efforts to protect children at risk involve a considerable amount of service that is purchased from for-profit agencies. Among the basic out-of-home services delivered in 1977, for example, public agencies contracted with for-profit providers to supply 35 per cent of residential treatment, 24 per cent of institutional care, and 28 per cent of group-home care. An examination of the overall pattern of contracting for these three types of services reveals that for-profit agencies were used as vendors more often than either voluntary non-profit agencies or public agencies (Born, 1983).

Health Care

Health care services in the United States have always been financed and delivered mainly through the private sector. In 1987, 76 per cent of the population was covered by some form of private health insurance, 10 per cent by government insurance, and 13 per cent were uninsured. Information published by the Census Bureau in October 1994, revealed that the number without health insurance for the whole of 1993 was 39.7 million – or 15.3 per cent of the population (US Bureau of the Census, 1994). The Clinton health reform proposals were intended to overcome the problem of non-insurance, but even before the landslide Republican victory in the mid-term elections in November 1994, the Bill had been considerably modified. The administration is now aiming at only a modest reform of health insurance. Those covered by private health insurance, however, benefited from government subsidies of about $US28 billion through tax expenditures for employee health insurance. In terms of health care expenditures, 60 per cent of the $US442.5 billion spent on health services and supplies in 1987 came from private sources and 40 per cent from government programmes (US Bureau of the Census, 1990).

Housing

More than health care, housing has been a predominantly private affair in the United States. Compared with the UK, where local public authorities own and maintain about 30 per cent of all housing units, less than 1.5 per cent of the housing stock in the US is publicly owned. But even in the US, the trend toward privatisation is evident. Up to and throughout the 1960s, federal funds for housing went mainly for the construction of units owned and managed by public authorities. Since the 1970s, however, the form of federal housing assistance has shifted from the construction of public housing to the provision of rent supplements for use in the private market, and rent subsidies tied to new, privately-constructed units.

Assumptions and Rationale

The privatisation of social welfare encompasses more than the design of indirect cash transfers via tax expenditures which subsidise private consumption and the use of public contracting with private enterprise for the delivery of in-kind welfare provisions. It represents a larger configuration of ideas and activities that include a renewed emphasis on the work ethic, reflected, for example, in the 'workfare' provisions initiated under the Family Support Act of 1988. There is also an increasing effort to adjust the moral balance of social welfare by weighing citizens' rights to public benefits against their obligations to perform as dependable members of the community (Mead, 1986). Finally, privatisation entails an infusion of the capitalist ethos, with its zeal for efficiency, consumer choice and entrepreneurial activity.

Several basic assumptions support the movement toward privatisation (Gilbert and Gilbert, 1989):

1 The cost, quality and accessibility of social welfare services will be beneficially affected by the introduction of competition, choice, the entrepreneurial spirit, profit-making, and business methods.
2 The tax system is a desirable vehicle for the transfer of income that may be applied toward the private purchase of social welfare provisions in the economic market.
3 There are limits to the affordability of desirable social welfare services, and no limit to the demand for them, so that the mode of financing, delivery, and usage of the recent past must be restructured to maintain fiscal health, to refine demand, and to maintain reasonable overall service levels.
4 In a capitalist society that has moved from an industrial and manu-facturing to a technology- and service-oriented economy, the growing production of services in the social market present a ready outlet for investment-hungry capital, as well as opportunities for employment.
5 Employment patterns of US workers, including those of traditional social service workers, must accommodate themselves to these new trends, even if it means moving into the more volatile and rootless mode of entrepreneurship and corporate life.

Underlying these assumptions is the popular belief that privatisation works because it is ultimately the most efficient approach to the production and delivery of welfare services. While many are sceptical of this view (Henig et al., 1988; Karger and Stoesz, 1990) the arguments for efficiency rest on two sets of explanations: one is macro-theoretical, focusing on institutional or structural analyses, while the other is micro-empirical, examining the evidence on intra-organisational or inter-sectoral levels. In examining the theoretical rationale for market provisions, there are at least five explanations for efficiency in privatisation. Since the case for privatisation is intricately linked with the failure of public provisions, it is not surprising to see that efficiency of privatisation is very often built upon the inefficiency of government.

Inefficiency from Irrationality of Interest-group Bargaining

Buchanan (1975) argues that a political system of interest-group bargaining will almost certainly produce very large inefficiencies in the allocation of a society's resources. If government can be pressured to provide greater goods and services for one particular group, the full benefits will flow to that group. Yet the costs are likely to be spread out over all taxpayers. Each interest group will then have a strong incentive to demand as much in goods and services from government as it can get. It will also have little incentive to oppose individual demands of other interest groups, because each of these demands would be too small to affect the overall budget and tax situation.

On the income side, each group will have an incentive to resist paying taxes levied on it. No interest group will have much individual incentive to support general taxes. With intense pressures to raise government delivery of goods and services and similar pressures to hold down taxes, interest-group interaction will act to make a great gap between costs of government and income collected. In addition, since future taxes are seen as less painful than current taxes, there is a strong bias in favour of raising government income through borrowing rather than direct taxation. This would lead to ever-growing budget deficits. As Linowes (1988) observes, this system of interest-group government would suggest that both the absolute magnitude and the distribution of goods and services provided by government are likely to be economically irrational and inefficient. Political exchanges achieved through democratic institutions are, in effect, a special kind of barter which lacks a common currency or prices to rationalise the system of exchange.

Inefficiency from Government Growth and Overload

Organised interest groups bargaining for resources from government create strong pressures toward government growth (Buchanan, 1977). Another source of pressure for growth comes from public bureaucracies which work outside the constraints of costs, efficiency and competition. Friedman (1962) observes that, once government programmes and organisations are instituted, they can rarely be dismantled. It is impossible to control bureaucracies from the outside, because they have far greater knowledge of their own operations. This built-in 'law' of bureaucratic growth underlines the popular belief that big government is bad government. The government becomes inefficient since it is also overloaded with demands made on it by interest groups and bureaucrats.

Inefficiency through the Paradox of Knowledge

According to Hayek (1976), social institutions have evolved over the centuries as a result of the spontaneous action and interaction of millions of people. As he sees it, society is not a product of design. Hayek warns not to tamper with social institutions, because people lack the knowledge that would enable them to shape society to their liking. The market system and voluntary interaction is a superior way of co-ordinating complex human activities to state direction. In short, Hayek opposes social engineering and central planning. This view is in line with what Glazer (1988) has called the paradox of knowledge: the more knowledge people acquire about social policy, the more uncertainty there is. Much of the attack on the state-centred approach to welfare is fuelled by disenchantment with scientific social engineering.

Efficiency from Competition

The argument for privatisation rests mainly on notions of efficiency and competition (Mishra, 1984; Hanke, 1987; Savas, 1989). The case is made in terms of the differing norms around which the public and private sectors are organised. There are also differing institutional arrangements which give expression to these norms. The driving force for private sector activity is said to be the profit motive. The competitive market provides an institutional structure for the pursuit of profit. A competitive environment provides strong incentives for firms to adopt cost-effective practices which reduce waste. Thus competition produces efficiency. By contrast, the public sector is said to be organised around political norms, including representation and accountability. These shape the institutions of policy-making and administration to be responsive to the multiple and conflicting preferences of individuals and groups in society. As Heilman and Johnson (1989) have observed, policy-making is a process which yields sub-optimisation, whereby the need to compromise among competing interests gives a solution that is acceptable but not optimal. The expected result is growth in regulation, paperwork, staff levels, programmes and budgets.

Efficiency from Property Rights

Another theoretical basis for efficiency comes from the property rights theory of the firm (Alchian, 1965). It posits that a top decision-maker of a single-proprietorship firm under private property rights will maximise utility by choosing the optimal combination of the non-pecuniary benefits of the firm (pleasant offices, colleagues and leisure, etc.) and the wealth of the firm. But if there is a non-profit constraint on the firm, which limits the amount of the firm's wealth that the owner can possess, the decision-maker will choose a new optimum which involves an increase in non-pecuniary benefits. In choosing this increase of non-pecuniary goods, he or she would lower the efficiency of the firm. This firm would be at a disadvantage when caught in a competitive market, because it would have to compete with profit-making firms. Although it might manage to survive with the help of substantial tax and regulatory advantages and subsidies from charitable donors (private or government), the inefficiency would linger on.

In sum, the rationale for privatisation suggests that private provisions of welfare services benefit from the results of competition, profit incentives and private property rights, while public provision of services suffer inherent problems of overload, irrationality and excessive growth. Those opposed to privatisation argue that competition based on consumer satisfaction is not replicated through third-party purchase-of-service arrangements; vulnerable populations served by social welfare agencies are often not well-informed consumers, and the incentive for profit promotes greed and low-quality services.

Proponents of privatisation claim that the theoretical justification for the advantages of the private market can be demonstrated by its performance (Savas, 1989). An examination of this claim which is grounded on empirical evidence is thus of importance.

Public Versus Private Provision: A Review of Performance

Efforts to compare the relative efficiency of public and private provision of social welfare services are beset with problems (Gilbert and Gilbert, 1989; Marmor et al., 1987; Savas, 1987). First, there is a lack of sufficient studies on relative efficiency in many areas of social welfare to draw any definitive conclusions. The field of social welfare is characterised by an imbalance of empirical findings tipped in favour of studies conducted in the health field. And when comparisons of relative efficiency are made, one runs into the following problems:

1 many studies rely only on individual or anecdotal experiences (Savas, 1987);
2 there are important intervening variables, sometimes overlooked, that can influence the outcome of any study (Johnson, 1987);
3 there is often no control over quality wh :n costs are measured (Millward and Parker, 1983);
4 there can be different criteria to assess costs and quality (Gilbert and Gilbert, 1989).

One of the most serious difficulties in measuring efficiency concerns the relationship between efficiency, quality, and effectiveness. Efficiency refers to the economically appropriate allocation of resources. It is the relationship between inputs and outputs, allowing for the influence of factors outside the control of the agencies in question (Hill, 1986). The most efficient arrangement is the one that produces the greatest output per unit of input – for example the lowest cost for a given level and quality of service (Savas, 1987; Deane and Kuper, 1988). On the other hand, effectiveness is the extent to which a service increases welfare. The most effective arrangement is the one whose output most nearly satisfies the need; for example a high quality of provision that meets the demand, produces the best results, and achieves customer satisfaction (Hill, 1986). It is easier to obtain a precise measure of the cost of inputs than of the quality and effectiveness of outputs. Thus there is a built-in tendency for measures of efficiency to be better at comparing the costs of input than the equivalence of output.

Despite the various obstacles to comparing the efficiency of public versus private social welfare provisions, a number of studies have been conducted in different service areas which bear on this issue. The largest body of research is in the area of hospital care, where some of the stickiest problems of measuring cost and quality are illustrated.

Hospitals

An early study by Clarkson (1972) predicted that hospitals under private and public ownership would perform differently. He compared for-profit hospitals with non-pecuniary hospitals (government and non-profit) in California. Non-pecuniary general hospitals were found to have different and more explicit rules than for-profit ones, but they did not care much about market price in their decisions. This led Clarkson to conclude that property rights theory was right to predict that the lack of incentive in non-pecuniary hospitals would make the decision-makers less conscious of the competitive market.

Spann (1977) examined the relative efficiency of public, non-profit and for-profit hospitals in the United States. He found that different kinds of provision did not appear to affect quality, but that private provision seemed to lower costs slightly. However, he emphasised that his conclusion was only tentative.

But the weight of evidence is hardly in one direction. Lewin et al. (1981) compared 53 non-profit hospitals with a matched set of for-profit hospitals in the South and the Southwest of the United States. They concluded that investor-owned hospitals were more expensive than non-profit hospitals, largely due to higher ancillary and administrative service costs. Also, investor-owned hospitals used fewer full-time-equivalent staff to provide care than did non-profit hospitals. A study by the Florida Hospital Cost Containment Board in 1980 compared 72 for-profit proprietary and 82 non-profit hospitals. It reported a 15 per cent higher charge for patient care and an 11 per cent higher collection rate by investor-owned hospitals over their non-profit counterparts. Data from the Health Care Finance Administration of the Department of Health and Human Services confirmed higher costs for investor-owned hospitals of nearly 20 per cent above that for government hospitals. Costs were measured for short-term hospital stay. A series of other studies also suggested lower costs for non-profit hospitals which ranged from 3 per cent to 24 per cent (Pattison and Katz, 1983; Eskoz and Peddecord, 1985; Gray and McNerney, 1986).

In one of the most comprehensive reviews of research in this area, the Institute of Medicine of the National Academy of Sciences concluded that there was 'no evidence to support the common belief that investor-owned organizations are less costly or more efficient than are not-for-profit organizations' (Gilbert and Gilbert, 1989). Many researchers would share this cautiously balanced view. Summarising the various findings, Marmor et al. (1987) observe that there are

> only small, inconsistent differences in reported costs of proprietary and non-profit facilities. Cost per day is usually higher in for-profit facilities. But shorter lengths of stay have led to their relative cost per admission being measured as lower in some studies, higher in others, and roughly equal in the rest.

Advocates of privatisation have tried to rely on different measurements of cost to argue for their case. Instead of looking at cost per day, cost per admission is emphasised. As Marmor et al. (1987) noted, there were cases where for-profit hospitals had lower costs per admission. Following this approach, Herzlinger and Krasker (1987) develop a strong case for for-profit hospitals on the basis that cost per admission was lower in for-profit hospitals. They found that the for-profit hospitals produced better results for society, and required virtually no societal investments. According to this study, for-profit hospitals were more efficient than non-profit hospitals. They re-invested their earnings in newer plant and equipment, and offered just as broad a range of services to a large number of patients, including the medically indigent. On the other hand, non-profit hospitals received more social subsidies, but they did not achieve better social results. They were oriented toward short-term results, replacing plant and equipment much more slowly than for-profits.

Other researchers suggest that, while there is slight difference between the two sectors, it is gradually levelling out. Karger and Stoesz (1990), for example, explain that many non-profit hospitals are being driven toward greater efficiency because of the increasing open-market competition with the for-profit hospitals.

In the case of multi-hospital systems, Ermann and Gabel (1984) found lower costs for the non-profit system compared to the for-profit one. In contrast, a study of a special public system, Veterans Administration Hospitals, provides evidence of high costs for non-profit hospitals. As Hanke (1985) reports, the Grace Commission's examination of veteran hospitals found the system to be highly inefficient by many measures: high operating costs, too many employees, longer length of stay, and higher inventory levels. This led the commission to recommend that the Veterans Administration phase out construction of hospitals, and contract out existing hospital management services to the private sector on a trial basis.

Overall, the field of hospital care has mixed empirical results. In efforts to measure efficiency in this field, one important question is whether cost per day or cost per admission forms a better basis for comparison and policy decisions. From the viewpoint of societal resources, cost per admission seems to offer the appropriate answer by allowing better use of resources. In the eyes of consumers, many would select the cost per admission measure, unless the illnesses are chronic. One difficulty with the cost per admission criterion is that it could lead to the discharge of patients 'sooner and sicker', as the US Congress Select Committee on Aging (1986) has charged. Policy-makers would have to balance the lower cost per admission against other social values in order to arrive at a conclusion. Thus the choice is not easy, and it varies with different criteria.

When the level of analysis moves from the hospital to individual hospital services, again findings reveal a mixed picture. For-profit providers appear to have lower costs in the provision of laboratory services (Danzon, 1982) and health insurance (Frech III, 1976), but to have equal or higher costs for renal dialysis centres (Held and Pauly, 1982) and health maintenance organisations (Schlesinger et al., 1986).

On the question of quality of care, the evidence suggests that for-profit hospitals do not have higher quality of care than non-profit hospitals. Marmor et al. (1987) indicate that there seem to be few, if any, measurable ownership-related differences in quality, and find no evidence to suggest that the profit motive influences the quality of medical practice by physicians. The same conclusion can be found in the field of mental health. Schlesinger and Dorwart (1984) concluded that for-profit providers, when compared with private non-profit providers devoted fewer staff resources to patient care, and offered fewer services with community-wide benefits.

As in many of the social services, there is a relation between quality and access. Certain kinds of cases are easier to cure, less messy, and simpler to manage. On the issue of access, the for-profit hospitals are criticised by Nutter (1984) as 'cream-skimming'. Nutter predicts that access to care will remain at risk for certain groups as the for-profit transformation continues and cost-containment programmes become more comprehensive.

Comparing hospital ownership with the care of uninsured and Medicaid patients, Frank et al. (1990) found that for-profit hospitals served significantly lower percentages of uninsured discharges than non-profit and public hospitals. The same pattern was observed with respect to Medicaid. On the whole, the results of the survey indicate that non-profit hospitals rendered greater public services in treating indigent patients than did for-profit hospitals. Other findings support this conclusion. Thus for-profit hospitals appear more likely to select patients on the basis of their ability to pay (Steinwald and Neuhauser, 1970). They are more likely to locate in areas with higher incomes (Kushman and Nuckton, 1977; Mullner and Hadley, 1984) and they tend to avoid offering services used most by indigent patients (Schlesinger et al., 1986; Frank et al., 1990). Since non-profit hospitals are often publicly subsidised, this result is not to surprising.

In addition to hospital care, comparative studies of for-profit and non-profit providers have been conducted on nursing homes, health insurance, day care, and other areas of service. The following is a brief survey of the findings in these areas.

Nursing Homes

Over a dozen studies have compared average costs of care in non-profit and for-profit nursing homes. There is a fair degree of agreement that for-profit nursing homes have lower costs. Marmor et al. (1987) found from 5 per cent to 15 per cent cost reduction in for-profit homes. Supporting this conclusion, the National Centre for Health Statistics found that non-profit nursing homes (both public and voluntary) charged more than the for-profit homes. In a study of nursing homes operated by the Veterans Administration, an extremely large difference in costs was seen by Lindsay (1975), who found that the average cost per patient day was 83 per cent higher than the cost of comparable care by privately-operated homes. Other studies have come up with similar findings of higher costs for non-profit nursing homes (Birnbaum et al., 1981; Frech III and Ginsburg, 1981; Hanke, 1985).

When quality of service is related to cost, however, Bishop (1980) found that the non-profit homes he studied in Massachusetts provided significantly more nursing hours per patient day than the for-profit homes. Thus it is possible that different patients and/or different services would account for the lower costs in for-profit homes. But reasons other than inferior quality of service have been put forth to explain the lower costs in for-profit homes. Both Bishop (1980) and Birnbaum et al. (1981)

attribute lower costs to the profit incentive. In their study of nursing homes in Illinois, Hill et al. (1986) suggest that competition and oversight were the factors that accounted for the lower costs among for-profits. Judge and Knapp (1985) explained this cost advantage in terms of the high degree of proprietorial involvement in the daily operations of owner-managed homes. The Moreland Commission (1976) accounted for the higher costs of non-profit providers by the existence of large employee fringe benefits in public nursing homes.

However, many other researchers regard lower quality as the main factor accounting for lower costs (Frech III and Ginsburg, 1981). And there is much evidence that supports this judgement. Fottler et al. (1981) found lower quality of care in for-profit nursing homes in Southern California. Weisbrod and Schlesinger (1981) discovered that profit-oriented homes employed fewer full-time registered nurses and full-time maintenance workers per patient than non-profit ones. There was also some evidence to suggest that drugs were used in place of more expensive labour costs for patient care. Among nursing homes studied in Wisconsin, Riportella-Mueller and Slesinger (1982) report that non-profit homes had fewer violations and complaints than those operated for profit. There is also evidence that for-profit homes are disproportionately represented among institutions offering the very lowest-quality care (Vladeck, 1980; Koetting, 1980; Smith, 1981).

The literature on nursing homes points to the importance of intervening variables, such as size of the facility and the presence of physicians, which might influence costs and quality. Holmberg and Anderson (1968), for example, found that the type of ownership did not influence the quality of nursing home care, but they suggested that size might be an important variable. Size of the facility was deemed to be a significant determinant of costs in Judge and Knapp's (1985) study. There are also indications that differences in costs occur in facilities where physicians' roles are relatively attenuated (Koetting, 1980). Marmor et al.(1987) suggest that professional standards and incentives mitigate the profit incentive for cost reduction when there is a strong professional presence.

Overall, the studies in this area reveal that, although for-profit homes seem to enjoy lower costs, it is not clear that they are delivering services of equivalent quality.

Health Insurance

There are two studies which look at this area from the viewpoint of ownership. Comparing the relative efficiency of public and private administration of health insurance in the US, Hsiao (1978) found that the processing cost per claim was higher for public than for private administration. This was explained by higher competition in the private sector, greater administrative complexity in the public sector, the profit incentive, and higher compensation in the public sector.

The second study compared for-profit and non-profit insurance companies under contract with the Social Security Administration to process Medicaid and Medicare claims. Here the research revealed that for-profit firms did the work faster and had a lower error rate (Frech III, 1980).

Public Housing

Few studies are found in this area. In the United States, housing is not a service that most people believe government should produce and manage. It is a private good that exemplifies consumer demands for variety which government is poorly equipped to meet (Starr, 1989). Moreover, public housing is an expensive approach to housing low-income households. The construction cost of an average unit of public housing is only 10 per cent lower than the median price of a new house, and is 25 per cent greater than the cost of comparable private housing (Weicher, 1980). In addition to the question of construction costs, the issue of public versus private management is germane to this area. A Department of Housing and Urban Development report (1983) compared nineteen public housing authorities that used contract management to similar authorities that managed their own projects. In general, the study found no significant difference in terms of cost and performance between public and private management.

Day Care

A study by the Comptroller General of the General Accounting Office in 1979 compared the cost of federally-funded day care centres to that of comparable private centres. Their data showed that federally-funded programmes (grant and contract arrangements) were more expensive than the private ones (market and voluntary arrangements). Among the private centres, for-profit providers were less costly than the voluntary non-profit ones. The cost differences were explained by the lower ratios of teachers and aides to children, less workers, lower wages, and fewer additional services in the for-profit centres. In other words, different inputs and quality of services accounted for variations in costs (US General Accounting Office, 1979). Examining the data on child care in North Carolina, Kahn and Kamerman (1989) observe that the private non-profit programmes were operated at lower cost than the public programmes, but suggest that these savings were related to lower staff/child ratios, larger groups, larger centres, less equipment and lower care-giver salaries. These two studies reveal the likelihood that lower costs in this highly labour-intensive service are achieved mainly at the price of quality.

Legal Aid

While very little research has been conducted in this area, a study by Hermann et al. (1977) indicates that poor defendants rated privately-retained lawyers higher than court-appointed lawyers. But an analysis of conviction and imprisonment rates showed fairly equal results for both groups.

Education

The literature on educational institutions that operate for profit is limited (Levy, 1987). Comparisons between public and non-profit educational institutions, though more plentiful, tend to focus on the issue of effectiveness. Coleman's education study is often cited as support for vouchers and tuition tax credits, since it finds that private high schools seem to provide a better education than public high schools, and are less segregated as well. (Coleman et. al., 1982). Accumulated, if scattered, evidence suggests an edge in the level of academic achievement of private over public institutions. This private edge is reflected in admissions to graduate school, graduate training, research, and awards received (Shils, 1973; Carnegie Council on Policy Studies in Higher Education, 1976).

When client satisfaction is used to measure the performance of private and public institutions, there is substantial evidence of a private advantage. The School Finance Project found that only 3 per cent of parents were dissatisfied with their child's private school (Williams et al., 1983). Other studies indicate a high level of satisfaction among the private students (Kraushaar, 1972) and a continued shift to the private sector (Cooper et al., 1983).

On the question of cost, a study by the New York City Comptroller (1978) examined the relative efficiency of in-house and contract work for handicapped children. It was found that the cost per pupil in public schools was slightly greater than in private schools. The public and private costs were $US4,785 and $US4,512 respectively for the non-severely handicapped and $US6,196 and $US4,730 for the severely handicapped.

Levy (1987) has emphasised that the private/public distinction in the field of education is 'diminished or blurred, less a result of the public sector emulating the private one than the private one becoming more public'. This is due to increased public funding and regulation.

In Support of Welfare Pluralism

Comparative studies of public and private provision in social welfare services are generally fewer and less robust than the studies of physical and commercial services. The available evidence seems to favour private provision of social welfare in areas such as nursing homes, health insurance administration, housing construction, and day care services, if cost is the only criterion. However, when the criteria of cost, quality and effectiveness are continued, the cost-advantage of services produced and delivered for profit fade in some areas. Overall, the relative merits of for-profit and non-profit service providers remain to be judged on a case-by-case basis, giving due consideration to intervening variables such as organisational size and client characteristics.

While a firm conclusion as to the precise value of public versus private provisions of welfare is out of reach, one can find an auspicious element in the recent trends. The heightened use of profit-oriented agencies to deliver welfare services, and the increasing allocation of benefits through indirect cash transfers, fuel a move toward privatisation, which has opened new avenues of thought and action to policy-makers. As public, voluntary/non-profit, and for-profit providers vie for a share of the social market, they stimulate more probing comparisons of access, cost, quality and outcomes of welfare services delivered under different auspices. Those who fear the excesses of either government bureaucracy or private enterprise can take solace as the search for an appropriate balance between public and private activity in the mixed economy of welfare unfolds.

References

Alchian, A.A. (1965) 'Some economies of property rights', *Il Politico*, no.30, pp.816–29.

Born, Catherine (1983) 'Proprietary firms and child welfare services: Patterns and implications', *Child Welfare*, March–April, p.112.

Birnbaum, H., Bishop, C., Lee, A. and Jensen G. (1981) 'Why do nursing home costs vary? The determinants of nursing home costs', *Medical Care*, vol.19.

Bishop, C. (1980) 'Nursing home cost studies and reimbursement issues', *Health Care Financing Review*, no. 2, Spring, pp.47–64.

Buchanan, James (1975) *The Limits of Liberty*, Chicago, The University of Chicago Press.

—— (1977) 'Why does government grow?', in Borcherding, T.E. (ed.), *Budgets and Bureaucrats: The Sources of Government Growth*, Durham, North Carolina, Duke University Press.

Carnegie Council on Policy Studies in Higher Education (1976) *The States and Higher Education*, San Francisco, Jossey-Boss.

Clarkson, K.W. (1972) 'Some implications of property rights in hospital management', *Journal of Law and Economics*, 15 October, pp.363–84.

Coleman, J., Hoffer, T. and Kilgore, S. (1982) *High School Achievement: Public, Catholic and Private Schools Compared*, New York, Basic Books.

Cooper,B.S., McLaughlin, D.H. and Bruno, V.M. (1983) 'The latest word on private-school growth' *Teacher College Record*, no.85, pp.88–98.

Danzon, P. (1982) 'Hospital's profits: The effects of reimbursement policies', *Journal of Health Economics*, no.1, May, pp.29–52.

Deane, P. and Kuper, J. (1988) *A Lexicon of Economics*, New York, Routledge & Kegan Paul.

Department of Housing and Urban Development (1983) *Public Housing Authority Experiences with Private Management: A Comparative Study*, Washington, DC, Office of Policy Development and Research.

Ermann, D. and Gabel, J. (1984) 'Multihospital systems: Issues and empirical findings', *Health Affairs*, vol.3, no.1, pp.50–64.

Eskoz, Robin and Peddecord, K. Michael (1985) 'The relationship of hospital ownership and service composition to hospital charges', *Health Care Financing Review*, Spring.

Florida Hospital Cost Containment Board (1980), quoted in Relman, A. (1983) 'Investor-owned hospitals and health care costs', *New England Journal of Medicine*, August, pp.370–1.

Fottler, M.D., Smith, H.L. and James, W.L. (1981) 'Profits and patient care quality in nursing homes: Are they compatible?', *The Gerontologist*, vol.21, no.5.

Frank, R.G., Salkever, D.S. and Mullann, F. (1990) 'Hospital ownership and the care of uninsured and Medicaid patients: findings from the National Hospital Discharge Survey 1979–1984', *Health Policy*, January/February, pp.1–11.

Frech III, H.E. (1976) 'The property rights theory of the firm: Empirical results from a natural experiment', *Journal of Political Economy*, no.84, pp.143–52.

—— (1980) 'Health insurance; private, mutuals and governments', in Clarkson, K.W. and Martin, D.L. (eds) (1980) *Proceedings of the Seminar on the Economics of Nonproprietary Organizations*, Connecticut, JAI Press.

Frech III, H.E. and Ginsberg, P. (1981) 'The cost of nursing home care in the United States: Government ownership, financing, and efficiency', in Van Der Gaag, J. and Perlman, M. (eds) (1981) *Health, Economics, and Health Economics*, New York, North-Holland.

Friedman, Milton (1962) *Capitalism, Freedom and Democracy*, Chicago,

University of Chicago Press.

Gilbert, Neil and Gilbert, Barbara (1989) *The Enabling State*, New York, Oxford University Press.

Glazer, N. (1988) *The Limits of Social Policy*, Cambridge, Mass., Harvard University Press.

Gray, Bradford and McNerney, Walter (1986) 'For-profit enterprise in health care: The institute of medicine study', *New England Journal of Medicine*, 5 June.

Hanke, Steve H. (1985) 'Privatization theory, evidence and implementation', in Harriss, C.L. (ed) (1985) *Control of Federal Spending, Proceedings of the Academy of Political Science*, vol.35, no.4, pp.101–13.

—— (ed.) (1987) *Privatization and Development*, California, International Center for Economic Growth.

Hayek, F. (1976) *The Road to Serfdom*, Chicago, The University of Chicago Press.

Heilman, John G. and Johnson, Gerald W. (1989) 'System and process in capital-intensive privatization: A comparative case study of municipal wastewater treatment works', *Policy Studies Review*, Spring, vol.8, no.3, pp.549–72.

Held, P. and Pauly, M. (1982) *An Economic Analysis of the Production and Cost of Renal Dialysis Treatments*, Working Paper 3064-03, Washington, DC, Urban Institute.

Henig, Jeffrey R., Hamnett, Chris and Feigenbaum, Harvey B. (1988) 'The politics of privatization: A comparative perspective', *Governance*, 1 October.

Hermann, R., Single, E. and Bolton, J. (1977) *Counsel For The Poor: Criminal Defense in Urban America*, Lexington, Mass., Lexington Books.

Herzlinger, R. and Krasker, W. (1987) 'Who profits from nonprofits?', *Harvard Business Review*, January–February.

Hill, B.S., Blaser, C.J. and Balmer, P.W. (1986) 'Oversight and competition in profit vs nonprofit contracts for home care', *Policy Sciences Review*, vol.5, no.3.

Hill, Michael (1986) *Analysing Social Policy*, Oxford, Basil Blackwell.

Holmberg, R. and Anderson, N. (1968) 'Implications of ownership for nursing home care', *Medical Care*, vol.6, July–August, pp.300–7.

Hsiao, W. (1978) 'Public and private administration of health insurance: A study in relative economic efficiency', *Inquiry*, vol.15, December, pp.379–87.

Johnson, Norman (1987) *The Welfare state in Transition: The Theory and Practice of Welfare Pluralism*, Sussex, Wheatsheaf Books.

Judge, K. and Knapp, M. (1985) 'Efficiency in the production of welfare:

The public and private sectors compared', in Klein R. and O'Higgins, M. (eds) (1985) *The Future of Welfare*, Oxford, Basil Blackwell, pp.139–40.

Kahn, A. and Kamerman, S. (eds) (1989) *Privatization and the Welfare State*, New Jersey, Princeton University Press.

Karger, H.J. and Stoesz, D. (1990) *American Social Welfare Policy: A Structural Approach*, New York, Longman.

Koetting, M. (1980) *Nursing-Home Organization and Efficiency*, Lexington, Mass., Lexington Books.

Kraushaar, Otto F. (1972) *American Non-Public Schools: Patterns of Diversity*, Baltimore, Johns Hopkins University Press.

Kristensen, O.P. (1983) 'Public versus private provision of government services: The case of Danish fire protection services', *Urban Studies*, no.20, pp.1–9.

Kushman, J.E. and Nuckton, C.F. (1977) 'Further evidence on the relative performance of proprietary and nonprofit hospitals', *Medical Care*, vol.15, no.3, pp.189–204.

Levy, D.C. (1987) 'A comparison of private and public educational organizations', in Powell, W. (ed.) (1987) *The Nonprofit Sector: A Research Handbook*, New Haven, Yale University Press, pp.258–76.

Lewin, Lawrence S., Derzon, Robert A. and Margulies, Rhea (1981) 'Investor-owneds and nonprofits differ in economic performance', *Hospitals*, July, pp.52–8.

Lindsay, C.M. (1975) *Veterans Administration Hospitals*, Washington, DC, American Enterprise Institute.

Linowes, David F. (1988) *Privatization: Toward More Effective Government*, Chicago, University of Illinois Press.

Marmor, Theodore R., Schlesinger, M. and Smithey, R.W. (1987) 'Nonprofit organizations and health care', in Powell, W. (ed.) (1987) *The Nonprofit Sector. A Research Handbook*, New Haven, Yale University Press.

Mead, Lawrence (1986) *Beyond Entitlement: The Social Obligations of Citizenship*, New York, Free Press.

Meyers, Marcia. (1990) 'The ABC's of child care in a mixed economy: A comparison of public and private sector alternatives', *Social Service Review*, vol.64, no.4, pp. 559–79.

Millward, R. and Parker, D.M. (1983) 'Public and private enterprise: Comparative behavior and relative efficiency', in Millward, Robert, et al. (eds) (1983) *Public Sector Economics*, New York, Macmillan, pp.199–264.

Mishra, Ramesh (1984) *The Welfare State in Crisis*, London, Wheatsheaf Publishers.

Moreland Commission (1976) 'Reimbursing operating costs: Dollars without sense', *Report of the New York Moreland Commission on Nursing Homes and Residential Facilities*, March.

Mullner, Ross and Hadley, Jack (1984) 'Interstate variations in the growth of chain-operated proprietary hospitals, 1973–82', *Inquiry*, vol.21, June, pp.144–57.

New York City Comptroller (1978) *Policy Analysis of the Cost and Financing of Special Education to Handicapped Children in New York City*, New York, Office of the Comptroller.

Nutter, D.O. (1984) 'Access to care and the evolution of corporate, for-profit medicine', *New England Journal of Medicine*, vol.311, pp.917–19.

Pattison, Robert V. and Katz, Hallie (1983) 'Investor-owned and not-for-profit hospitals: A comparison based on California data', *New England Journal of Medicine*, 11 August, pp.347–53.

Riportella-Mueller, R. and Slesinger, D. (1982) 'The relationship of ownership and size to quality of care in Wisconsin nursing homes', *Gerontologist*, no.22, Winter, pp.429–34.

Savas, E.S. (1987) *Privatization: The Key to Better Government*, Chatham, NJ, Chatham Publishers.

—— (1989) Introduction, in Sherrod, J. (ed.) (1989) *Privatization: A Sourcebook*, Michigan, Omnigraphics.

Schlesinger, M. and Dorwart, R. (1984) 'Ownership and mental health services: a reappraisal', *New England Journal of Medicine*, vol.311, pp.959–65.

Schlesinger, M., Blumenthal, D. and Schlesinger, E. (1986) 'Profits under pressure: The economic performance of investor-owned and nonprofit Health Maintenance Organizations', *Medical Care*, vol.24, no.7, pp.615–27.

Shils, Edward (1973) 'The American private university', *Minerva*, no.11, pp.6–29.

Smith, D. (1981) *Long-Term Care in Transition: The Regulation of Nursing Homes*, Washington, DC, AUPHA Press.

Spann, R.M. (1977) 'Public versus private provision of government services', in Borcherding, T.E. (ed.) (1977) *Budgets and Bureaucrats: The Sources of Government Growth*, Durham, NC, Duke University Press.

Starr, Paul (1989) 'The meaning of privatization', in Sherrod, J. (ed.) (1989) *Privatization: A Sourcebook*, Michigan, Omnigraphics.

Steinwald, B. and Neuhauser, D. (1970) 'The role of the proprietary hospital', *Journal of Law and Contemporary Problems*, vol.35, pp.817–38.

US Bureau of the Census (1990) *Statistical Abstract of the United States, 1990*, Washington, DC, US Government Printing Office.

—— (1981) *Statistical Abstract of the United States, 1981*, Washington DC, US Government Printing Office.

—— (1994) *Annual Report on Poverty and Income Trends*, Washington, DC, US Government Printing Office.

US Congress, Select Committee on Aging (House of Representatives) (1986) *Out 'Sooner and Sicker': Myth or Medicare Crisis?* Washington, DC, Government Printing Office.

—— US General Accounting Office (1979) *Report on the National Day Care Study: Report by the Controller General of the United States*, Washington, DC, US Government Printing Office.

Vladeck, B.C. (1980) *Unloving Care*, New York, Basic Books.

Weicher, J.C. (1980) *Housing: Federal Policies and Programs*, Washington DC, American Enterprise Institute.

Weisbrod, B.C. and Schlesinger, M. (1981) 'Benefit-cost analysis in the mental health area: issues and directions for research', *Economics and Mental Health*, National Institute of Mental Health Series EN no.1, DHHS Publication No. (ADM) 81-1114, Washington DC, US Government Printing Office, pp. 8–28.

Williams, M.F., Addison, L., Hancher, K.S., Hunter, A., Kutner, M.A., Sherman, J.D. and Trow, E.O. (1983) *Private Elementary and Secondary Education*, vol.2 of a final report to Congress of the Congressionally Mandated Study of School Finance, July.

–11–

Conclusion
Norman Johnson

The most obvious feature of the accounts of the situation in individual countries in this book is the variety of experiences relating to markets. The scope of markets in health and welfare varies from the United States – with the greatest reliance upon markets – to Sweden, where market penetration has made least progress. The other countries are ranged on a continuum between these two. However, although the size of the market sector is important, as is indicated in the discussion which follows, concentration on size alone will obscure some of the less obvious variations.

Models

To some degree, the different size and scope of the market sector depends upon general attitudes to the provision of welfare, and in particular upon the support for state provision. A number of writers have attempted to construct models of welfare to explain the very different rates of development of state welfare in different countries.

An early attempt was made by Wilensky and Lebeaux (1965), and although this model was elaborated many years ago, and a decade before the alleged crisis in welfare, it still has relevance. Wilensky and Lebeaux identify:

> two conceptions of social welfare: . . . the residual and the institutional. The first holds that social welfare institutions should come into play only when the normal structures of supply break down. The second, in contrast, sees the welfare services as normal, 'first line' functions of modern industrial society. (p.138)

The residual system implies a minimum role for the state in the provision of welfare. It is expected that most people's needs will be met through the family, charitable bodies or the market, state welfare being brought into play only when these fail. In a residual welfare system, state services are provided at minimal levels on the basis of means tests, and are highly –

and quite deliberately – stigmatising. The principal means of the distribution of rewards are based on work or desert. There is a strong tendency to blame the victim. In these circumstances there is a powerful disincentive to avoid the use of state services, and anyone who can possibly do so will resort to the market.

Wilensky and Lebeaux assign the United States to the residual category, describing it as a reluctant Welfare State. They argue that the principal reasons for the US's reluctance lie in the dominant cultural values of US society: individualism, private property and the free market. These three closely related values lead to a fourth – a distrust of government and a preference for one which adopts a non-interventionist stance.

Racial, ethnic and religious heterogeneity and political decentralisation are cited by Wilensky and Lebeaux as additional reasons for relatively underdeveloped government welfare provision in the United States.

It is true that Wilensky and Lebeaux's analysis pre-dated the expansion of health and welfare provision, and of federal involvement in it, which occurred in the 1960s and the early 1970s, but in 1981 Higgins was still characterising the United States as a reluctant Welfare State. Interestingly, Higgins also highlights cultural heterogeneity and political decentralisation as being important influences upon the US approach to welfare.

Institutional welfare systems have extensive and well-developed public services which are seen as one of the main means by which people's needs will be met. Universalism, well-articulated citizenship rights and an avowed aim of reducing stigma are features of institutional forms of welfare. Wilensky and Lebeaux see most of the countries of Western Europe as falling into this category, although the archetypal examples are Sweden and the other Scandinavian countries.

Furniss and Tilton (1977) emphasise the archetypal nature of the Swedish welfare state:

> For more than a generation Sweden has been both celebrated and condemned as the society most closely approximating the ideals of the welfare state ... Estimates of the moral worth of Swedish society clearly vary, but neither enthusiasts nor detractors doubt that Sweden is the archetype of the modern welfare state. (p.122)

Furniss and Tilton's explanation of the success of the Swedish Welfare State is what they claim to be a unique blend of paternalism, Christian charity and an acceptance of the economic benefits of welfare provision with the socialist ideals of 'liberty, equality, solidarity, democracy, economic efficiency and personal security' (p.123). It should be noted, however, that this rosy picture may be changing, as Sven Olsson Hort and Daniel Cohn indicate in Chapter 9. Sweden's economy is faltering, with zero growth in 1990 and a fall in GDP in 1991 and 1992. Profits and investment shrank, and unemployment (while still low by the standards of the UK and Italy, for example) rose quickly. The right-of-centre government, elected in 1991, instituted severe cuts in public expenditure. Towards the end of 1992 the economic indicators began to point to an improvement in the Swedish economy. A report in the *European* (21 July 1994) showed that, whereas the Gross Domestic Product had fallen by 5.1 per cent in the first quarter of 1992, the corresponding figure for 1993 showed a fall of only 0.3 per cent. The same report also recorded a fall in unemployment during 1993, but at 7.4 per cent, this was still high by Swedish standards.

Titmuss (1974) produced a model consisting of three categories: (1) residual; (2) industrial achievement-performance; (3) institutional. The first and third correspond to the categories used by Wilensky and Lebeaux. The industrial achievement-performance model 'incorporates a significant role for social welfare institutions as adjuncts of the economy. It holds that social needs must be met on the basis of merit, work performance and productivity' (p.31). The industrial achievement-performance model places great emphasis on occupational and private welfare, and public provision is on the basis of means tests and desert. Economic policy takes precedence over social policy, and health and welfare services are expected to support rather than subvert the market economy.

There are elements of this position in most of the countries covered in this book. It is perhaps paradoxical that, in Hungary, Poland and Slovenia, economic restructuring has been given a much higher priority than social welfare reform. Social policy is quite firmly subordinate to economic policy, and what are seen as the economic imperatives determine the pace and character of developments in the spheres of health and welfare. The UK, Canada, France, Italy, Sweden and the United States have all experienced economic downturns in their economies during the 1980s and the early 1990s. The tendency at such times has been to blame excessive public expenditure, especially social expenditure, and to propose cuts. Even the Socialist President Mitterand, after going on a spending spree in 1981, had to introduce stringent cuts in public expenditure in 1982.

Kohl (1981) makes an interesting distinction between public consumption expenditures and transfer expenditures. He distinguishes between countries which follow the Scandinavian pattern – with an emphasis on public consumption expenditures and the direct provision of services by public agencies – and those which follow the Continental pattern, emphasising transfer incomes. The UK falls clearly into the Scandinavian camp, as does Sweden itself. France and Italy follow the Continental pattern, although in one respect Italy diverges from this pattern in having (like Sweden and the UK) a national health service based on direct provision of services, financed almost entirely from general taxation.

It is more difficult to place Canada and the United States within this schema. Canada more closely approximates to the Continental pattern in that, although it has a universal health care system, it is based on a state insurance scheme which is 90 per cent funded by the state. The United States relies on transfer payments, and, apart from Medicare and Medicaid, its health care system is chiefly based on various forms of private insurance. Historically, the three Eastern European countries provided services directly, although frequently through the workplace. In Hungary, however, as Orosz notes, the public nature of the medical services was considerably modified by the system of 'gratitude payments'. Poland, Hungary and Slovenia are now moving towards insurance-based health care.

The reason for this extended discussion of Scandinavian and Continental patterns of provision is that it is usually claimed that transfer payments are more encouraging of private markets than is direct provision. As Kohl (1981) says:

> The Continental pattern emphasises the redistribution of cash income relegating final consumption decisions to individual preferences. While this may be an effective way to achieve income maintenance or greater equality, cash transfers encourage reliance on the market provision of social services and thereby reinforce private modes of producing and delivering such services . . . The Scandinavian pattern, on the other hand, favours the public provision of services whereby collective choice more directly shapes the structure of supply and the mode of control. (pp.313–4).

While there is a good measure of truth in this claim, there are several factors which may modify the outcome in some countries. For example, a great deal will depend on the scope for private practice within a publicly-provided system, and on the use of direct financial inducements in the form of subsidies and tax relief. The health care system and the pension scheme in the UK might serve as examples. Equally, much will depend upon the standard of the public service and how readily available it is: a system denied adequate resources may lead to an exodus of the better-off users who will be able to pay for a superior service in the marketplace.

A model which is particularly helpful in explaining variations in market provision is Esping-Andersen's (1990) *Three Worlds of Welfare Capitalism.* One of its drawbacks is its exclusion of Eastern Europe, but with a little ingenuity the theory can be adapted to encompass former communist bloc countries. The work highlights two key Welfare State variables: commodification/de-commodification and social stratification.

Esping-Andersen recognises the central importance of social citizenship in Welfare States, but argues that the concept is better understood when it is tied in with the granting of inalienable social rights unrelated to performance which 'will entail a de-commodification of the status of individuals *vis-à-vis* the market' (p.21). In addition, it is necessary to consider how status as a citizen relates to class position.

The spread of industrial capitalism and its attendant markets meant that people's survival depended entirely on the sale of their labour, and their welfare became a function simply of the cash nexus. People became commodities. However, 'the introduction of modern social rights implies a loosening of the pure commodity status. De-commodification occurs when a service is rendered as a matter of right , and when a person can maintain a livelihood without reliance on the market' (pp.20–1).

The relevance of this analysis to markets in health and welfare should now be clear. Market dependence is the central issue, and de-commodification is the means by which the dominance of market relations is weakened. It should also be apparent that contemporary Welfare States are unequally de-commodifying; as the individual chapters in this book demonstrate, dependence on markets varies considerably from one country to another. Esping-Andersen says that the mere existence of benefit systems does not guarantee de-commodification. The forms in which the benefits are delivered and the rules of entitlement are also important. Thus, in residual Welfare States, predominantly based on assistance as opposed to insurance, the receipt of very low levels of benefits is dependent upon needs and means tests; the system debases those who use it. The result, according to Esping-Andersen, is 'actually to strengthen the market since all but those who fail in the market will be encouraged to contract private-sector welfare' (p.22). Insurance-based systems render benefits dependent upon contributions and work status, and their de-commodifying potential is thus reduced. Similarly, universal systems of the Beveridge type offer only limited de-commodification because benefits tend to be meagre.

The second key factor which differentiates Welfare States is social stratification. Esping-Andersen, in common with many other writers, views Welfare States as systems of social stratification, but claims that the nature of social stratification varies internationally, depending upon the kind of regime which predominated in particularly formative periods. Countries that had conservative regimes – Italy and France in our sample – developed corporatist, paternalistic class structures, with welfare systems which tended to confirm and strengthen status differences. One consequence is the development of myriad separate pension and other benefits, with different entitlements and preferential treatment for state functionaries. Countries with a liberal regime – the United States and pre-war UK, for example – have class systems that are based on 'the competitive individualism that the market supposedly cultivates' (p.64). However, the Labour government's legislative programme after the war, while it presented no long-lasting challenge to a capitalist market economy, nevertheless modified the free play of market forces to an extent unmatched in the United States. The third group of countries identified by Esping-Andersen are those where what he calls 'socialist' regimes have been influential. The social policy that emerged in such countries as Sweden was based on comparatively generous universal benefits.

Putting the two key variables together, Esping-Andersen says: 'As we survey international variations in social rights and welfare-state stratification, we will find qualitatively different arrangements between state, market and family' (p.26). If Esping-Andersen's conclusion is correct, it clearly has considerable significance for a study of private markets in health and welfare. How do the countries covered in this book conform to the pattern that emerges from Esping-Andersen's analysis?

There is a strong tendency for Welfare States to cluster by regime-types. Esping-Andersen identifies three clusters: the liberal Welfare State; the conservative corporatist Welfare State and the social democratic Welfare State. The liberal Welfare State corresponds to the residual Welfare State identified by Titmuss (1974) and Wilensky and Lebeaux (1965). Such a Welfare State provides modest benefits, with a heavy reliance on means tests and the deliberate imposition of stigma as a deterrent to the 'workshy'. De-commodification is minimal and market provision is extensive. A dual system of welfare develops, with poorer people dependent on state benefits and the better-off buying services on the private market. Esping-Andersen cites both the United States and Canada as archetypal examples of this model.

The conservative corporatist model includes France and Italy. There is a reliance on state insurance schemes, with benefits related to class and status. Because the form of such regimes is influenced by the Church, there is a strong commitment to traditional nuclear families. The influence of the Catholic Church is much more obvious in Italy than in France.

The social democratic regimes, represented in our sample by Sweden, provide high-quality services on a universal basis, with rights enjoyed by all social classes. Esping-Andersen says that this model 'crowds out the market' (p.28), and certainly market provision of health and welfare is currently of only marginal significance in Sweden. The success of the social democratic regimes is that they were able to win the loyalty of the middle classes by raising the quality of state provision to the levels demanded by better-off citizens. There was little incentive to seek a market alternative to state services. This contrasts very strongly with the liberal regimes, in which the state services were generally of a quality poor enough to impel the middle classes towards the market.

Esping-Andersen examines the potential of these clusters of Welfare State regimes for de-commodification which, it will be recalled, is concerned with freeing people from dependence on the market: the greater the de-commodification, the less the significance of markets. Esping-Andersen devises a set of criteria for measuring de-commodification and for ranking Welfare States according to the amount of de-commodification they allow. In an attempt to capture the degree of market-independence for the average worker, the scoring system is applied to pensions, unemployment benefits and sickness benefits. One of the weaknesses of the analysis is that it concentrates on income transfers, and takes no account of direct services in kind which might also serve to reduce dependence on the market. However, the results of applying the criteria are revealing. The clustering of Welfare States into three groups is clearly demonstrated.

The United States, Canada and the United kingdom are in a group with low de-commodification scores. The United States has a much lower score than Canada, which scores slightly lower than the United Kingdom. The second group of nations includes France and Italy and other conservative corporatist regimes. France achieves more de-commodification than Italy, but both out-score the countries in the first group. The final group achieves the highest scores for de-commodification, with Sweden achieving the highest score of all. Thus the North American and Western European nations covered in this book are ranked in terms of their capacity for de-commodification in the following ascending order: the United States, Canada, the United Kingdom, Italy, France, Sweden.

So far nothing has been said of Eastern European countries, and Esping-Andersen excludes them from his analysis. This exclusion is not surprising, given that the book was published in 1990 and was concerned with welfare capitalism. However, Deacon et al. (1992) demonstrate that the models do have some relevance for the former communist countries. The great uncertainty in Eastern Europe – only a relatively short time after considerable political and economic upheaval – makes prediction hazardous. Another problem is the lack of the necessary data. Deacon (1992), while recognising that entirely new forms of welfare may emerge in Eastern Europe, believes that variants of the models in North America and Western Europe are the most likely outcome.

Deacon (1992, p.168) says that:

> with varying degrees of speed and conviction all the countries of Eastern Europe and, trailing behind, the former Soviet Union are trying to replace their centralized command economies and their one-party political systems with economies governed by the rules of the market and by political systems that provide for a degree of democracy.

Markets were never entirely absent from the grey economies in Poland, Slovenia, and particularly Hungary, under the communist regimes. The crucial importance of 'gratitude money' in the Hungarian health system is identified by Orosz (see Chapter 5), who claims that income from this source far exceeded the doctors' salaries. Markets are gradually becoming more prominent, although as yet their progress in the health and welfare systems of all three countries has been slight.

Using the terminology of Esping-Andersen, Deacon (1992) says that, although benefits were dependent upon work record, the old system was highly de-commodified. He argues that:

> the new system is and will become highly commodified, will generate a new system of inequalities, and will place far greater reliance on the marketplace for pensions and other provisions . . . The market and, perhaps to a lesser extent private property extending into the welfare sphere have been seen by all social groups as the requirements for economic and social development. (p.178)

Many of the characteristics of liberal Welfare State regimes are emerging in Eastern Europe, and Deacon expects both Hungary and Slovenia to adopt regimes of this type. Lack of resources alone will prevent extensions of state welfare. When lack of resources is combined with a suspicion of the central state, then the unlikelihood of the emergence of a social democratic Welfare State regime is confirmed. Ferge (1992) identifies the forces combining to produce a liberal welfare state in Hungary:

> Following the lead of Esping-Andersen, one may discern, in the field of forces shaping social policy, very strong *conservative* and some *liberal* (libertarian) tendencies in the governing parties, and a powerful *liberal* orientation in two liberal opposition parties. As far as *socialist* or social democratic values are concerned, they are very weak, and on the defensive, both in Parliament and in other spheres of policy-making. (p.19) [Emphases in the original.]

However, the liberal welfare state does not have to be the final position. It may be possible, over a long period, to move towards a social democratic welfare state, as Ferge herself (1990) once argued.

Poland is in a rather different position, and what may result there is a modified version of conservative corporatism. Deacon (1992, pp.179–80) explains that Poland has 'a nomenklatura turned capitalist and a strong working class resistant to accepting the privatization of capitalism', and that both of these may 'see their interests represented in a particular Polish variant of post-communist authoritarian conservatism with strong populist tendencies'. In Western Europe, the development of conservative corporatism was greatly influenced by the Church, and the Catholic Church has always been of considerable significance in Poland.

The models we have looked at, then, have explanatory value in both the established capitalist democracies and the post-communist countries of Eastern Europe. The main focus has been on the balance between the market and the state in the provision of health and welfare services. In the countries covered in this study, more pluralist forms of provision have been developing with a greater role for the market. The term 'welfare pluralism' has been used to describe the shifting balance in the mixed economy of welfare.

Welfare Pluralism

Chapter 10 on the United States by Gilbert and Tang ends with the observation that 'Those who fear the excesses of either government bureaucracy or private enterprise can take solace as the search for an appropriate balance between public and private activity in the mixed economy of welfare unfolds.' It is clear from the other chapters that Welfare Pluralism is a characteristic of all Welfare States in Western Europe and North America, and that it is now likely to become the dominant mode in the former communist countries of Central and Eastern Europe.

Welfare pluralism is by no means a new phenomenon; it has a history as long as the Welfare State itself, and private markets have always constituted one of its components. Even in Hungary, Poland and Slovenia, before the changes of 1989/90, private markets were never entirely absent: housing in all three countries had a substantial private sector, in Hungary much health care was provided on the basis of payments, and there is evidence of a small but significant 'grey' market in the Slovenian health system.

The term 'welfare pluralism' simply means the provision of health and welfare services by a variety of suppliers: it may be used neutrally, implying no preference for a particular mix of providers. However, the term first came into general currency in the late 1970s and early 1980s as a response, at least in part, to the alleged crisis in the Welfare State. Governments began to look for ways of reducing social expenditure and curtailing the role of the state. This was particularly obvious in the UK and the United States during the Thatcher and Reagan administrations, although policies initiated then were carried forward in a modified form by both Major and Bush. President Clinton has not substantially changed the direction of US social policy. Private markets in health and welfare retain their prominent role. Plans to reform the health care system, for example, were always market-oriented and this has become more pronounced as a result of dilution and compromise. Whatever the eventual fate of Clinton's plan to introduce universal coverage, the US health care system will continue to be dominated by the powerful health insurance industry. The term 'welfare pluralism' ceased to be used neutrally, and changes in the welfare mix in the UK stemmed not so much from pragmatic or efficiency considerations as from an ideological commitment to privatisation and competition in what Mrs Thatcher liked to be known as the 'enterprise society'. The movement from description to prescription in the use of the term 'welfare pluralism' is illustrated by two UK writers:

> In one sense welfare pluralism can be used to convey the fact that social and health care may be obtained from four different sectors – the statutory, the voluntary, the commercial and the informal. More prescriptively, welfare pluralism implies a less dominant role for the state, seeing it as not the only possible instrument for the collective provision of welfare services. (Hatch and Mocroft, 1983, p.2)

Clearly, if the state is to provide less, then the other three sectors have to provide more. It should be noted, however, that the emphasis so far in this discussion has been on *provision*, and it is possible for the state to provide less, while simultaneously increasing its role in terms of finance and regulation.

This book is concerned with markets, and the notion of welfare pluralism directs attention towards the interweaving of private markets with other forms of provision. The remainder of this section will be concerned with the relationship of private markets in health and welfare with the other three sectors. We begin with the state.

Markets and the State

Here we will address two major issues: the ways in which governments can and do influence the development of private provision, and the role of government in regulating the private sector.

Governments may encourage the development of private market provision by regulatory or legislative change. A few examples drawn from the individual chapters in this book will serve to illustrate this point. The Health Care Bill in Slovenia is specifically aimed at changing the balance in health care provision by increasing opportunities for private practice. In Poland the Law on Establishments, passed in 1991, allowed state funds to be paid to private medical practitioners and companies. Law 412 in Italy increased charges, and other provisions will have the effect, according to Vicarelli and David, of encouraging private practice, both within the National Health Service and in entirely private establishments. In the UK the National Health Service and Community Care Act of 1990 has produced a purchaser/provider split in community care so that local authority social services departments are expected to be enablers rather than providers; there is an additional expectation built into these new arrangements that local authorities will make the maximum feasible use of independent suppliers.

Another way of encouraging private provision is by introducing or increasing charges for public services, thereby altering the comparative costs of using private as opposed to public facilities. In the United States during the 1980s, the system of cost-sharing was extended. This is a system in which service-users are required to bear part of the cost; this affected both Medicare and Medicaid patients. Greater cost-sharing has also been a feature of French health care, and charges have been increased in most other countries, including those in Eastern Europe.

Reducing the scale or scope of public services, or restricting their growth, also has the effect of increasing the attractiveness of private services. All of the Western European countries reported inadequate and reducing resources, but the situation in Eastern Europe is even more precarious. Resources for the development – and even for the maintenance – of services are stretched to their limits, and all three countries are facing economic crises. A mass exodus of people to the private sector is unlikely, however, since most consumers do not have the necessary income to pay for services in the marketplace. The imposition of stigmatising eligibility criteria, or branding claimants as scroungers, or the harsh application of workfare schemes, all serve to reduce the attractiveness of public services. Only those who can afford nothing else will use such services, and this will further emphasise the provision of poor services for poor people.

Governments may encourage markets in health and welfare by giving direct financial support to for-profit enterprises. An example of this is the use of public funds to purchase services or to pay the fees of those utilising private services of various kinds. This happens just about everywhere, but it has been a particular feature of developments in the UK during the 1980s, and it has been common in the United States for much longer. Frequently these arrangements take the form of a system of contracting which again has been particularly prominent in the United States and has gained ground in the UK and other Western European countries during the last ten years. There is very little contracting with commercial agencies at present in Eastern Europe, but such a development seems probable in the future.

All of the chapters on Europe and North America refer to contracting, and it would appear, therefore, to be a widespread practice. It is notable that Sweden is now moving in this direction, although developments so far have not been extensive. The Canadian case is interesting, not least because of considerable divergence among the provinces. British Columbia and Ontario have encouraged contracting with for-profit companies, whereas other provinces have been much more cautious.

Fiscal measures represent an alternative to direct subsidies as a means of stimulating private markets in health and welfare; they include the granting of tax concessions to private suppliers, and arrangements which allow consumers to claim tax relief against expenditure on such things as private pensions, private health insurance or house purchase. The fullest discussion of fiscal welfare (to use Titmuss's phrase) is in Chapter 10, on the United States, where there has been a very rapid growth in tax expenditures and credit subsidies since 1970. The US authors note that tax expenditures constitute part of a general move to provide benefits in cash rather than in kind, and that this mode of provision is more in keeping with markets, since people can buy services from a variety of suppliers. This relates to the distinction made earlier between the Scandinavian model and the Continental model.

It is clear, then, that the state has at its disposal a variety of means by which it can stimulate market provision. Once markets have become firmly established, however, their regulation presents a number of problems. This assumes, of course, that regulation is thought to be desirable; the radical right would certainly not share this view. It must be recognised, too, that tight and extensive regulation of market provision is inconsistent with the forms of robust capitalism pursued in the UK and the United States in the Thatcher/Reagan era, when the emphasis appeared to be on deregulation. However, deregulation was less extensive than the rhetoric might lead one to suppose, and the dangers of totally unregulated markets in health and welfare were usually recognised, and the need for some form of control was therefore accepted. An extra incentive for introducing controls, at least in the UK, was the desire to limit the open-ended commitment involved in the payment of residential and nursing home fees through the social security system.

Regulation may serve several purposes: controlling the costs to public funders of the for-profit sector; controlling its territorial or geographical distribution; controlling its size; attempting to preserve the 'shape' of the service, and monitoring standards.

We have seen how governments may encourage the development of the for-profit sector through various forms of subsidies. However, in the interests of controlling public expenditure, some form of regulation may be thought necessary. As long as services continue to be publicly financed (no matter who provides them) regulation linked to cost control may be inevitable.

Controlling the geographical distribution of for-profit services is not usually attempted, because of the enormous problems involved. It is clear from all the chapters in this book that information about the distribution of private services is sparse and unreliable, but what knowledge we do have indicates a very uneven distribution. It is a feature of markets that they open up outlets where the biggest and most assured profits are available. On the whole, it appears that urban areas are better served than rural areas, and that middle-class districts are better served than working-class districts. The distribution varies according to the service being considered. In the UK, for example, the south coast is over-provided with residential and nursing home accommodation for older people, and there is a surplus of private hospital facilities in London and elsewhere. In 1988, Higgins noted that: 'the problem of over-bedding' which had been apparent in London for some time had now, 'extended to the West Midlands and Wessex Regions where several private sector developments all came on stream at the same time' (Higgins, 1988 p.119). The problems of trying to control the distribution of for-profit provision are highlighted by Parker (1990, p.295):

> Governments find it difficult to control or influence the location of private services: financial incentives are expensive and the assumption of powers of direction unattractive; but even if governments could influence where new private services are established there remains the problem of their existing disposition.

The lack of geographical control may be compounded by functional distortion, in the sense that, in the absence of regulation, there is a rapid development of the most profitable specialisms. Chapter 4 on France indicates that, in the area of health care, surgery and obstetrics have been particularly prominent in the private sector. In Chapter 5, Orosz identifies distortion in the distribution of resources in the Hungarian health service, as a result of the rapid development of dialysis treatment by a private company working independently and under contract to the state. The same example shows the almost coincidental way in which such developments come about. The development of dialysis treatment occurred when an entrepreneurial engineer with important political contacts began manufacturing dialysis equipment ten years ago. Since the revolution the company has expanded quickly and appears to be subject to only minimal regulation.

The French contributors also point to the unregulated growth of private complementary medicine – a feature of the private sector that is not by any means restricted to France. The issue of complementary medicine raises the whole question of monitoring standards. This is hampered by imperfect knowledge of what the private sector is actually doing, and for whom they are doing it, and the position is not improved by the difficulty of devising and resourcing effective mechanisms. Higgins (1988, p.235) argues that:

> The best means of controlling private sector developments fairly and efficiently are by no means self-evident and the experience of different countries reveals flaws in many of the possible options . . . attention must be given not only to the control of planned developments but also to monitoring standards of care and accreditation procedures in both institutional and non-institutional settings.

It is probably easier to monitor institutional provision than domiciliary services. At least with the former there is tangible evidence in the form of buildings. Even in the case of institutional care, however, there are problems of ensuring that visits of inspection occur frequently and are of sufficient duration to enable the work to be done thoroughly. Furthermore, it is easier to frame and enforce regulations about physical conditions than it is to measure and evaluate the quality of relationships.

Formal contractual relationships may facilitate the monitoring and evaluation of market provision. Contracts may specify in some detail what is to be provided and how the quality is to be judged. Contracted providers have to report on their activities, and deviations from the terms of the contract usually have to have prior approval from the funding authority. Contracts frequently require providers to seek the views of users.

A number of the countries included in this book have experimented with various forms of regulation, and experienced similar problems. One of the problems, which comes over most strongly in the Italian and French accounts, is the power of professional groups to resist and evade regulation. Renewed attempts have been made in France to secure the co-operation of the medical profession in a corporatist form of regulation covering the determination of regional objectives, allowable costs and a revised fee structure. In the past, French doctors have managed to subvert attempts to implement more stringent regulation, and it is still too early to say whether the new system will be any more successful. In Italy, the medical profession is frequently in dispute with the health authorities. Governments have made sporadic – and not always consistent – attempts to limit the power of the medical profession, but they have not been notably successful.

One of the reasons for attempting to control private markets in health and welfare in a pluralist system is that powerful private suppliers might damage the voluntary, non-profit sector. It is therefore important to look at the relationship between the for-profit and the voluntary (or non-profit) sectors.

Markets and the Voluntary Sector

It was suggested above that powerful private suppliers might damage the voluntary sector. This could come about either through direct takeover, or the diversion of funds. Gilbert (1984, p.64), writing of the United States, says: 'Once an almost exclusive preserve of voluntary nonprofit organizations, . . . the private sector of social welfare has been penetrated by an increasing number of proprietary agencies dedicated to service at a profit.' Judging by Chapter 10 on the United States, the penetration has intensified since 1984.

Contracting involves competition between competing suppliers; this could very well bring voluntary and for-profit agencies into competition. The for-profit suppliers are not bound to win contracts, and it is possible that some public agencies prefer to award contracts to voluntary associations. This appears to be the case, for example, in the Canadian province of Quebec. Most of the contracts under the new community care arrangements in the UK have, initially at least, gone to voluntary agencies. This may be because of the uncertain profitability in domiciliary provision and the relatively small number of private operators in this area. In the United States, the small-business lobby has complained about unfair competition because of the tax-exempt status of non-profit organisations, and has called for much more stringent criteria for the conferment of tax exemption; it has also urged tighter control of commercial activities by non-profit groups.

In Eastern Europe the newly-emerging voluntary organisations will also find themselves in competition with commercial undertakings. The voluntary sector in Hungary, aided by liberal regulation and generous tax concessions, is growing more quickly than it is in other parts of Eastern and Central Europe (Kuti, 1992). However, the voluntary sector in the former communist countries is hampered by lack of recent experience, and the generally low incomes of potential donors. It is significant that, in Hungary, it is foundations that have experienced the most substantial growth, and Kuti (1992) claims that a number of them – especially corporate foundations – take on the legal status of foundations as a means of avoiding tax, and are virtually indistinguishable from for-profit enterprises. The relationships between the voluntary sector and markets are still to be established, but, if markets become really powerful, the voluntary sector could suffer.

Because the voluntary sector has had to compete with the for-profit sector, it has felt obliged to change its practices so that they more closely resemble those which predominate in commercial undertakings. For example a trend identified in the UK and a number of other countries is increased reliance on fees. Taylor (1990, pp.37–8) identifies the possible consequences of this trend:

> If a growing number of service providing organisations come to rely on fee income, services may well be moved away from those most in need towards those who can pay ... At a time when government is shifting responsibility for the relief of need on to voluntary organisations, to force the voluntary sector to operate under market conditions will leave its most disadvantaged clientele totally without support.

The structure and character of voluntary organisations have also changed with the greater prominence given to market principles. Among the changes are: increased size; more bureaucratic and complex structures;

greater professionalisation and greater departmental specialisation; increased market orientation with entrepreneurial and competitive cultures; greater collaboration with business and government, and emphasis on results and the development of systems of evaluation (Darlington, 1989; Butler and Wilson, 1990; Kramer, 1990; Nathan, 1990; Taylor, 1990).

It is becoming increasingly difficult to make a clear-cut distinction between these new-style voluntary organisations and for-profit enterprises. Almost certainly, some users will not fully appreciate the distinction, especially if the voluntary organisation is charging fees.

Markets and the Family

There is very little to say about the relationships in this area, largely because – although families buy services such as childminding, home helps and other welfare services – much of it is unrecorded. More formal market provision of domiciliary services is, in most countries, still relatively under-developed. The most extensive development appears to have been in the United States. At present the vast bulk of home-based services for elderly and disabled people is provided by families, but if market provision does expand, carers who can afford the fees may choose to purchase services rather than provide them themselves. This will be a source of inequality and inequity. Carers who can buy services will find it easier to continue working, which will be financially advantageous, and they will also avoid the isolation which is so often the fate of those with heavy caring responsibilities.

There will need to be careful vetting and regulation of companies providing domiciliary services, although the risk of exploitation or poor quality is reduced when services are provided under contract to a third party (usually a public agency).

Concluding Remarks

The analysis of Welfare State models and of welfare pluralism helps to explain the variations in the role of markets in different Welfare States. But in all Welfare States, including the newly-emergent ones in Central and Eastern Europe, there appears to be a readiness to accept that markets have a part to play in the provision of health and welfare services. It is equally the case that markets have become more prominent in this sphere since the mid-1970s.

In looking at models, we applied Esping-Andersen's (1990) classification into regime types, and we were able to allocate the countries covered in this study to one of the three main categories or clusters: liberal Welfare States, conservative corporatist Welfare States and social democratic Welfare States. In making this allocation, great importance was attached to Esping-Andersen's notion of de-commodification. This has particular significance for an analysis of markets in health and welfare, since it is an indicator of the degree of dependence on markets.

Too rigid a categorisation has to be avoided, because most Welfare States have liberal, conservative and social democratic elements. It is the balance between these elements that determines the clusters. Furthermore, any categorisation of Hungary, Poland and Slovenia has to be provisional only.

It is clear that Esping-Andersen's typology has some relevance for pluralist analyses of welfare, especially in what it has to say about state–market–family relations. In the previous section the relationships between markets and the state, voluntary and informal sectors were examined individually, but in welfare pluralism the focus is on the inter-relatedness of all four sectors. The balance between the sectors and the ways in which they are interwoven vary from country to country, and from service to service within countries. Within this welfare mix, the control of the size of the market sector and the regulation of commercial suppliers of health and welfare have been identified as important issues.

One of the main arguments advanced by proponents of greater private market provision is based on the enlargement of choice. In a market-led approach, however, choice is extended only for those who can afford to pay the market price. Choice for those who cannot afford to pay for services, on the other hand, may contract as resources follow fees.

The development of health and welfare markets is connected to a wider debate about consumerism in both the private and public sectors. Beresford (1988) argues that the consumerist approach in public services has been influenced by the expansion of commercial social services provision. Service users are seen as consumers or customers, and the vocabulary of the marketplace – market preferences, consumer rights and product developments – is employed (p.38). This can only be conceived of as an improvement, but it perhaps envisages a rather passive consumer. Consumerism, in its fullest sense, involves the active involvement of service-users in both policy and practice, and possibly in the management of services and facilities. Consumers in such a system would have the opportunity to participate in the identification of need and to fully express their views on resources, on the speed and method of delivery, and on the quality and quantity of provision.

Competition from the market may have the effect of encouraging public services to become more responsive to the views of their customers, and less dominated by bureaucrats and professionals. There has certainly been much recent discussion in social policy about empowerment, which has implications for both attitudes and strategy.

Among the necessary attitudes is a respect for all service-users, and the recognition by professionals and bureaucrats that service-users have not only the right to be heard, but also the right to participate in policy formulation and service delivery. Another desirable attitude concerns freedom of information, which should not be withheld simply because a social worker or doctor believes that disclosure would be harmful to the person concerned. There may be instances where the denial of disclosure is justified, but a strong case must be made before sanctioning such a course of action. The information on which policy is based, and by which it may be judged, should also be readily available.

A full discussion of strategies for empowerment is beyond the scope of this book, but it is necessary to stress that, no matter what strategies are employed, empowerment without some control over resources is meaningless. Chapter 1 included a discussion of autonomy, and strategies for empowerment may be judged by the degree to which they facilitate greater autonomy, especially among those groups to whom it has long been denied. Jordan (1990, p.71), in common with many other writers, makes a connection between autonomy and citizenship, which:

> contains elements of both the sharing out of rights and resources in order to give each individual his or her due measure of autonomy, and sharing in the quality of life promoted by the common culture, environment, political institutions and public amenities of the society.

Other writers see the values of citizenship as being at odds with the values of the marketplace (Harris, 1987; Lister, 1990).

On the other hand, the values of the market and those of citizenship can be reconciled, or at least co-exist, and a number of writers cited in Chapter 1 (Miller, 1990; Gray, 1992) emphasise the importance of autonomy, and argue that markets are essential to its realisation. The unequal capacity to participate in markets, and therefore the inability of some members of society to secure autonomy, raises questions of equity.

However, market economies are currently enjoying considerable popularity, not least in Central and Eastern Europe. Some of this enthusiasm in the former communist countries may evaporate if the economic problems accompanying the move to markets persist.

Markets of one sort or another are virtually universal, and the possibility of replacing them simply does not arise. The question is how far markets should extend. Are there spheres in which the role of markets should be limited? Since the mid-1970s they have become more prominent in health and welfare services, and it seems likely that they will remain a feature of mixed economies of welfare in the foreseeable future. The issues to be addressed in every Welfare State are: what share of total provision should

Conclusion

be allowed to the market, and what forms of regulation will be necessary to guarantee acceptable standards?

Another danger to be guarded against is the effect markets might have in reducing pressure for improvements in the public sector if most of the better-off choose to go private. Conversely, as Sweden demonstrates, high-quality public services used by the vast majority of the population reduce the scope for markets.

The debate about the most appropriate role for markets in health and welfare is far from over, and, indeed, what is thought to be appropriate is subject to constant revision. It is also clear that the approaches adopted by individual countries will, as this study indicates, vary with their different cultural and political histories, and with their present and future social, political and economic circumstances.

References

Beresford, P. (1988) 'Consumer views: Data collection or democracy?', in Allen, I. (ed.) (1988) *Hearing the Voice of the Consumer*, London, Policy Studies Institute.

Butler, R. and Wilson, D. (1990) *Managing Voluntary and Non-Profit Organizations: Strategy and Structures*, London, Routledge.

Darlington, T. (1989) *Management Learning and Voluntary Organisations*, London, National Council for Voluntary Organisations.

Deacon, B. (1992) 'The future of social policy in Eastern Europe', in Deacon et al. (1992), pp.167–91.

Deacon, B., Castle-Kancrova, M., Manning, N., Millard, F., Orosz, E., Szalai, J. and Vidinova, A. (1992) *The New Eastern Europe: Social Policy Past, Present and Future*, London, Sage.

Esping-Andersen, G. (1990) *The Three Worlds of Welfare Capitalism*, Cambridge, Polity Press.

Ferge, Z. (1990) 'The fourth road: The future for Hungarian social policy', in Deacon, B. and Szalai, J. (eds) (1990) *Social Policy in the New Eastern Europe*, Aldershot, Avebury, pp.103–18.

—— (1992) 'Social change in Eastern Europe – Social citizenship in the new democracies', Paper prepared for the First European Conference of Sociology, Sociological Perspectives on a Changing Europe, Vienna.

Furniss, N. and Tilton, T. (1977) *The Case for the Welfare State: From Social security to Social Equality*, Bloomington, Indiana University Press.

Gilbert, N. (1984) 'Welfare for profit: Moral, empirical and theoretical perspectives', *Journal of Social Policy*, vol. 13, part. 1, pp.63–74.

Gray, J. (1992) *The Moral Foundations of Market Institutions*, London, Institute of Economic Affairs Health and Welfare Unit.

Harris, D. (1987) *Justifying State Welfare: The New Right versus the Old Left*, Oxford, Blackwell.

Hatch, S. and Mocroft, I. (1983) *Components of Welfare*, London, Bedford Square Press.

Higgins, J. (1981) *States of Welfare*, Oxford, Blackwell and Robertson.

—— (1988) *The Business of Medicine*, London, Macmillan.

Jordan, B. (1990) *Social Work in an Unjust Society*, Hemel Hempstead, Harvester Wheatsheaf.

Kohl, J. (1981) 'Trends and problems in postwar public expenditure development in Western Europe and North America', in Flora, P. and Heidenheimer, A.J. (eds) (1981) *The Development of Welfare States in Europe and America*, New Brunswick, Transaction Books, pp.307–44.

Kramer, R.M. (1990) 'Change and continuity in British voluntary organisations, 1976–1988', *Voluntas*, vol.1, no.2, pp.127–38.

Kuti, E. (1992) 'Scylla and Charybdis in the Hungarian nonprofit sector' in Kuhnle, S. and Selle, P. (eds) (1992) *Government and Voluntary Organizations*, Aldershot, Avebury, pp.185–97.

Lister, R. (1990) *The Exclusive Society: Citizenship and the Poor*, London, Child Poverty Action Group.

Miller, D. (1990) *Market, State and Community: Theoretical Foundations of Market Socialism*, Oxford, Clarendon Press.

Nathan, Lord (1990) *Effectiveness and the Voluntary Sector*, London, National Council for Voluntary Organisations.

Parker, R. (1990) 'Care and the private sector', in Sinclair, I., Parker, R., Leat, D. and Williams, J. (1990) *The Kaleidoscope of Care*, London, HMSO, pp.293–348.

Taylor, M. (1990) *New Times, New Challenges: Voluntary Organisations Facing 1990*, London, National Council for Voluntary Organisations.

Titmuss, R.M. (1974) *Social Policy: An Introduction*, London, Allen and Unwin.

Wilensky, H.L. and Lebeaux, C.N. (1965) *Industrial Society and Social Welfare*, New York, The Free Press.

INDEX